The 365 CROCK POT EXPRESS™ Cookbook

365 Delicious Recipes for

Every Day of the Year

Patrick King

Copyright

TABLE OF CONTENTS

INTRODUCTION

The Crock-Pot Express Multi-Cooker™ is Amazing! You can cook virtually anything in a pressure cooker — from meats and main courses to rice, potatoes, vegetables of every description, dessert to even yogurt. Better yet, pressure cooking allows you to prepare foods up to 70 percent faster, on average, than conventional cooking methods do, which means you save energy in addition to your precious time!

Since the pressure cooker came into my life close to ten years ago, I've eaten better and saved money as well as time. Now I'd like to share with you all that I've learned.

If you are one of those "hurry-up" cooks who dreams of getting a delicious meal on the table in 30 minutes or less, you'll love this book. I love good meals, but I'm not patient about waiting a long time for it to be done.

In this book, we'll explore the surprising variety of easy dishes you can make with your electric pressure cooker.

For healthy, homemade fast food, the pressure cooker is the best option. We'll explore a wide variety of dishes, from pasta, fish, risottos, meatloafs, and cheesecakes, to all of the splendid soups, stews, ribs, and pot roasts, using wholesome and healthy ingredients in the process.

I invite you to experience the surprise and delight that awaits every cook who unlocks the lid of a pressure cooker and sees what magic has transpired within.

A pressure cooker is a real kitchen partner.

Let's see what the Crock-Pot Express™ can do!

Happy Cooking!

HERITAGE OF FOOD: A FAMILY GATHERING

To survive, we need to eat. As a result, food has turned into a symbol of loving, nurturing and sharing with one another. Recording, collecting, sharing and remembering the recipes that have been passed to you by your family is a great way to immortalize and honor your family. It is these traditions that carve out your individual personality. You will not just be honoring your family tradition by cooking these recipes but they will also inspire you to create your own variations, which you can then pass on to your children's.

The recipes are just passed on by everyone and nobody actually possesses them. I too love sharing recipes. The collection is vibrant and rich as a number of home cooks have offered their inputs to ensure that all of us can cook delicious meals at our home. I am thankful to each one of you who has contributed to this book and has allowed their traditions to pass on and grow with others. You guys are really wonderful!

I am also thankful to the cooks who have evaluated all these recipes. You're, as well as, the comments that came from your family members and friends were really invaluable.

If you have the time and inclination, please consider leaving a short review wherever you can, we would love to learn more about your opinion.

https://www.amazon.com/review/review-your-purchases/

TIME SELECTION FOR EACH RECIPE

The Crock-Pot Express™ does not have a "Manual" function setting. However, the manufacturer recommends using the "Beans/Chili" function when using a recipe that calls for "Manual" adjustments. This function allows you to adjust the pressure to LOW or HIGH and set cook times from 5 minutes to 2 hours.

Also, you can set the time using the following table:

COOKING GUIDE

Cooking Function	Default Setting	Pressure Adjustments	Temperature Adjustments	Cook Time Range
SLOW COOK	High temp / 4 hours	N/A	Low-High	30 minutes – 20 hours
STEAM	High pressure / 10 minutes	Low-High	N/A	3 minutes – 1 hour
BROWN/ SAUTÉ	High temp / 30 minutes	N/A	Low-High	5 minutes – 30 minutes
KEEP WARM	Warm temp / 4 hours	N/A	Warm	30 minutes – 4 hours
MEAT/STEW	High pressure / 35 minutes	Low-High	N/A	15 minutes – 2 hours
BEANS/CHILI	High pressure / 20 minutes	Low-High	N/A	5 minutes – 2 hours
RICE/ RISOTTO	Low pressure / 12 minutes	Low-High	N/A	6 minutes – 30 minutes
YOGURT	Low temp / 8 hours	N/A	Low-High	Low: 6 hours - 12 hours High: N/A
POULTRY	High pressure / 15 minutes	Low-High	N/A	15 minutes – 2 hours
DESSERT	Low pressure / 10 minutes	Low-High	N/A	5 minutes – 2 hours
SOUP	High pressure / 30 minutes	Low-High	N/A	5 minutes – 2 hours
MULTIGRAIN	High pressure / 40 minutes	Low-High	N/A	10 minutes – 2 hours

Main Dishes – Breakfast

1. Egg and Cheese Breakfast

Prep: 5 minutes • pressure: 4 minutes • total: 9 minutes • pressure level: high • release: quick - Serves: 2

Ingredients
1 teaspoon-unsalted butter, at room temperature, divided
2 large eggs
¼ teaspoon kosher salt, divided
Freshly ground black pepper
2 tablespoons grated aged Cheddar or Parmesan cheese, divided
1-cup water, for steaming
2 English muffins

Directions
1. Preparing the Ingredients. Using ½ teaspoon of butter each, coat the insides of 2 heatproof custard cups or small ramekins. Crack 1 egg into each cup, and carefully pierce the yolks in several places to make sure the yolk cooks through evenly. Sprinkle each with ⅛ teaspoon of kosher salt, some pepper, and 1 tablespoon of Cheddar cheese, covering the eggs. Cover the cups with aluminum foil, crimping it around the sides.
   Add water and insert the steamer basket or trivet. Place the cups on the insert.
2. High pressure for 4 minutes. Lock the lid in place, and bring the pot to high pressure for 4 minutes. To get 4-minutes cook time, press the "Steam" button and use the COOK TIME SELECTOR button to adjust the cook time to 4 minutes.
3. Pressure Release After the timer reaches 0, the cooker will automatically enter **Keep warm** mode. Press the Stop button and carefully release the pressure.
4. Finish the dish Toast the English muffins while the eggs cook.
   Unlock but *don't remove* the lid for another 30 seconds; this helps ensure that the whites are fully cooked. Using tongs, remove the cups from the cooker and peel off the foil.
   Using a small offset spatula or knife, loosen the eggs, then tip each one out onto the bottom half of one of the English muffins.
5. Top with the other half, and enjoy.

PER SERVING: CALORIES: 241; FAT: 9G; SODIUM: 682MG; CARBOHYDRATES: 26G; FIBER: 2G; PROTEIN: 14G

2. Quinoa Breakfast Bowl

Prep: 15 minutes • pressure: 7 minutes • total: 22 minutes • pressure level: high • release: natural - Serves: 4

Ingredients

1-cup (173 g) quinoa
1 1/2 cups (350 ml) water
3/4 teaspoon kosher salt, divided
1-pint cherry tomatoes (25 to 30 tomatoes)
1-tablespoon (15 ml) extra-virgin olive oil
1/4 teaspoon freshly ground black pepper
2 scallions (white and light green parts), thinly sliced
2 tablespoons (8 g) chopped fresh flat-leaf parsley
1 avocado
2 large eggs, hard-boiled, cooled, and peeled

Directions

1. Preparing the Ingredients Using a fine-mesh strainer, rinse the quinoa, then place into the Crock-Pot Multi-Cooker®. Add the water and 1/2 teaspoon of the salt.
2. High pressure for 7 minutes. Close the lid and Cook for 7 minutes. To get 7-minutes cook time, press the "Steam" button and use the TIME ADJUSTMENT button to adjust the cook time to 7 minutes.
3. Pressure Release Use the "Natural Release" method for 5 minutes, then vent any remaining steam and open the lid.
   Fluff with a fork. Press Start/Stop, lock the lid, and let sit for 5 minutes more.
4. Finish the dish While the quinoa is cooking, preheat broiler. On a small rimmed baking sheet, toss the tomatoes with the olive oil, pepper, and the remaining 1/4 teaspoon salt. Broil until the tomatoes begin to burst, about 3 minutes. Toss with the scallions and parsley.
   Pit, peel, and dice the avocado. Divide the quinoa among bowls, top with the tomatoes and avocado, and then coarsely grate the eggs on top.
5. Serve and Enjoy!

3. Bulgur, Oat, And Walnut Porridge

Prep: 5 minutes • pressure: 25 minutes • total: 29 minutes • pressure level: high • release: quick - Serves: 6

Ingredients

½ cup steel-cut oats
½ cup bulgur
½ cup chopped walnuts
½ cup maple syrup
½ teaspoon ground cinnamon
½ teaspoon salt

Directions

1. Preparing the Ingredients. Mix everything with 4 cups water in the Crock-Pot Multi-Cooker®.
2. High pressure for 25 minutes. Close the lid and the pressure valve and then cook for 25 minutes. To get 25-minutes cook time, press "Beans/Chili" button and use the TIME ADJUSTMENT button to adjust the cook time to 25 minutes.
3. Pressure Release. Use the quick-release method to bring the pot's pressure back to normal.
4. Finish the dish. Unlock and remove the lid. Turn the electric cooker to its browning function. Bring to a simmer, stirring often. Cook, stirring constantly, until slightly thickened, about 2 minutes.
5. Serve and Enjoy!

4. French Toast Bread Pudding

Prep: 5 minutes • pressure: 15 minutes • total: 20 minutes • pressure level: high • release: quick - Serves: 6

Ingredients
2 large eggs, at room temperature
1 cup whole or low-fat milk
¼ cup sugar
¼ cup orange marmalade
2 teaspoons vanilla extract
½ teaspoon ground cinnamon
5 cups of 1-inch bread cubes (about 7 ounces)
¼ cup raisins

Directions
1. Preparing the Ingredients. Lightly butter a 2-quart, high-sided, round baking or soufflé dish; set aside. Place the pressure cooker rack inside the Crock-Pot Multi-Cooker®; pour in 2 cups water.
   Whisk the eggs, milk, sugar, marmalade, vanilla, and cinnamon in a big bowl until smooth, with no bits of egg visible. Add the bread cubes and raisins; toss well to soak up the liquids. Pour the entire mixture into the prepared baking dish; cover and seal the dish with aluminum foil. Make a foil sling, set the filled baking dish on it, and lower the baking dish in the sling onto the rack. Fold the ends of the sling so they'll fit inside the cooker.
2. High pressure for 15 minutes. Lock the lid onto the cooker, bring the cooker to high pressure by pressing the "Poultry" button and cook for 15 minutes.
3. Pressure Release. Use the quick-release method to bring the pot's pressure back to normal.
4. Finish the dish. Unlock the lid and open the cooker. Use the foil sling to transfer the hot baking dish to a wire rack. Uncover and cool for 5 minutes before dishing it up by the big spoonful.

5. Soft, Medium, And Hard-Boiled Eggs

Prep: 5 minutes • pressure: 3 minutes • total: 8 minutes • pressure level: high • release: various - Serves: 1-12

Ingredients
1–12 cold, large eggs (straight from the refrigerator)

Directions
1. Preparing the Ingredients. Set a large metal vegetable steamer in the Crock-Pot Multi-Cooker®; Add about 2 inches of water to the cooker—not so much that it comes through the holes of the steamer. Set one or more eggs in the steamer.

For soft-boiled eggs—Lock the lid onto the pot.

High pressure for 1 1/2 minutes. Bring the cooker to high pressure by pressing the "Steam" button. Allow to cook for 1 1/2 minute and press START/STOP.

Pressure Release. Use the quick-release method to bring the pressure in the pot back to normal.

For medium-boiled eggs—Lock the lid onto the pot.

High pressure for 3 minutes. Close the lid and the pressure valve and then cook for 3 minutes. To get 3-minutes cook time, press "Steam" button.

Pressure Release Use the quick-release method to bring the pot's pressure back to normal—but do not open the pot. Set the cooker aside, covered, for 1 minute. Use the quick-release method to bring the pot's pressure fully back to normal.

For hard-boiled eggs—Lock the lid onto the pot.

High pressure for 3 minutes. Close the lid and the pressure valve and then cook for 3 minutes. To get 3-minutes cook time, press "Steam" button and use the TIME ADJUSTMENT button to adjust the cook time to 3 minutes.

Pressure Release. Turn off the machine or unplug it; set aside for 8 minutes. Use the quick-release method to bring the pot fully back to normal pressure.

For all eggs—Unlock and remove the lid. Transfer the eggs to a large bowl. Cut the top off a soft-boiled egg and serve it in an egg cup; peel the other kinds of eggs while still warm.

6. "Softboiled" Eggs

Prep: 5 minutes • pressure: 3 minutes • total: 8 minutes • pressure level: high • release: quick • Serves: 2

Ingredients
2 teaspoons unsalted butter, at room temperature, divided
2 large eggs
¼ teaspoon kosher salt, divided
Freshly ground black pepper
1-cup water, for steaming
2 slices of toast (optional)

Directions
1. Preparing the Ingredients Using ½ teaspoon of butter each, coat the insides of 2 heatproof custard cups or small ramekins. Crack 1 egg into each cup, and sprinkle each with ⅛ teaspoon of kosher salt and some pepper. Divide the remaining 1teaspoon of butter in half, and top each egg with one piece. (You can omit the butter on top of the egg, but it is delicious. Don't skip buttering the dish, though, or the egg won't come out.) Cover the cups with aluminum foil, crimping it down around the sides.
   Add the water and insert the steamer basket or trivet. Carefully transfer the cups to the steamer insert.
2. High pressure for 3 minutes Close the lid and the pressure valve and then cook for 3 minutes. To get 3-minutes cook time, press "Steam" button and use the TIME ADJUSTMENT button to adjust the cook time to 3 minutes.
3. Pressure Release Use the quick-release method.
4. Finish the dish Unlock but *don't remove* the lid for another 30 seconds; this will help ensure that the whites are fully cooked. Using tongs, remove the cups from the cooker and peel off the foil. Scoop each egg out onto a slice of toast (if desired).
5. Serve and Enjoy!

PER SERVING: CALORIES: 105; FAT: 9G; SODIUM: 388MG; CARBOHYDRATES: 0G; FIBER: 0G; PROTEIN: 3G

7. Mini Fritatas

Prep: 5 minutes • pressure: 5 minutes • total: 10 minutes • pressure level: normal • release: quick • Serves: 5

Ingredients
5 eggs
Splash of milk (I use almond milk)
Spices such as salt and pepper
Desired mix in's: cheese, veggies, meats, the options are endless!

Directions
1. Preparing the Ingredients .Mix eggs, milk, and mix-in's in a dish.
   Pour mixture into individual baking molds, I use silicone molds.
   Place molds on rack in Crock-Pot Multi-Cooker ® with 1 cup of water.
2. High pressure for 5 minutes. Close the lid and the pressure valve and then cook for 5 minutes. To get 5-minutes cook time, press "Beans/Chili" button and use the TIME ADJUSTMENT button to adjust the cook time to 5 minutes.
3. Pressure Release Use the quick-release method when the timer goes off and cooking is done.
4. Enjoy!

8. Grits with Cranberries Breakfast

Prep: 5 minutes • pressure: 10 minutes • total: 15 minutes • pressure level: high • release: quick • Serves: 4

Ingredients
¾ cup grits or polenta (not quick cook or instant)
3 cups water
⅛ teaspoon kosher salt
½ cup dried cranberries
1 tablespoon unsalted butter
1 tablespoon heavy (whipping) cream
2 tablespoons honey
½ cup slivered almonds, toasted

Directions
1. Preparing the Ingredients. In the Crock-Pot Multi-Cooker® combine the grits, water, kosher salt, and dried cranberries.
2. High pressure for 10 minutes. Lock the lid in place, and bring the cooker to high pressure by pressing "Steam" button and cook for 10 minutes.
3. Pressure Release. Use the quick-release method.
4. Finish the dish. Unlock and remove the lid. Quickly add the butter, heavy cream, and honey, and stir vigorously with a wooden spoon or paddle until smooth and creamy. Spoon into bowls, top with the toasted almonds, and serve.

PER SERVING: CALORIES: 251; FAT: 11G; SODIUM: 62MG; CARBOHYDRATES: 35G; FIBER: 3G; PROTEIN: 5G

9. Cinnamon, Vanilla and Banana Bread

Prep: 5 minutes • pressure: 40 minutes • total: 45 minutes • pressure level: high • release: quick • Serves: 6

Ingredients
1/4 cup (1/2 stick, or 60 g) unsalted butter, melted, plus more for the pan
1 cup (120 g) all-purpose flour
1/2 teaspoon baking powder
1/4 teaspoon baking soda
1/2 teaspoon kosher salt
1/8 teaspoon ground cinnamon, plus more for dusting
2 large eggs
1/3 cup (65 g) sugar
1/3 cup (77 g) sour cream
1/2 teaspoon pure vanilla extract
1 large ripe banana, mashed
1/2 cup (55 g) pecans, chopped

Directions
1. Preparing the Ingredients. Insert the steam rack into the Crock-Pot Multi-Cooker® and add 1 1/2 cups (350 ml) water. Butter a 6 × 3-inch (15 × 7.5 cm) round cake pan.
    In a medium bowl, whisk together the flour, baking powder, baking soda, salt, and cinnamon.
    In a second medium bowl, whisk together the eggs, sugar, sour cream, melted butter, and vanilla. Mix in the banana. Add the dry ingredients and mix to combine; stir in the pecans.
    Scrape the batter into the prepared pan and cover with aluminum foil. Place the pan on the steam rack. Lock the lid.
2. High pressure for 40 minutes. Close the lid and the pressure valve and then cook for 40 minutes. To get 40 minutes cook time, press "Multigrain" button.
3. Pressure Release .Use the "Quick Release" method.
4. Serve and Enjoy!

10. Bacon and Onions Quiche

Prep: 5 minutes • pressure: 8 minutes • total: 13 minutes • pressure level: high • release: quick • Serves: 2

Ingredients

Butter, at room temperature, for coating
2 bacon slices, diced
¼ cup thinly sliced onion
¼ teaspoon kosher salt, plus additional for seasoning
2 large eggs
2 tablespoons whole milk
2 tablespoons heavy (whipping) cream
Freshly ground black or white pepper
1-cup water, for steaming

Directions

1. Preparing the Ingredients. Using a small amount of butter, coat the insides of 2 heatproof custard cups or small ramekins.
   Set the Crock-Pot Multi-Cooker® to"brown,"add the bacon.
   Cook for 2 to 3 minutes, stirring occasionally, until the bacon renders most of its fat and is mostly crisp. Add the onion, and sprinkle with a pinch or two of kosher salt. Cook for about 3 minutes, stirring, until the onions just begin to brown. Transfer the bacon and onions to paper towels to drain briefly. Wipe out the inside of the Crock-Pot Multi-Cooker®. If you prefer, sauté the bacon and onions in a small skillet, and you won't have to clean out the Crock-Pot Multi-Cooker®.
   Into a small bowl, crack the eggs. Add the milk, heavy cream, and ¼ teaspoon of kosher salt, and season with the pepper. Whisk until the mixture is homogeneous; no streaks of egg white should remain. Pour one-quarter of the egg mixture into each cup or ramekin. Sprinkle half of the bacon and onions over each, and evenly divide the remaining egg over the bacon and onions.
   Add the water and insert the steamer basket or trivet. Carefully transfer the custard cups to the steamer insert. Place a sheet of aluminum foil over the cups. You don't have to crimp it down; it's just to keep steam from condensing on top of the custard.
2. High pressure for 7 minutes. Lock the lid in place, and bring the pot to high pressure, cook at high pressure for 7 minutes. To get 7-minutes cook time, press the "Steam" button and use the TIME ADJUSTMENT button to adjust the cook time to 7minutes.
3. Pressure Release Use the quick-release method.
4. Finish the dish. Unlock and remove the lid. Using tongs, carefully remove the custard cups from the Crock-Pot Multi-Cooker®. Cool for 1 to 2 minutes before serving. If you want to unmold the quiches, run the tip of a thin knife around the inside edge of the cups. One at a time, place a small plate over the top of the cups, and invert the quiches onto the plate.

5. Enjoy!

PER SERVING: CALORIES: 144; FAT: 12G; SODIUM: 392MG; CARBOHYDRATES: 3G; FIBER: 0G; PROTEIN

11. Cinnamon Honey Applesauce

Prep: 5 minutes • pressure: 6 minutes • total: 11 minutes • pressure level: high • release: natural • Serves: 6-8

Ingredients

3 pounds medium-tart baking apples, such as McIntosh, cored, peeled, and roughly chopped
¾ cup unsweetened apple juice
⅓ cup honey
1-tablespoon fresh lemon juice
½ teaspoon ground cinnamon
½ teaspoon salt

Directions

1. Preparing the Ingredients. Mix everything in the Crock-Pot Multi-Cooker ®.
2. High pressure for 6 Minutes. Lock the lid onto the pot. Set the Crock-Pot Multi-Cooker to cook at high pressure for 6 minutes, using the "Rice/Risotto" Button and use the TIME ADJUSTMENT button to adjust the cook time to 6 minutes. Turn off the Crock-Pot Multi-Cooker ® or unplug it so it doesn't flip to its keep-warm setting.
3. Pressure Release. Reduce the pressure with Natural Release Method. Unlock and open the Crock-Pot Multi-Cooker.
4. Finish the dish. Use an immersion blender or a potato masher right in the pot to puree the apples into a thick sauce.
5. Serve warm and enjoy!

12. Apples And Cinnamon Oatmeal

Prep: 5 minutes • pressure: 12 minutes • total: 17 minutes • pressure level: high • release: natural • Serves: 4

Ingredients
3 cups water
2 tablespoons packed brown sugar
½ teaspoon ground cinnamon
¼ teaspoon kosher salt
¾ cup steel-cut oats
1 small apple, peeled, cored, and diced
1 teaspoon unsalted butter
1-tablespoon heavy (whipping) cream

Directions
1. Preparing the Ingredients. In the Crock-Pot Multi-Cooker®, stir together the water, brown sugar, cinnamon, and kosher salt, dissolving the salt and sugar. Pour in the oats, add the apple, and stir again.
2. High pressure for 12 minutes. Lock the lid in place, cook for 12 minutes. To get 12 minutes cook time, press the "Rice/Risotto" button. When the time is up turn the Crock-Pot Multi-Cooker off. ("Keep warm" setting, turn off).
3. Pressure Release. Use the natural release method. Unlock and open the Crock-Pot Multi-Cooker ®.
4. Finish the dish. Stir the oats, and taste; if you like them softer, place the lid on the cooker, but *don't lock* it. Let the oats sit for 5 to 10 minutes more. When they are ready to serve, stir in the butter and heavy cream.
5. Serve and Enjoy!

PER SERVING: CALORIES: 181; FAT: 4G; SODIUM: 157MG; CARBOHYDRATES: 31G; FIBER: 4G; PROTEIN: 5G

13. Apple, bacon And Grits Casserole

Prep: 15 minutes • pressure: 20 minutes • total: 35 minutes • pressure level: normal • release: quick • Serves: 4-6

Ingredients

2 tablespoons unsalted butter, plus more for buttering the dish
8 ounces Canadian bacon, chopped
1 medium tart green apple, such as Granny Smith, peeled, cored, and chopped
4 medium scallions, green and white parts, trimmed and sliced into thin bits
1 teaspoon dried thyme
¾ cup quick cooking or instant grits
2 large eggs, lightly beaten
½ cup shredded Cheddar cheese (about 2 ounces)

Directions

1. Preparing the Ingredients. Melt the butter in the Crock-Pot Multi-Cooker ® turned to the Browning function. Add the Canadian bacon; cook, stirring often, for 1 minute. Add the apple, scallions, and thyme; cook for 1 minute, stirring constantly. Scrape the contents of the cooker into a large bowl. Wipe out the cooker with a damp paper towel. Turn the Crock-Pot Multi-Cooker® to its Browning mode. Add 3 cups water and bring to a boil. Whisk in the grits and cook, whisking all the while, until thickened, about 5 minutes. Scrape the grits into the bowl with the bacon mixture; cool for 10 minutes. Wash and dry the cooker.
Set the rack inside the cooker and pour in 2 cups water. Make a foil sling and set a 2-quart, high-sided, round baking or soufflé dish on top of it. Lightly butter the inside of the dish.
Stir the eggs and cheese into the grits mixture until uniform and well combined. Spread the mixture in the prepared baking dish; cover and seal with foil. Lower the dish onto the rack in the cooker with the sling. Fold the ends of the sling so they'll fit inside the cooker.
2. High pressure for 22 minutes. Lock the lid onto the pot and cook at high pressure for 22 minutes. To get 22 minutes cook time, press the "Beans/Chili" button and then use the"time adjustment" button to adjust to 22 minutes.
3. Pressure Release.Use the quick-release method.
4. Finish the dish. Unlock and open the cooker. Use the sling to transfer the baking dish to a wire cooling rack, steadying the dish as necessary. Uncover, cool a couple of minutes, and spoon the casserole onto individual plates to serve.

14. Banana Oatmeal

Prep: 5 minutes • pressure: 18 minutes • total: 24 minutes • pressure level: high • release: natural • Serves: 4

Ingredients
½ cup steel-cut oats
½ cup packed light brown sugar
2 ripe bananas, chopped
2 teaspoons vanilla extract
½ teaspoon ground cinnamon
¼ teaspoon salt
¼ cup heavy cream

Directions
1. Preparing the Ingredients. Mix the oats, brown sugar, bananas, vanilla, cinnamon, and salt with 2¼ cups water in the Crock-Pot Multi-Cooker® until the brown sugar dissolves.
2. High pressure for 18 minutes. Lock the lid onto the pot and cook at high pressure for 18 minutes. To get 18 minutes cook time, press the "Poultry" button and use the TIME ADJUSTMENT button to adjust the cook time to18 minutes.
3. Pressure Release. Turn off the Crock-Pot Multi-Cooker® or unplug it so it doesn't flip to its keep-warm setting. Allow the pot's pressure to come to normal naturally, 10 to 12 minutes.
   If the pot's pressure hasn't returned to normal within 12 minutes, use the quick-release method to bring it back to normal.
4. Finish the dish Unlock and open the cooker. Stir in the cream and set aside for 1 minute to warm before serving.

Main Dishes – Beef and Lamb

15. Classic Pot Roast

Prep: 5 Minutes • Pressure: 90 Minutes • Total: 95 Minutes • Pressure Level: High • Release: Quick And Natural • Serves: 6

Ingredients
1 tablespoon olive oil
One 3- to 3½-pound boneless beef chuck roast
1 teaspoon salt
½ teaspoon ground black pepper
1 large yellow onion, chopped
2 teaspoons minced garlic
Up to 1½ cups beef broth
3 tablespoons tomato paste
One 4-inch rosemary sprig
½ ounce dried mushrooms, preferably porcini
1½ pounds small white or yellow potatoes

Directions
1. Preparing the Ingredients Heat the oil in the Crock-Pot Multi-Cooker®. Turn on the pressure cooker to the Sauté setting then wait for it to boil.
   Season the roast with the salt and pepper; brown it on both sides, turning once, about 10 minutes. Transfer the meat to a large bowl.
   Add the onion; cook, stirring often, until translucent, about 4 minutes. Add the garlic; cook, stirring constantly, until aromatic, about 30 seconds. Pour 1¼ cup broth in the Crock-Pot Multi-Cooker®. Add the tomato paste and stir well until dissolved. Tuck the rosemary into the sauce and crumble in the mushrooms. Nestle the meat into the sauce, adding any juices in the bowl.
2. High pressure for 60 minutes. Close the lid and the pressure valve and then cook for 60 minutes. To get 60-minutes cook time, press "Multigrain" button and use the TIME ADJUSTMENT button to adjust the cook time to 60 minutes.
3. Pressure Release Use the quick-release method.
   Unlock and open the cooker; sprinkle the potatoes around the meat.
4. High pressure for 30 minutes. Close the lid and the pressure valve again and cook for 30 minutes. To get 30-minutes cook time, press "Soup" Button.
5. Pressure Release Use the natural-release method -20 to 30 minutes.

6. **Finish the dish.** Transfer the roast to a cutting board; set aside for 5 minutes. Discard the rosemary sprig. Slice the meat into 2-inch irregular chunks and serve these in bowls with the vegetables, mushrooms, and broth.
7. Serve and Enjoy¡

16. Korean Braised Short Ribs

Prep: 10 minutes • pressure: 45 minutes • total: 55 minutes • pressure level: high • release: natural • Serves 4-6

Ingredients
1 teaspoon vegetable oil
2 green onions cut into 1-inch lengths
3 cloves garlic, smashed
3 quarter-sized slices of ginger
4 pounds beef short ribs, about 3 inches thick, cut into 3 rib portions
1/2-cup water
1/2-cup soy sauce
1/4-cup rice wine (or dry sherry)
1/4-cup pear juice (or apple juice)
2 teaspoons sesame oil
Minced green onions
Gochujang sauce

Directions
1. Preparing the Ingredients Heat the vegetable oil in the Crock-Pot Multi-Cooker® using the "Sauté" function, until the oil is shimmering. Add the green onion, garlic, and ginger, and sauté for 1 minute, or until you can smell garlic. Add the short ribs, water, soy sauce, rice wine, pear juice and sesame oil. Stir until the ribs are completely coated.
2. High pressure for 45 minutes. Lock the lid on the Crock-Pot Multi-Cooker® and then cook for 45 minutes. To get 45-minutes cook time, press ""meat/stew"" button and use the TIME ADJUSTMENT button to adjust the cook time to 45 minutes.
3. Pressure Release Let the pressure to come down naturally for at least 15 minutes, then quick release any pressure left in the pot.
4. Finish the dish Remove the short ribs from the pot with a slotted spoon.
5. Serve the ribs with the degreased sauce.

17. Thai Red Beef Curry

Prep: 15 minutes • pressure: 45 minutes • total: 60 minutes • pressure level: medium • release: natural • Serves 6-8

Ingredients
1 tablespoon vegetable oil
1 medium onion, peeled, and sliced into 1/2 inch wedges
1 red bell pepper, cored, stemmed, and sliced into 1/2 inch strips
3 cloves garlic, crushed
1/2 inch piece of ginger, peeled and crushed
Cream from the top of a (13.5 ounce) can coconut milk
4 tablespoons red curry paste (a whole 4 oz. can)
8-ounce can bamboo shoots, drained
2 pounds flat iron steak (or chuck blade steak), cut into 2 inch by 1/2 inch strips
1 teaspoon Diamond Crystal kosher salt or 2 teaspoons fine sea salt
1/2 cup chicken stock or water
1 tablespoon fish sauce (plus more to taste)
1 tablespoon soy sauce (plus more to taste)
Juice from 1 lime
Minced cilantro
Minced basil (preferably Thai basil)
Lime wedges
Jasmine rice

Directions
1. Preparing the Ingredients. Heat the vegetable oil in the Crock-Pot Multi-Cooker® using the "Sauté" function, until the oil is shimmering. Stir in the onion, red bell pepper, garlic, and ginger, and sauté until the onion starts to soften, about 3 minutes.
   Fry the curry paste: Scoop the cream from the top of the can of coconut milk and add it to the pot, then stir in the curry paste. Cook, stirring often, until the curry paste darkens, about 5 minutes.
   Sprinkle the beef with the kosher salt. Add the beef to the pot, and stir to coat with curry paste. Stir in the rest of the can of coconut milk, bamboo shoots, chicken stock, fish sauce, and soy sauce.
2. High pressure for 12 minutes. Lock the lid on the Crock-Pot Multi-Cooker® and then cook for 12 minutes. To get 12-minutes cook time, press Rice/Risotto button.
3. Pressure Release. Let the pressure to come down naturally for at least 20 minutes, then quick release any pressure left in the pot.
4. Finish the dish. Remove the lid from the Crock-Pot Multi-Cooker®. Stir in the lime juice, and then taste the curry for seasoning, adding more fish sauce or brown sugar as needed. Ladle the curry into bowls, sprinkle with minced cilantro and basil, and serve with Jasmine rice.
5. Serve and Enjoy!

18. Beef Ribs

Prep: 10 minutes • pressure: 60 minutes • total: 70 minutes • pressure level: high • release: normal • Serves 4-6

Ingredients
1 tablespoon sesame oil
2 cloves garlic, peeled and smashed
1" knob fresh ginger, peeled and finely chopped
1 pinch red pepper flakes
¼ cup rice vinegar (or white balsamic vinegar)
⅓ cup raw sugar
⅔ cup soy sauce
⅔ cup salt-free (home made) beef stock
4 pounds (2k) beef ribs (about 8, ask butcher to saw or chop them in half
2 tablespoons cornstarch
1-2 tablespoons water

Directions
1. Preparing the Ingredients Turn on the Crock-Pot Multi-Cooker® to "Sauté" mode.
   Add sesame oil garlic, ginger and red pepper flakes and sauté for a minute.
   Then, de-glaze with vinegar, mix-in the sugar, soy sauce and beef stock - mix well.
   Add the ribs to the Crock-Pot Multi-Cooker® coating them with the mixture.
2. High pressure for 60 minutes. Close and lock the lid of the Crock-Pot Multi-Cooker®, cook at high pressure for 60 minutes. To get 60-minutes cook time, press ""meat/stew"" button and use the TIME ADJUSTMENT button to adjust the cook time to 60 minutes.
3. Pressure Release Use the Natural release method (20 minutes).
4. Finish the dish Remove the ribs, and place on a cookie sheet and slide under the broiler for about 5 minutes to brown. Make a slurry with the corn starch and water and then mix into the rib cooking liquid in the Crock-Pot Multi-Cooker®."Sauté" the mixture until it reaches the desired consistency.
5. Serve and Enjoy!

Per Serving Calories: 307.3; Carbohydrates: 8.6g; Fat: 10.7g; Fiber: 10.6g; Protein: 32.3g; Sodium: 1654.6mg; Cholesterol: 89.2g

19. Sausage And Peppers

Prep: 5 minutes • pressure: 10 minutes • total: 15 minutes • pressure level: high • release: quick • Serves 6

Ingredients
  2 tablespoons olive oil
  2½ pounds sweet Italian sausages in their casings
  4 large red bell peppers, stemmed, seeded, and cut into strips
  1 medium red onion, halved and thinly sliced
  2 medium garlic cloves, slivered
  1 cup red (sweet) vermouth
  2 tablespoons balsamic vinegar
  ¼ teaspoon grated nutmeg

Directions
1. Preparing the Ingredients. Heat the oil in a Crock-Pot Multi-Cooker®, turned to the browning function. Prick the sausages with a fork, add them to the pot, and brown on all sides, about 6 minutes. Transfer to a large bowl.
   Add the peppers and onion; cook, stirring almost constantly, just until the pepper strips glisten, about 2 minutes. Add the garlic, cook a few seconds, then stir in the vermouth, vinegar, and nutmeg. Nestle the sausages into the mixture.
2. High pressure for 10 minutes. Lock the lid on the Crock-Pot Multi-Cooker® and Cook for 10 minutes. To get 10-minutes cook time, press the "Steam" button.
3. Pressure Release Use the quick-release method to bring the pot's pressure back to normal.
4. Unlock and open the pot. Stir well before serving.

20. Spicy Sausage And Chard Pasta Sauce

Prep: 5 minutes • pressure: 6 minutes • total: 11 minutes • pressure level: high • release: quick • Serves 6

Ingredients
  2 tablespoons olive oil
  1 medium red onion, chopped
  Up to 3 small hot chiles, such as cherry peppers or Anaheim chiles, stemmed, seeded, and chopped
  1 tablespoon minced garlic
  1 pound mild Italian pork sausage meat, any casings removed
  ½ cup dry red wine, such as Syrah
  ½ cup canned tomato paste
  ¼ cup chicken broth

1 tablespoon dried basil

2 teaspoons dried oregano

4 cups stemmed and chopped Swiss chard

Directions

1. Preparing the Ingredients. Heat the oil in a Crock-Pot Multi-Cooker®, turned to the browning function.

   Add the onion and cook, stirring often, until softened, about 4 minutes. Add the chiles and garlic; cook until aromatic, stirring all the while, about 1 minute.

   Crumble in the sausage meat, breaking up any clumps with a wooden spoon. Stir until it loses its raw color. Stir in the wine, tomato paste, broth, basil, and oregano until the tomato paste dissolves. Add the chard and stir well.

2. High pressure for 6 minutes. Lock the lid onto the cooker, set the machine's timer to cook at high pressure for 6 minutes. To get 6-minutes cook time, press the Stew button and use the TIME ADJUSTMENT button to adjust the cook time to 6 minutes.

3. Pressure Release. Use the quick-release method to drop the pressure back to normal.

4. Unlock and open the pot. Stir well before serving.

21. Ground Beef Stew

Prep: 5 minutes • pressure: 5 minutes • pressure level: high • release: quick
• Serves 4

Ingredients
1 tablespoon olive oil
1½ pounds lean ground beef (about 93% lean)
1 large yellow onion, chopped
1 large sweet potato (about 1 pound), peeled and shredded through the large holes of a box grater
1 teaspoon ground cinnamon
1 teaspoon ground cumin
½ teaspoon dried sage
½ teaspoon dried oregano
½ teaspoon salt
½ teaspoon ground black pepper
2 tablespoons yellow cornmeal
2 tablespoons honey
2½ cups beef broth

Directions

1. Preparing the Ingredients. Heat the oil in the Crock-Pot Multi-Cooker® turned to the "Browning" function. Crumble in the ground beef; cook, stirring occasionally, until it loses its raw color and browns a bit, about 5 minutes. Add the onion; cook, stirring often, until softened, about 3 minutes.
   Stir in the sweet potato, cinnamon, cumin, sage, oregano, salt, and pepper. Cook for 1 minute, stirring constantly. Stir in the cornmeal and honey; cook for 1 minute, stirring often, to dissolve the cornmeal. Stir in the broth.
2. High pressure for 5 minutes. Lock the lid on the Crock-Pot Multi-Cooker® and then cook for 5 minutes. To get 5-minutes cook time, press "Steam" button and use the TIME ADJUSTMENT button to adjust the cook time to 5 minutes.
3. Pressure Release Use the quick-release method to drop the pot's pressure to normal.
4. Unlock and open the lid. Stir well and set aside, loosely covered, for 5 minutes before serving.

22. Meatballs and Tomato Sauce

Preparation time: **10 minutes** | Cooking time: **10 minutes** | Servings: **6**

Ingredients:
1 onion, peeled and chopped

⅓ cup Parmesan cheese, grated
½ cup bread crumbs
½ teaspoon dried oregano
Salt and ground black pepper, to taste
½ cup milk
1 pound ground meat
1 tablespoon extra virgin olive oil
1 egg, whisked
1 carrot, peeled and chopped
½ celery stalk, chopped
2¾ cups tomato puree
2 cups water

Directions:
1. In a bowl, mix the bread crumbs with cheese, half of the onion, oregano, salt, and pepper, and stir. Add the milk and meat and stir well. Add the egg and stir again.
2. Set the Crock pot Express™ on "Brown/Sauté" mode, add the oil, and heat it up. Add the onion, stir, and cook for 3 minutes. Add the celery and carrot, tomato puree, water, and salt and stir again. Shape the meatballs and add them to the Crock pot Express™, toss them to coat, cover, and cook on the ""meat/stew"" setting for 5 minutes. Release the pressure naturally for 10 minutes, and serve with your favorite spaghetti.

Nutrition: **Calories: 150, Fat: 3, Fiber: 1, Carbs: 4 , Protein: 8**

23. Crock Pot Express™ Beef Roast

Preparation + Cook Time: 70 minutes | Servings: 8

Ingredients:
4 pounds beef chuck roast, cut into cubes (2 inches)
1 cup beef broth
5 minced garlic cloves
1 peeled and chopped Granny Smith apple
1 thumb of grated ginger
½ cup soy sauce
Juice of one big orange
2 tbsp olive oil
Salt and pepper to taste

Directions:

1. Season the roast with salt and pepper. Turn on your Crock Pot Express™ to "BROWN/SAUTÉ".
2. When hot, pour in the olive oil and brown the roast all over.
3. Move the meat to a plate.
4. Pour in the beef broth and scrape any stuck bits of meat.
5. Pour in soy sauce and stir.
6. Put the roast back into the pot.
7. Arrange the cut apple, garlic, and ginger on top.
8. Pour in the orange juice. Close the pressure cooker lid.
9. Select "BEANS/CHILI" and cook for 45 minutes at HIGH pressure.
10. Press CANCEL and quick-release the pressure when the timer beeps. Serve!

24. Corned Beef

Preparation time: **10 minutes** - Cooking time: **60 minutes** - Servings: **6**

Ingredients:
4 pounds beef brisket
2 oranges, sliced
2 garlic cloves, peeled and minced
2 yellow onions, peeled and sliced thin
11 ounces celery, sliced thin
1 tablespoon dried dill
3 bay leaves
4 cinnamon sticks, cut into halves
Salt and ground black pepper, to taste
17 ounces water

Directions:
1. Put the beef in a bowl, add some water to cover, set aside to soak for a few hours, drain and transfer to the Crock pot Express™.
2. Add the celery, orange slices, onions, garlic, bay leaves, dill, cinnamon, dill, salt, pepper, and water. Stir, cover the Crock pot Express™ and cook on the "meat/stew" setting for 50 minutes. Release the pressure, set the beef aside to cool for 5 minutes, transfer to a cutting board, slice, and divide among plates. Drizzle the juice and vegetables from the Crock pot Express™ over beef, and serve.

25. The Ultimate Pot Roast

Preparation + Cook Time: 50 minutes | Servings: 6

Ingredients:
2-3 pounds beef, chuck roast
4 potatoes, large-sized, cut into large cubes
4 carrots, chopped
3 tbsp steak sauce, optional
3 cloves garlic
2 tbsp olive oil
2 tbsp Italian Seasonings
2 stalks celery, chopped
1 onion
1 cups beef broth
1 cup red wine

Directions:
1. Press the "BROWN/SAUTÉ" key of your Crock Pot Express™.
2. Pour in the olive oil. Add the roast beef and cook each side for about 1 to 2 minutes or until browned.
3. Transfer the browned beef into a plate.
4. Put the celery, carrots, and potatoes in the pot. Top with the garlic and onion.
5. Pour the beef broth and the wine in the pot. Put the roast on top of the vegetables.
6. Spread the seasonings over the top of the roast and then spread with the steak sauce.
7. Press the CANCEL key to stop the "BROWN/SAUTÉ" function. Cover and lock the lid. Turn the steam valve to Sealing.
8. Press the "Beans/Chili" key, set the pressure to HIGH, and set the timer for 35 minutes.
9. When the Crock Pot Express™ timer beeps, release the pressure naturally for 10-15 minutes or until the valve drops.
10. Turn the steam valve to Venting to release remaining pressure. Unlock and carefully open the lid. Serve!

26. Beef Curry

Preparation time: **10 minutes** - Cooking time: **20 minutes** - Servings: **4**

Ingredients:
2 pounds beef steak, cubed
2 tablespoons extra virgin olive oil
3 potatoes, diced
1 tablespoon Dijon mustard
2½ tablespoons curry powder
2 yellow onions, peeled and chopped
2 garlic cloves, peeled and minced
10 ounces canned coconut milk
2 tablespoons tomato sauce
Salt and ground black pepper, to taste

Directions:

Set the Crock pot Express™ on "Brown/Sauté" mode, add the oil, and heat it up. Add the onions and garlic, stir and cook for 4 minutes. Add the potatoes and mustard, stir, and cook for 1 minute. Add the beef, stir and brown on all sides. Add the curry powder, salt and pepper, stir, and cook for 2 minutes. Add the coconut milk and tomato sauce, stir, cover the Crock pot Express™ and cook on the "meat/stew" setting for 10 minutes. Release the pressure, uncover the Crock pot Express™, divide curry among plates, and serve.

27. Balsamic Maple Beef

Preparation + Cook Time: 55 minutes | Servings: 6

Ingredients:

3 pounds chuck steak, boneless, fat trimmed, sliced into ½-inch strips
2 tbsp avocado oil OR olive oil
½ cup balsamic vinegar
1 tsp ground ginger
1 tsp garlic, finely chopped
1 cup maple syrup
1 cup bone broth
1 ½ tsp salt

Directions:

1. Trim the fat off from the joint the beef and slice the meat into 1/2-inch thin strips. In a bowl, mix the ground ginger with the salt. Season the meat with the ginger mix.
2. Press the "BROWN/SAUTÉ" key of the Crock Pot Express™. Put the oil in the pot and heat.
3. When the oil is hot and shimmery, but not smoking, add the beef and cook until all sides are browned – you will have to cook in batches.
4. Transfer the browned beef into a plate and set aside. Put the garlic in the pot and sauté for about 1 minute.
5. Add the broth, maple syrup, and balsamic vinegar. Stir to mix. Return the browned beef into the pot.
6. Press the CANCEL key to stop the "BROWN/SAUTÉ" function. Cover and lock the lid.
7. Press the "Beans/Chili" key, set the pressure to HIGH, and set the timer for 35 minutes.
8. When the Crock Pot Express™ timer beeps, turn the steam valve to Venting to quick release the pressure.
9. Unlock and carefully open the lid. If desired, you can thicken the sauce. Press the "BROWN/SAUTÉ" key.
10. Mix 4 tablespoons arrowroot or tapioca starch with 4 tablespoons water until smooth and then add into the pot; cook for about 5 minutes or until the sauce is thick.

11. Serve!

28. Beef Chili

Preparation time: **10 minutes** - Cooking time: **40 minutes** - Servings: **6**

Ingredients:
1½ pounds ground beef
1 sweet onion, peeled and chopped
Salt and ground black pepper, to taste
16 ounces mixed beans, soaked overnight and drained
28 ounces canned diced tomatoes
17 ounces beef stock
12 ounces beer
6 garlic cloves, peeled and chopped
7 jalapeño peppers, diced
2 tablespoons vegetable oil
4 carrots, peeled and chopped
3 tablespoons chili powder
1 bay leaf
1 teaspoon chili powder

Directions:
1. Set the Crock pot Express™ on "Brown/Sauté" mode, add half of the oil and heat it up.
2. Add the beef, stir, brown for 8 minutes and transfer to a bowl. Add the rest of the oil to the Crock pot Express™ and heat it up. Add the carrots, onion, jalapeños and garlic, stir, and sauté for 4 minutes. Add the beer and tomatoes and stir.
3. Add the beans, bay leaf, stock, chili powder, chili powder, salt, pepper, and beef, stir, cover and cook on the Bean/Chili setting for 25 minutes. Release the *pressure naturally, uncover the Crock pot Express™, stir chili, transfer to bowls, and serve.*

29. Classic Corned Beef and Cabbage

Preparation + Cook Time: 1 hour 35 minutes | Servings: 6

Ingredients:
3 pounds cabbage, cut into eight wedges
1 quartered onion
1 quartered celery stalk
1 corned beef spice packet
4 cups water

1 ½ pounds new potatoes, quartered
1 pound carrots, peeled and cut to 2.5 inches in length

Directions:
1. Rinse the beef. Put in the Crock Pot Express™ along with onion and celery.
2. Add in the spice packet and pour in water. Close and seal the lid.
3. Press "Beans/Chili" and cook for 90 minutes at HIGH pressure.
4. When time is up, press CANCEL and very carefully quick-release the pressure.
5. Plate beef and keep celery and onion in the pot.
6. Add potatoes, carrots and cabbage in the pot. Close and seal lid again.
7. Select "BEANS/CHILI" and cook for 5 minutes at HIGH pressure.
8. When time is up, turn off cooker and quick-release. Move veggies to plate with the corned beef.
9. Pour pot liquid through a gravy strainer.
10. Serve beef and veggies with a bit of broth on top, and the rest in a gravy boat.

30. Beef and Vegetables

Preparation time: **10 minutes** - Cooking time: **30 minutes** - Servings: **4**

Ingredients:
2 tablespoons extra virgin olive oil
1½ pounds, beef chuck roast, cubed
4 tablespoons flour
1 yellow onion, peeled and chopped
2 tablespoons red wine
2 garlic cloves, peeled and minced
2 cups water
2 cups beef stock
Salt and ground black pepper, to taste
1 bay leaf
½ teaspoon dried thyme
2 celery stalks, chopped
2 carrots, peeled and chopped
4 potatoes, chopped
½ bunch parsley, chopped

Directions:
1. Season the beef with salt and pepper and mix with half of the flour.
2. Set the Crock pot Express™ on "Brown/Sauté" mode, add the oil and heat it up. Add the beef, brown for 2 minutes, and transfer to a bowl. Add the onion to the Crock pot Express™, stir, and cook for 3 minutes. Add the garlic, stir, and cook for 1 minute.

Add the wine, stir well, and cook for 15 seconds. Add the rest of the flour and stir well for 2 minutes. Return the meat to the Crock pot Express™,

3. Add the stock, water, bay leaf, and thyme, stir, cover and cook on the "meat/stew" setting for 12 minutes. Release the pressure, uncover the Crock pot Express™, add the carrots, celery, and potatoes, stir, cover the Crock pot Express™ and cook on the "Steam" setting for 5 minutes. Release the pressure naturally for 10 minutes, uncover the Crock pot Express™, divide among plates, and serve with parsley sprinkled on top.

31. Very Tender Pot Roast

Preparation + Cook Time: 50 minutes | Servings: 6

Ingredients:
2-3 pounds beef, chuck roast
4 potatoes, large-sized, cut into large cubes
4 carrots, chopped
3 tbsp steak sauce, optional
3 cloves garlic
2 tbsp olive oil
2 tbsp Italian Seasonings
2 stalks celery, chopped
1 onion
1 cup beef broth
1 cup red wine

Directions:
1. Press the "BROWN/SAUTÉ" key of your Crock Pot Express™. Pour in the olive oil.
2. Add the roast beef and cook each side for about 1 to 2 minutes or until browned. Transfer the browned beef into a plate.
3. Put the celery, carrots, and potatoes in the pot. Top with the garlic and onion.
4. Pour the beef broth and the wine in the pot. Put the roast on top of the vegetables.
5. Spread the seasonings over the top of the roast and then spread with the steak sauce. Press the CANCEL key to stop the "BROWN/SAUTÉ" function. Cover and lock the lid.
6. Press the "BEANS/CHILI" key, set the pressure to HIGH, and set the timer for 35 minutes.
7. When the Crock Pot Express™ timer beeps, release the pressure naturally for 10-15 minutes or until the valve drops.
8. Turn the steam valve to release remaining pressure. Unlock and carefully open the lid. Serve!

32. Beef Stroganoff

Preparation time: **10 minutes** - Cooking time: **25 minutes** - Servings: **4**

Ingredients:
10 pounds beef, cut into small cubes
1 yellow onion, peeled and chopped
2½ tablespoons vegetable oil
1½ tablespoons white flour
2 garlic cloves, peeled and minced
4 ounces mushrooms, sliced
1½ tablespoon tomato paste
Salt and ground black pepper, to taste
3 tablespoons Worcestershire sauce
13 ounces beef stock
8 ounces sour cream
Egg noodles, already cooked, for serving

Directions:
Put the beef, salt, pepper and flour in a bowl and toss to coat. Set the Crock pot Express™ on "Brown/Sauté" mode, add the oil, and heat it up. Add the meat and brown it on all sides. Add the onion, garlic, mushrooms, Worcestershire sauce, stock, and tomato paste, stir well, cover the Crock pot Express™ and cook on the "meat/stew" setting for 20 minutes. Release the pressure, uncover the Crock pot Express™, add the sour cream, more salt and pepper, stir well, divide among plates on top of egg noodles and serve.

33. Cheesy Beef Pasta

Preparation + Cook Time: 30 minutes | Servings: 8

Ingredients:
1 ¼ pounds ground beef
1 pound elbow macaroni
1 packet onion soup mix
3 ½ cups hot water
3 beef bouillon cubes
8 ounces sharp cheddar

Directions:
1. Press the "BROWN/SAUTÉ" key of the Crock Pot Express™. Add the beef and sauté until browned.

2. While the beef is cooking, combine the bouillon cubes with the hot water, and onion soup mix in a bowl and stir until well mixed.
3. When the beef browned, add the liquid mixture and the pasta in the pot and stir well to combine. Cover and lock the lid.
4. Press the "BEANS/CHILI" key, set the pressure to HIGH, and set the timer for 5 minutes.
5. When the Crock Pot Express™ timer beeps, press the CANCEL key. Turn the steam valve to quick release the pressure. Unlock and carefully open the lid.
6. Add the shredded cheese, press the "BROWN/SAUTÉ" key, and sauté for about 1 to 2 minutes or until the meat cheese is melted. Serve immediately.

34. Beef and Pasta Casserole

Preparation time: **10 minutes** - Cooking time: **20 minutes** - Servings: **4**

Ingredients:
17 ounces pasta
1 pound ground beef
13 ounces mozzarella cheese, shredded
16 ounces tomato puree
1 celery stalk, chopped
1 yellow onion, peeled and chopped
1 carrot, peeled and chopped
1 tablespoon red wine
2 tablespoons butter
Salt and ground black pepper, to taste

Directions:
1. Set the Crock pot Express™ on "Brown/Sauté" mode, add the butter and melt it. Add the carrot, onion, and celery, stir, and cook for 5 minutes.
2. Add the beef, salt and pepper, and cook for 10 minutes. Add the wine, stir and cook for 1 minute. Add the pasta, tomato puree, and water to cover pasta, stir.
3. Cover and cook on the "BEANS/CHILI" setting for 6 minutes. Release the pressure, uncover the Crock pot Express™, add the cheese, stir, divide everything among plates, and serve.

35. Pasta with Meat Sauce

Preparation + Cook Time: 15 minutes | Servings: 4

Ingredients:

1 ½ pounds ground beef
8-ounces dried pasta
24-ounces pasta sauce
12-ounces water
Italian seasoning to taste

Directions:
1. Turn your cooker to "BROWN/SAUTÉ".
2. Add ground beef to brown, breaking it up with a spatula as it cooks.
3. When browned, press CANCEL and pour in pasta, sauce, and water. You'll probably have to break the pasta in half.
4. Close and lock the lid. Select "BEANS/CHILI" and cook at HIGH pressure for 5 minutes.
5. When time is up, press CANCEL and use a quick release.
6. Season with Italian seasoning to taste and serve!

36. Chili Con Carne

Preparation time: **10 minutes** - Cooking time: **30 minutes** - Servings: **4**

Ingredients:
1 pound ground beef
1 yellow onion, peeled and chopped
4 tablespoons extra virgin olive oil
Salt and ground black pepper, to taste
2 garlic cloves, peeled and minced
1 bay leaf
4 ounces kidney beans, soaked overnight and drained
1 teaspoon tomato paste
8 ounces canned diced tomatoes
1 tablespoon chili powder
½ teaspoon cumin
5 ounces water

Directions:
1. Set the Crock pot Express™ on "Brown/Sauté" mode, add 1 tablespoon oil and heat it up. Add the meat, brown for a few minutes and transfer to a bowl.
2. Add the rest of the oil to the Crock pot Express™ and also heat it up. Add the onion and garlic, stir, and cook for 3 minutes. Return the beef to pot, add the bay leaf, beans, tomato paste, tomatoes, chili powder, cumin, salt, pepper, and water, stir,
3. Cover, and cook on the Bean/Chili setting for 18 minutes. Release the pressure, uncover the Crock pot Express™, discard bay leaf, divide chili among bowls, and serve.

37. Stuffed Rigatoni

Preparation + Cook Time: 45 minutes | Servings: 6

Ingredients:
1 pound rigatoni, cooked
½ pound ground beef
½ pound hot sausage
16 ounces mozzarella
16 ounces ricotta cheese
2 eggs
1 tbsp garlic powder
1 tbsp parsley
32 ounces of your favorite sauce
Equipment:
Spring-form pan

Directions:
1. In a large-sized bowl, mix the ricotta cheese with the mozzarella cheese, 2 eggs, parsley, and garlic powder. Set aside.
2. Press the "BROWN/SAUTÉ" key of the Crock Pot Express™.
3. Brown the sausage and the ground beef in the pot, breaking up the sausages in the process.
4. Add into the bowl with the sauce and mix well. Turn off the pot for the time being.
5. Coat the bottom of the spring-form pan with the meat-sauce mix. In a standing up position, place the pasta in the pan.
6. Spoon the cheese mix into a plastic bag. Poke a hole in one corner of the plastic bag and squeeze the cheese mix inside each rigatoni. Top the sauce mix with additional mozzarella cheese.
7. Set a trivet in the Crock Pot Express™ and pour in 1 cup of water. Place the spring-form pan in the trivet. Cover and lock the lid.
8. Press the "BEANS/CHILI" key, set the pressure to HIGH, and set the timer for 20 minutes.
9. When the Crock Pot Express™ timer beeps, turn the steam valve to quick release the pressure.
10. Unlock and carefully open the lid. Let the pan sit in the pot for 10 minutes or until the dish settles. Serve!

38. Beef and Broccoli

Preparation time: **10 minutes** - Cooking time: **10 minutes** - Servings: **4**

Ingredients:
3 pounds beef chuck roast, cut into thin strips
1 tablespoon peanut oil
1 yellow onion, peeled and chopped
½ cup beef stock
1 pound broccoli florets
2 teaspoons toasted sesame oil
2 tablespoons potato starch

For the marinade:
1 cup soy sauce
1 tablespoon sesame oil
2 tablespoons fish sauce
5 garlic cloves, peeled and minced
3 red peppers, dried and crushed
½ teaspoon Chinese five spice powder
White rice, already cooked, for serving
Toasted sesame seeds, for serving

Directions:
1. In a bowl, mix the soy sauce with the fish sauce, 1 tablespoon sesame oil, garlic, five spice powder, and crushed red peppers and stir well.
2. Add the beef strips, toss to coat, and set aside for 10 minutes. Set the Crock pot Express™ on "Brown/Sauté" mode, add the peanut oil and heat it up. Add the onions, stir, and cook for 4 minutes. Add the beef and marinade, stir, and cook for 2 minutes.
3. Add the stock, stir, cover the Crock pot Express™ and cook on the "Beans/Chili" setting for 5 minutes. Release the pressure naturally for 10 minutes, uncover the Crock pot Express™, add the cornstarch with ¼ cup liquid from the Crock pot Express™, add the broccoli to the steamer basket, cover the Crock pot Express™ again, and cook for 3 minutes on "BEANS/CHILI" mode. Release the pressure, uncover the Crock pot Express™, divide the beef into bowls on top of rice, add the broccoli on the side, drizzle the toasted sesame oil, sprinkle with sesame seeds, and serve.

39. Cheesy Taco Pasta

Preparation + Cook Time: 10 minutes | Servings: 8

Ingredients:
1 pound ground beef
1 packet taco seasoning
16 ounces salsa
16 ounces pasta (I used ruffles)

16 ounces canned black beans
2 cups Doritos
16 ounces cheddar cheese
3 cups water
Sour cream, for topping

Directions:
1. Press the "BROWN/SAUTÉ" key of the Crock Pot Express™.
2. Put the beef in the pot and add the taco seasoning. Sauté for about 1 to 2 minutes or until the beef is just crumbled.
3. Add the salsa, and black beans/ refried beans, uncooked pasta and water in the pot.
4. Press the CANCEL key to stop the "Brown/Sauté" function. Cover and lock the lid.
5. Press the "BEANS/CHILI" key, set the pressure to HIGH, and set the timer for 4 minutes.
6. When the Crock Pot Express™ timer beeps, press the CANCEL key and unplug the Crock Pot Express™. Turn the steam valve to quick release the pressure. Unlock and carefully open the lid.
7. Add 1/2 of the cheese and stir. Crumble the Doritos and line the bottom of the baking pan.
8. Pour the pasta over the Doritos, top with the rest of the cheddar cheese, and then with crumbled Doritos.
9. Bake in a preheated oven 350F for about 3-4 minutes or until the cheese is just melted.

40. Lamb Curry

Preparation time: **10 minutes** - Cooking time: **25 minutes** - Servings: **6**

Ingredients:
1½ pounds lamb shoulder, cut into medium chunks
2 ounces coconut milk
3 ounces dry white wine
3 tablespoons pure cream
3 tablespoons curry powder
2 tablespoons vegetable oil
3 tablespoons water
1 yellow onion, peeled and chopped
1 tablespoon parsley, chopped
Salt and ground black pepper, to taste

Directions:
1. In a bowl, mix half of the curry powder with the salt, pepper, and coconut milk, and stir well. Set the Crock pot Express™ on "Brown/Sauté" mode, add the oil and heat it up. Add the onion, stir, and cook for 4 minutes. Add the rest of the curry powder, stir, and

cook for 1 minute. Add the lamb, brown them for 3 minutes, and mix with water, salt, pepper, and wine. Stir,

2. Cover the Crock pot Express™ and cook on the "meat/stew" setting for 20 minutes. Release the pressure, set the Crock pot Express™ to "BEANS/CHILI" mode, add the coconut milk mixture, stir, and boil for 5 minutes. Divide among plates, sprinkle parsley on top, and serve.

41. Easy Teriyaki Beef
Preparation + Cook Time: 45 minutes | Servings: 4-6

Ingredients:
1 cup water, plus 1 tbsp
¼ cup sodium-reduced soy sauce
2 tbsp brown sugar
3 cloves garlic, crushed
1 inch fresh ginger, grated
½ tsp pepper, plus more
1 tbsp extra virgin olive oil
1 small onion, sliced into sticks
1 small red pepper, sliced
1 small yellow pepper, sliced
Salt to taste
1 lb stewing beef cubes
1 tbsp cornstarch
2 green onions, sliced

Directions:
1. Whisk together the 1 cup of water, the soy sauce, brown sugar, garlic, ginger and ½ teaspoon pepper (no salt); set aside.
2. Set your Crock Pot Express™ to "BROWN/SAUTÉ" and add in the olive oil, when it's hot add the onion and peppers; season with salt and pepper.
3. Sauté for 2-3 minutes, just until the veggies start to soften and then set the veggies aside in a bowl.
4. Add the beef to the Crock Pot Express™ to brown (with the setting still on "Brown/Sauté") working in batches if needed; season with salt and pepper.
5. Give the soy mixture a quick mix and then add it to the pot, gently scraping the bottom of the pot to release any yummy bits.
6. Cover with the lid and lock it. Select "BEANS/CHILI" and cook at HIGH pressure for 45 minutes. Use a quick release.
7. Whisk together the 1 tbsp water and the cornstarch until completely smooth, it should look like white water.

8. Take the lid off the pot, set the pot back to "BROWN/SAUTÉ" and when the liquid comes to a boil add in the cornstarch/water slurry; let it bubble until the sauce thickens.
9. Turn the pot off and add in the reserved peppers, onion and the green onion; mix well.
10. Taste and adjust seasoning before serving.
11. Serve on your favorite rice or noodles.

Notes: Use any combination of peppers you'd like. Feel free to add in more veggies of your choosing

42. Moroccan Lamb

Preparation time: **10 minutes** - Cooking time: **25 minutes** - Servings: **8**

Ingredients:
2½ pounds lamb shoulder, chopped
3 tablespoons honey
3 ounces almonds, peeled and chopped
9 ounces prunes, pitted
8 ounces vegetable stock
2 yellow onions, peeled and chopped
2 garlic cloves, peeled and minced
1 bay leaf
Salt and ground black pepper, to tastes
1 cinnamon stick
1 teaspoon cumin
1 teaspoon turmeric
1 teaspoon ground ginger
1 teaspoon ground cinnamon
Sesame seeds, for serving
3 tablespoons extra virgin olive oil

Directions:
1. In a bowl, mix the ground cinnamon with ginger, cumin, turmeric, garlic, and 2 tablespoons olive oil, and stir well. Add the meat and toss to coat. Put the prunes in a bowl, cover them with hot water and set aside. Set the Crock pot Express™ on "Brown/Sauté" mode, add the rest of the oil, and heat it up. Add the onions, stir, cook for 3 minutes, transfer to a bowl and set aside. Add the meat to the Crock pot Express™, and brown it for 10 minutes. Add the stock, cinnamon stick, and bay leaf, and return the onions, stir,
2. Cover the Crock pot Express™ and cook on the "meat/stew" setting for 25 minutes. Release the pressure naturally, uncover the Crock pot Express™, add the prunes, salt, pepper, and honey, and stir. Set the Crock pot Express™ on "BEANS/CHILI" mode, cook

everything for 5 minutes, and discard the bay leaf and cinnamon stick. Divide among plates, and serve with almonds and sesame seeds on top.

43. Texas-Style Beef Chili

Preparation + Cook Time: 55 minutes | Servings: 4

Ingredients:

1 pound beef, grass-fed, organic
1 onion, large-sized, diced
1 green bell pepper, seeds removed and diced
1 tbsp fresh parsley, chopped
1 tbsp Worcestershire sauce
1 tsp garlic powder
1 tsp onion powder
1 tsp paprika
1 tsp sea salt
½ tsp ground black pepper
26 ounces tomatoes, finely chopped
4 carrots, large-sized, chopped into small pieces
4 tsp chili powder
Pinch cumin
For serving, optional:
Jalapenos, sliced
Onions, diced
Sour cream, dairy-free

Directions:

1. Press the "BROWN/SAUTÉ" key. Add the ground beef into the Crock Pot Express™ and cook until browned.
2. Add the remaining ingredients and mix well to combine. Lock the lid and close the steam valve.
3. Press CANCEL to stop the "Brown/Sauté" function. Press MEAT/ STEW key. It will automatically be set for 35 minutes.
4. When the timer beeps, let the pressure release naturally. Enjoy!

44. Lamb Ragout

Preparation time: **15 minutes** - Cooking time: **1 hour** - Servings: **8**

Ingredients:

1½ pounds mutton, bone-in
2 carrots, peeled and sliced

½ pounds mushrooms, sliced
4 tomatoes, cored and chopped
1 yellow onion, peeled and chopped
6 garlic cloves, peeled and minced
2 tablespoons tomato paste
1 teaspoon vegetable oil
Salt and ground black pepper, to taste
1 teaspoon dried oregano
½ cup parsley, diced

Directions:
1. Set the Crock pot Express™ on "Brown/Sauté" mode, add the oil, and heat it up. Add the meat and brown it on all sides. Add the tomato paste, tomatoes, onion, garlic, mushrooms, oregano, carrots, and water to cover everything. Add the salt and pepper, stir,
2. Cover the Crock pot Express™, and cook on the "meat/stew" setting for 1 hour. Release the pressure, take the meat out of the Crock pot Express™ , discard the bones, and shred it. Return the meat to pot, add the parsley and stir. Add more salt and pepper, if needed, and serve.

45. Easy Seasoned Italian Beef

Preparation + Cook Time: 1 hour 55 minutes | Servings: 6

Ingredients:
3 pounds of grass-fed chuck roast
6 garlic cloves
1 cup beef broth
¼ cup apple cider vinegar
2 tsp garlic powder
1 tsp oregano
1 tsp onion powder
1 tsp Himalayan pink salt
1 tsp marjoram
1 tsp basil
½ tsp ground ginger

Directions:
1. Cut a series of slits in the meat, and press the garlic cloves inside.
2. In a bowl, mix the onion powder, garlic powder, salt, ginger, basil, oregano, and marjoram.

3. Rub into the meat and put in your Crock Pot Express™. Pour in the apple cider vinegar and broth.
4. Close and lock the lid. Press "BEANS/CHILI" and cook at HIGH pressure for 90 minutes.
5. When time is up, press CANCEL and wait for a natural release.
6. When all the pressure is gone, open the lid and shred the beef on a plate.
7. Serve over salad, cauliflower rice, cooked sweet potatoes, and so on.

46. Mexican-style Lamb

Preparation time: **10 minutes** - Cooking time: **50 minutes** - Servings: **4**

Ingredients:
3 pounds lamb shoulder, cubed
19 ounces enchilada sauce
3 garlic cloves, peeled and minced
1 yellow onion, peeled and chopped
2 tablespoons extra virgin olive oil
Salt, to taste
½ bunch fresh cilantro, diced
warm corn tortillas, for serving
lime wedges, for serving
refried beans, for serving

Directions:
1. Put the enchilada sauce in a bowl, add the lamb and marinade for 24 hours. Set the Crock pot Express™ on "Brown/Sauté" mode, add the oil, and heat it up. Add the onions and garlic, stir, and cook for 5 minutes. Add the lamb, salt, and marinade, stir, bring to a boil,
2. Cover the Crock pot Express™, and cook on the "meat/stew" setting for 45 minutes. Release the pressure, take the meat and put it on a cutting board and set aside to cool down for a few minutes. Shred the meat and put it in a bowl. Add the cooking sauce to it and stir. Divide the meat on tortillas, sprinkle cilantro on each, add the beans, sprinkle with lime juice, roll, and serve.

47. Beef Tacos with Chili Sauce

Preparation + Cook Time: 1 hour 15 minutes | Servings: 6

Ingredients:
3 pounds beef short ribs or beef chuck roast, boneless, cut into 1-inch strips
3 dried guajillo chilies, stemmed, seeded, and rinsed (or 2 more ancho chilies)

3 cloves garlic, peeled

2 dried ancho chilies, stemmed, seeded, and rinsed

½ cup beer (preferably Negra Modelo) OR water

1 tbsp Worcestershire sauce

1 tbsp soy sauce

1 onion, large-sized, sliced

1 dried chipotle chili, stemmed, seeded, and rinsed or

1 canned chipotle en adobo

1 ½ tsp kosher salt (I used Diamond Crystal)

Directions:
1. Season the short ribs with salt and stack them in the Crock Pot Express™.
2. Top with the garlic, onions, and peppers.
3. Pour in the beer, Worcestershire sauce, and soy sauce. Cover and lock the lid.
4. Press the "BEANS/CHILI" key, set the pressure to HIGH, and set the timer for 40 minutes.
5. When the Crock Pot Express™ timer beeps, release the pressure naturally for 10-15 minutes or until the valve drops. Turn the steam valve to Venting to release remaining pressure. Unlock and carefully open the lid.
6. With a slotted spoon or with tongs, transfer the beef into a plate and set aside.
7. Pour the cooking liquid through a strainer set on a fat separator. Transfer the solids – garlic, onions, and pepper in blender.
8. When the fat surfaces, pour the de-fatted cooking liquid in the blender.
9. Starting from low power, blend the cooking liquid, slowly increasing to the highest speed, blending for 1 minute or until the sauce is very smooth.
10. Shred the beef and pour in the sauce.
11. Toss to coat the beef with the sauce.
12. Taste and adjust salt as needed.

48. Beef Meatloaf

Preparation time: **10 minutes** - Cooking time: **25 minutes** - Servings: **8**

Ingredients:
2 pounds ground beef

3 bread slices

½ cup milk

¾ cup Parmesan cheese, grated

Salt and ground black pepper, to taste

2 tablespoons dried parsley

2 cups water

8 bacon slices

3 eggs, whisked
½ cup barbecue sauce

Directions:
1. In a bowl, mix the bread slices with milk and set aside for 5 minutes. Add the meat, cheese, salt, pepper, eggs, and parsley and stir well. Shape into a loaf, place on aluminum foil, arrange bacon slices on top, tuck them underneath, and spread half of the barbecue sauce all over. Put the water in the Crock pot Express™, place the meatloaf in the steamer basket of the Crock pot Express™,
2. Cover and cook on "meat/stew" mode for 20 minutes. Release the pressure, uncover the Crock pot Express™, transfer meatloaf to a pan and spread the rest of the sauce over it. Introduce under a preheated broiler for 5 minutes, transfer to a platter, and slice.

49. Lamb Shanks

Preparation time: **10 minutes** - Cooking time: **45 minutes** - Servings: **4**

Ingredients:
4 lamb shanks
2 tablespoons extra virgin olive oil
2 tablespoons white flour
1 yellow onion, peeled and diced
3 carrots, peeled and chopped
2 garlic cloves, peeled and minced
2 tablespoons tomato paste
1 teaspoon dried oregano
1 tomato, cored and chopped
2 tablespoons water
4 ounces red wine
Salt and ground black pepper, to taste
1 beef bouillon cube

Directions:
1. In a bowl, mix the flour with salt and pepper. Add the lamb shanks and toss to coat. Set the Crock pot Express™ on "Brown/Sauté" mode, add the oil and heat it up. Add the lamb, brown on all sides, and transfer to a bowl. Add the onion, oregano, carrots, and garlic to the Crock pot Express™, stir and cook for 5 minutes. Add the tomato, tomato paste, water, wine, and bouillon cube, stir and bring to a boil. Return the lamb to pot, stir,

2. Cover, and cook on "BEANS/CHILI" mode for 25 minutes. Release the pressure, uncover the Crock pot Express™, divide the lamb among plates, pour cooking sauce all over, and serve.

50. Beef 'n Bean Pasta Casserole

Preparation + Cook Time: 20 minutes | Servings: 4

Ingredients:
1 pound lean ground beef
One 28-ounce can of diced tomatoes
2 cups corn kernels
One 15-ounce can of drained and rinsed kidney beans
One 12-ounce bottle brown ale
8-ounces pasta shells
1 chopped yellow onion
1 seeded and chopped green bell pepper
2 tbsp sweet paprika
1 tbsp olive oil
1 tbsp minced garlic
1 tsp dried oregano
1 tsp ground cumin
½ tsp chipotle pepper
½ tsp salt

Directions:
1. Heat your oil in the Crock Pot Express™ on the "BROWN/SAUTÉ" setting.
2. When hot, add garlic, bell pepper, and onion. Stir until the onion becomes clear.
3. Add the ground beef, breaking it up with a spatula if necessary.
4. Keep stirring and browning, which should take about 4 minutes.
5. Add the corn, tomatoes, beans, and seasonings. Pour in the beer. Stir until the beer foam has gone down.
6. Add the pasta and stir so it becomes coated. Close and seal the lid.
7. Select "BEANS/CHILI" and cook at HIGH pressure for 8 minutes.
8. When time is up, hit CANCEL and carefully quick-release the pressure. Stir the casserole before serving.

51. Pulled BBQ Beef Sandwiches

Prep: 10 minutes • pressure: 35 minutes • total: 45 minutes • pressure level: high • release: normal • Serves 2-4

Ingredients
    2 pounds – Beef of choice
    2 cps – Water
    4 cps – Finely shredded Cabbage (the secret ingredient and you'll never know it's in there.)
    1/2 cup – Of your favorite BBQ Sauce
    1 cup – Ketchup
    1/3 cup – Worcestershire Sauce
    1 tblsp – Horse Radish
    1 tblsp – mustard

    Directions
1. Preparing the Ingredients. Add and stir in ingredients to your Crock-Pot Multi-Cooker®.
2. High pressure for 35 minutes. Lock the lid on the Crock-Pot Multi-Cooker ® and then cook for 35 minutes. To get 35-minutes cook time, press "meat/stew" button.
3. Pressure Release. Use natural release method.
4. Finish the dish Set the beef aside. Set the Crock-Pot Multi-Cooker® to a "Sauté" mode, Sauté the sauce until it reaches the desired consistency.
5. Serve and Enjoy.

52. One Pot Chinese Beef Stew

Prep: 12 minutes • pressure: 30 minutes • total: 42 minutes • pressure level: high • release: normal • Serves 4-6

Ingredients
    1-2 Tsps. oil
    2 medium onions sliced
    ½ tsp sugar
    2 tsps. Rice wine or sherry
    1 Tb soy sauce
    1 kg beef round, cubed into one inch pieces
    2 tsps. cornstarch
    Pinch of smoked Paprika
    1-2 tsp garlic powder
    Salt and pepper
    ½ cup broth, preferably beef
    1 Tb Worcestershire sauce
    1 can of mushrooms
    1-2 tsps. Fresh ginger chopped finely
    1-2 tsps. Cornstarch slurry if needed

    Directions
1. Preparing the Ingredients. Place sugar, rice wine and soy sauce into Power Pressure Cooker® using the "Sauté" mode fry for 30 seconds.

Add beef broth and Worcestershire sauce, stir and close the lid.

2. High pressure for 30 minutes. Lock the lid on the Crock-Pot Multi-Cooker® and then cook for 30 minutes. To get 30-minutes cook time, press "meat/stew" button and use the TIME ADJUSTMENT button to adjust the cook time to 30 minutes.
   Leave on keep warm for 3 minutes.
3. Pressure Release. Release pressure using the Natural Release Method.
4. Finish the dish When meat is done, add chopped ginger, mushrooms (optional) and more salt and pepper (if needed).
   Sauté for another minute.
   Add cornstarch slurry to thicken to desired taste (if needed).
5. Serve with rice and stir fried greens or fresh cut veggies.
   Enjoy!

53. Braised Beef Shank in Soybean Paste
Preparation + Cook Time: 60 minutes | Servings: 6-8

Ingredients:
2 - 2½ pounds beef shank
2 tbsp olive oil
1 tbsp chili bean paste
1 tbsp sweet soybean paste
2 green onions chopped to 2-inch length
1 tsp Ginger sliced fresh
5-6 cloves garlic crushed
1 tsp Chinese cooking wine
1 tbsp light soy sauce
1 tbsp dark soy sauce
2 tsp sugar
1/3 tsp salt
3-4 tbsp water

Directions:
1. Soak beef in cold water for 30 minutes and then drain. Dice the beef into 1-inch pieces.
2. Heat 1 tablespoon of olive oil in the Crock Pot Express™ on the "BROWN/SAUTÉ" setting and add beef.
3. Sauté for a few minutes until water evaporates and beef turns brown. Transfer beef in a bowl and set aside.
4. Add another 1 tablespoon of olive oil in the pot. Sauté chili bean paste and sweet soybean paste for about 30 seconds.
5. Add chopped green onion, ginger and garlic; continue to sauté for 30 seconds.

6. Put the beef back into the pot, and sauté for 1 minute, then add the cooking wine, both soy sauces, sugar, salt, and water.
7. Press the CANCEL key to stop "BROWN/SAUTÉ" function.
8. Cover the lid and place the pressure valve in Sealing position. Select "BEANS/CHILI" and cook at HIGH pressure for 38 minutes. When the program is done, wait another 5 minutes.
9. Slowly release the pressure then open the lid. Select "BROWN/SAUTÉ" and set temperature to More, stir occasionally until the sauce is reduced to 1/3 its volume.
10. Transfer the braised beef shank into to a serving bowl, serve immediately over rice. Enjoy!

54. Lamb And Eggplant Pasta Casserole

Prep: 10 minutes • pressure: 8 minutes • total: 18 minutes • pressure level: high • release: quick • Serves 4

Ingredients
   2 tablespoons olive oil
   1 medium red onion, chopped
   1 tablespoon minced garlic
   1½ pounds lean ground lamb
   One small eggplant (about ¾ pound), stemmed and diced
   ¾ cup dry red wine, such as Syrah
   2¼ cups chicken broth
   ½ cup canned tomato paste
   1 teaspoon ground cinnamon
   ½ tablespoon dried oregano
   ½ teaspoon dried dill
   ½ teaspoon salt
   ½ teaspoon ground black pepper
   8 ounces dried spiral-shaped pasta, such as rotini

Directions
1. Preparing the Ingredients. Heat the oil in the Crock-Pot Multi-Cooker® turned to the "Browning" function. Add the onion and cook, stirring often, until softened, about 4 minutes. Add the garlic and cook until aromatic, less than 1 minute.
   Crumble in the ground lamb; cook, stirring occasionally, until it has lost its raw color, about 5 minutes. Add the eggplant and cook for 1 minute, stirring often, to soften a bit. Pour in the red wine and scrape up any browned bits in the pot as it comes to a simmer. Stir in the broth, tomato paste, cinnamon, oregano, dill, salt, and pepper until everything is coated in the tomato sauce. Stir in the pasta until coated.
2. High pressure for 8 minutes. Lock the lid on the Crock-Pot Multi-Cooker® and then cook for 8 minutes. To get 8-minutes cook time, press "Steam" button and use the TIME ADJUSTMENT button to adjust the cook time to 8 minutes.

3. Pressure Release. Use the quick-release method.
4. Unlock and open the pot. Stir well before serving.

55. Marinated Steak

Preparation + Cook Time: 45 minutes | Servings: 4

Ingredients:
2 pounds flank steak
2 tbsp onion soup mix, dried
¼ cups apple cider vinegar
½ cups olive oil
1 tbsp Worcestershire sauce

Directions:
1. Press the "BROWN/SAUTÉ" key of the Crock Pot Express™.
2. Put the flank steak in the pot and cook each side until browned.
3. Add the Worcestershire sauce, vinegar, onion soup mix, and olive oil.
4. Press the CANCEL key to stop the "Brown/Sauté" function. Cover and lock the lid.
5. Press the MEAT/ STEW key, and set the timer for 35 minutes.
6. When the Crock Pot Express™ timer beeps, turn the steam valve to quick release the pressure.
7. Unlock and carefully open the lid. Serve!

56. Lamb Shanks Provençal

Prep: 10 minutes • pressure: 40 minutes • total: 50 minutes • pressure level: high • release: natural • Serves 6

Ingredients
    2 large (12-ounce) lamb shanks
    1 teaspoon kosher salt, plus additional for seasoning
    Freshly ground black pepper
    1 tablespoon olive oil
    1 cup sliced onion
    2 garlic cloves, finely minced
    2 medium plum tomatoes, coarsely chopped, or ½ cup diced canned tomatoes, drained
    ½ cup dry white wine or dry white vermouth
    1 cup Chicken Stock or low-sodium broth
    1 bay leaf
    1 lemon, sliced very thin
    ⅓ cup pitted Kalamata olives
    2 tablespoons coarsely chopped fresh parsley

Directions

1. Preparing the Ingredients. Sprinkle the lamb shanks with 1 teaspoon of kosher salt and several grinds of pepper. The longer ahead of the cooking time you can do this, the better. Cover and let sit for 20 minutes to 2 hours at room temperature or refrigerate for up to 24 hours.

    Heat the vegetable oil in the Crock-Pot Multi-Cooker® using the "Sauté" function, until the oil is shimmering and flows like water. Add the lamb shanks, and brown on all sides, about 6 minutes total. Remove them to a plate. Add the onion and garlic, and sprinkle with a pinch or two of kosher salt. Cook, stirring, for about 3 minutes, or until the onions just begin to brown. Add the tomatoes, and cook until most of their liquid evaporates.

    Add the white wine, and stir, scraping up the browned bits from the bottom of the cooker.

    Cook for 2 to 3 minutes, or until the wine reduces by about half; then add the Chicken Stock and bay leaf. Return the lamb shanks to the cooker, and place the lemon slices over them.

2. High pressure for 40 minutes. Lock the lid on the Crock-Pot Multi-Cooker® and then cook for 40 minutes. To get 40-minutes cook time, press "Multigrain" button.

3. Pressure Release. After cooking, use the natural method to release pressure.

4. Finish the dish. Unlock and remove the lid. Transfer the lamb to a cutting board or plate, and tent it with aluminum foil. Strain the sauce into a fat separator, and let it rest until the fat rises to the surface.

    If you don't have a fat separator, let the sauce sit for a few minutes, then spoon or blot off any excess fat from the top and discard. Pour the defatted sauce back into the cooker along with the strained vegetables. If you want a thicker sauce, simmer the liquid for about 5 minutes, or until it reaches the desired consistency.

    Stir in the olives and parsley. Place the shanks in shallow bowls, pour the sauce and vegetables over the lamb, and serve.

    Lamb shanks benefit from salting in advance, which makes them much more flavorful and helps them brown beautifully. If you have the time, salt them up to 24 hours in advance. Place them on a tray and refrigerate, covered loosely with foil.

57. Steak Fajitas

Preparation + Cook Time: 1 hour 45 minutes | Servings: 4

Ingredients:
2 pounds Ribeye roast
1 tbs soy sauce
1 tbs worcestershire sauce
½ tsp lime juice
1 tbs olive oil – plus more for sautéing
1 tsp cumin
1 tsp chili powder
1 tsp salt
1 tsp pepper
1 tsp minced garlic
½ red bell pepper
½ green pepper
½ yellow onion
Tortillas and Mexican cheese for serving

Directions:
1. Make marinade out of liquids and seasoning and marinade meat for at least 1 hour, cube into 2-inch chunks
2. Turn Crock Pot Express™ to "BROWN/SAUTÉ" and brown the meat on either side
3. Chop vegetables into strips, remove meat from Crock Pot Express™ and sauté vegetables for 3-5 minutes
4. Place meat on top of veggies and pour out remaining marinade over the meat
5. Press "MEAT/STEW" on Crock Pot Express™ and set timer for 35 minutes
6. Serve on tortillas with some cheese

58. Glorious Beef Stew

Prep: 25 minutes • pressure: 60 minutes • total: 70 minutes • pressure level: high • release: normal • Serves 4-6

Ingredients
    2 pounds beef stew meat
    2 packets McCormick Stew Seasoning (or stew seasoning of your choice for 2 pounds meat)
    4 cups water
    5 scrubbed medium-sized potatoes chopped
    1 cup carrots chopped
    1 onion chopped

4 stalks celery
1 cup raw green beans

Directions

1. Preparing the Ingredients Add the beef Stew meet, McCormick Stew Seasoning Packets, and the water to the Crock-Pot Multi-Cooker ®
2. High pressure for 45 minutes. Lock the lid on the Crock-Pot Multi-Cooker® and then cook for 45 minutes. To get 45-minutes cook time, press "meat/stew" button and use the TIME ADJUSTMENT button to adjust the cook time to 45 minutes.
3. Pressure Release. Release the pressure using Natural Release.
   Remove the lid and stir.
4. Add vegetables below the maximum fill line, put lid back on.
5. High pressure for 15 minutes. Lock the lid on the Crock-Pot Multi-Cooker® and cook for 15 minutes. To get 15-minutes cook time, press "Poultry" button.
6. Pressure Release. Use Natural Release Method.
7. Serve and enjoy.

59. Round Roast and Veggies

Preparation + Cook Time: 40 minutes | Servings: 6

Ingredients:
2-3 pound round roast (top or bottom)
1 large white onion, sliced or diced however you prefer to eat them
2-3 cups sliced mushrooms
1 pound potatoes, quartered or cubed
3 cups vegetable or beef broth
2 tbsp minced garlic
2 tbsp olive oil
1 tbsp thyme
Generous pinch of salt and pepper

Directions:
1. Add all wet ingredients and spices to the Crock Pot Express™ and stir to combine.
2. Add in meat and veggies, excluding potatoes.
3. Seal the lid and set the timer for 15 minutes on HIGH pressure.
4. Do a quick release and add in the potatoes.
5. Cook for another 10 minutes on HIGH pressure.
6. Do another quick release
7. Remove and enjoy!

60. Brisket With Veggies

Prep: 10 Minutes • Pressure: 60 Minutes • Total: 70 Minutes • Pressure Level: High • Release: Quick • SERVES 6

Ingredients
2 tbs. olive oil
5 or 6 red potatoes
2 lb. or larger regular brisket, rinsed and patted dry
Fresh ground black pepper
3 tbs. heaping chopped garlic
1 lg. yellow onion
2 c. large chunks carrots
2-½ c. home made beef broth, or make from Knorr Beef Base
3 tbs. Worcestershire Sauce
4 bay leaves
5 or 6 red potatoes

Granulated garlic
Knorr Demi-Glace sauce
½ c. dehydrated onion
2 stalks celery in 1" chunks

Directions

1. Preparing the Ingredients Put the Crock-Pot Multi-Cooker® on the sauté setting. Put in 1 tbs. (more if needed) of the oil and caramelize the onions. Once golden, remove from pot, put in a bowl, and set aside. But keep the Crock-Pot Multi-Cooker® on the "Sauté" setting.
Rub the freshly ground pepper on both sides of the brisket. Do the same with the granulated garlic. Add 1tbs. olive oil (or more) and only lightly sear the brisket on all sides.
Add back the onions, garlic, Worcestershire sauce, bay leaves, dehydrated onion and beef broth.
2. High pressure for 50 minutes. Close the lid and the pressure valve and then cook for 50 minutes. To get 50-minutes cook time, press "meat/stew" button and use the TIME ADJUSTMENT button to adjust the cook time to 50 minutes.
While the meat is cooking, peal and cut up all the veggies. When the meat is done, use the quick pressure release feature, and then remove the lid. Add all of the veggies, replace the lid and cook at high pressure for to 10 minutes. To get 10-minutes cook time, press "Steam" button
3. Pressure Release When the time is up, turn the pot off, use the quick release again, and remove the lid.
4. Finish the dish. Use a platter to remove the veggies and meat. Use the "Sauté" setting and bring the broth to a boil, then add the Knorr Demi-Glace mixing with a Wisk. Adjust seasonings as needed. Serve with Cole Slaw or other salad, home made rolls or Italian garlic bread. Be sure to remove the bay leaves before serving.
5. Serve and Enjoy

Per Serving Calories: 425; Total Carbohydrates: 50g; Saturated Fat: 3.6g; Trans Fat: 0g; Fiber: 10.6g; Protein: 30.5g; Sodium: 490mg

61. Shredded Pepper Steak

Preparation + Cook Time: 1 hour 40 minutes | Servings: 6

Ingredients:

3-4 pounds beef (cheap steak or roast cuts will all work)
1 16-oz jar Mild Pepper Rings (banana peppers or pepperoncini)
½ cup salted beef broth
1 tbsp garlic powder
Red chili flakes to taste

Directions:

1. Season beef with garlic powder and red chili flakes before adding to cooker.
2. Pour peppers (including juice) and broth into cooker, too. Seal the lid.
3. Select "BEANS/CHILI" and cook at HIGH pressure for 70 minutes.
4. When the timer beeps, press CANCEL and wait for a natural pressure release.
5. When safe, open the cooker and shred the meat. Serve!

Notes: The jarred peppers can typically be found in the "Italian" foods section of your grocery store.

62. Lamb Shanks With Pancetta

Prep: 15 minutes • pressure: 60 minutes • total: 75 minutes • pressure level: high • release: natural • Serves 4

Ingredients
   2 tablespoons olive oil
   One 6-ounce pancetta chunk, chopped
   Four 12-ounce lamb shanks
   1 small yellow onion, chopped
   One 28-ounce can diced tomatoes, drained (about 3½ cups)
   1 ounce dried mushrooms, preferably porcini, crumbled
   3 tablespoons packed celery leaves, minced
   2 tablespoons minced chives
   2 cups dry, light white wine, such as Sauvignon Blanc
   2 tablespoons all-purpose flour
   ½ teaspoon ground black pepper

Directions

1. Preparing the Ingredients. Heat the oil in the Crock-Pot Multi-Cooker ®, turned to the "Browning" function. Add the pancetta and brown well, about 6 minutes, stirring often. Use a slotted spoon to transfer the pancetta to a large bowl.
   Add two of the shanks to the cooker; brown on all sides, turning occasionally, about 8 minutes. Transfer them to the bowl and repeat with the remaining shanks.
   Add the onion to the pot; cook, stirring often, until softened, about 4 minutes. Stir in the tomatoes, dried mushroom crumbles, celery leaves, and chives. Cook until bubbling, about minutes, stirring often.
   Whisk the wine, flour, and pepper in a medium bowl until the flour dissolves; stir this mixture into the sauce in the pot. Cook until thickened and bubbling, about 1 minute. Return the shanks, pancetta, and their juices to the cooker.

2. High pressure for 60 minutes. Close the lid and the pressure valve and then cook for 60 minutes. To get 60-minutes cook time, press "meat/stew" button and use the TIME ADJUSTMENT button to adjust the cook time to 60 minutes.
   Turn off the Crock-Pot Multi-Cooker ® or unplug it so it doesn't jump to its keep-warm setting.
3. Pressure Release. Let its pressure return to normal naturally, 20 to 30 minutes.
4. Finish the dish. Unlock and open the cooker. Transfer a shank to each serving bowl. Skim any surface fat from the sauce with a flatware spoon. Ladle the sauce and vegetables over the lamb shanks.

63. Beef Stroganoff

Preparation + Cook Time: 10 minutes | Servings: 4

Ingredients:
1 pound steak, thin-cut
1 cup sour cream
1 onion, small-sized
16 ounces egg noodles
4 cups beef broth
4 tbsp butter
8 ounces mushrooms, sliced

Directions:
1. Dice the onion into small-sized pieces. Cut the steak into thin pieces. Press the "BROWN/SAUTÉ" key of the Crock Pot Express™.
2. Add the butter, onion, and steak and wait until the butter is melted.
3. Add the mushrooms, broth, and egg noodle.
4. Press the CANCEL key to stop the "Brown/Sauté" function. Cover and lock the lid. Press the "BEANS/CHILI" key, set the pressure to HIGH, and set the timer for 4 minutes.
5. When the Crock Pot Express™ timer beeps, turn the steam valve to quick release the pressure. Unlock and carefully open the lid.
6. Stir in the sour cream and serve.

64. Lamb Casserole

Prep: 15 minutes • pressure: 35 minutes • total: 50 minutes • pressure level: high • release: normal • Serves 6-8

Ingredients
1 pound of baby potatoes
1 pound rack of lamb

2 carrots

1 large onion

2 stalks of celery

1-2 teaspoons of salt depending on the salt content of the chicken stock

2 medium size tomatoes

2 cups of chicken stock

3-4 large cloves of garlic

2 teaspoon of cumin powder

2 teaspoon of Paprika

A pinch of dried rosemary

A pinch of dried oregano leaves

2 table spoons of ketchup

3 table spoons of sherry or red wine

A splash of beer if you have one in hand

Directions

1. Preparing the Ingredients Dice the tomatoes, onion and garlic, cut potatoes and carrots, cut the rack of lamb to two halves. Put all the ingredients, in the Crock-Pot Multi-Cooker®.
2. High pressure for 35 minutes. Lock the lid on the Crock-Pot Multi-Cooker® and then cook for 35 minutes. To get 35-minutes cook time, press "meat/stew" button.
3. Pressure Release Use Natural-Release Method for 10 minutes, and then Quick-Release.
4. Serve and Enjoy!

Per Serving Calories: 407.3; Carbohydrates: 6.6g; Fat: 11.7g; Fiber: 8.6g; Protein: 35.3g; Sodium: 1640.6mg; Cholesterol: 77.2

65. Beef and Broccoli

Preparation + Cook Time: 50 minutes | Servings: 4

Ingredients:

1 pound stew beef meat, grass fed

1 bag (10-12 ounces) frozen broccoli, preferably organic

1 clove garlic, large-sized, pressed

1 onion, quartered

1 tsp ground ginger

½ cup beef or bone broth

½ tsp salt

¼ cup coconut aminos (or soy sauce)

2 tbsp fish sauce

Directions:

1. Except for the broccoli, put the rest of the ingredients in the Crock Pot Express™. Cover and lock the lid.
2. Press the "MEAT/STEW" key, and cook on pre-set time.
3. When the Crock Pot Express™ timer beeps, press the CANCEL key and turn the steam valve to quick release the pressure. Unlock and carefully open the lid.
4. Add the broccoli, loosely cover with the lid, and let sit for 15 minutes. Serve!

66. Garlic Teriyaki Beef

Preparation + Cook Time: 55 minutes | Servings: 4

Ingredients:
1 piece (2 pounds) flank steak
2 cloves garlic, finely chopped
For the teriyaki sauce:
2 tbsp fish sauce
¼ cup maple syrup, preferably organic grade B or higher
¼ cup coconut aminos OR soy sauce instead
1 tbsp raw honey
1 ½ tsp ground or fresh ginger, optional

Directions:
1. Slice the flank steak into 1/2-inch strips.
2. In a bowl, put all of the teriyaki sauce and mix until combined.
3. Put the steak strips and the sauce in the Crock Pot Express™ – there is no need to brown the meat. Add garlic. Cover and lock the lid.
4. Press the "BEANS/CHILI" key, set the pressure to HIGH, and set the timer for 40 minutes.
5. When the Crock Pot Express™ timer beeps, turn the steam valve to quick release the pressure. Unlock and carefully open the lid.
6. Serve and enjoy!

67. Barbecued Baby Back Ribs

Prep: 5 minutes • pressure: 32 minutes • total: 37 minutes • pressure level: high • release: natural • Serves 4

Ingredients

¼ cup canned tomato paste

2 tablespoons cider vinegar

1 tablespoon sweet paprika

½ tablespoon coriander seeds

½ tablespoon fennel seeds

1 teaspoon onion powder

1 teaspoon dried thyme

½ teaspoon ground allspice

½ teaspoon salt

½ teaspoon ground black pepper

¼ teaspoon celery seeds

One 4-pound rack baby back ribs, cut into 2 or 3 sections to fit in the cooker

Directions

1. Preparing the Ingredients Whisk the tomato paste, vinegar, paprika, coriander and fennel seeds, onion powder, thyme, allspice, salt, pepper, and celery seeds with ¾ cup water in an electric pressure cooker until the tomato paste dissolves. Add the ribs; toss to coat thoroughly and evenly in the sauce.

2. High pressure for 32 minutes. Lock the lid on the Crock-Pot Multi-Cooker® and then cook for 32 minutes. To get 32-minutes cook time, press "meat/stew" button and use the TIME ADJUSTMENT button to adjust the cook time to 32 minutes.

3. Pressure Release Let the pressure to come down naturally for at least 15 minutes, then quick release any pressure left in the pot.

4. Finish the dish Unlock and open the pot. Transfer the rib rack sections to a large rimmed baking sheet. Set the electric one to its browning function. Bring the sauce to a simmer. Cook, stirring occasionally, until the sauce has thickened, 3 to 5 minutes. Position the oven rack 4 to 6 inches from the broiler; heat the broiler. Brush a light coating of the sauce onto the ribs, then broil until glazed and hot, 6 to 8 minutes, turning once. Slice the racks between the bones to make individual ribs. Serve with the extra sauce on the side.

68. Beef Roast with Potatoes and Carrots

Preparation + Cook Time: 60 minutes | Servings: 6

Ingredients:

2-4 pound beef roast no longer than the width of the pressure cooker

1½ cups chicken stock

1 tbsp olive oil

2 pounds potatoes roughly cubed

1 pound carrots peeled

1 bunch parsley chopped

1 cup red wine

4 tbsp butter unsalted

2 tbsp thyme fresh

4 tbsp pistachio chopped

Optional Crust:

4 ounces pistachio nuts crushed, shelled and salted

1 tbsp black pepper

2 tbs fresh thyme

Directions:

1. Optional crusting: Start by making the rub. Crush the nuts well, and mix the pistachio powder with the black pepper and thyme. Reserve a quarter of the rub to garnish the roast after cooking. Press as much of the crust on the roast - some may fall off during cooking - but you will add another layer when the roast is finished. Reserve half of the rub to garnish the roast after cooking.
2. Preheat the Crock Pot Express™ by using the "Brown/Sauté" function. When "Hot" appears on the display, add a swirl of olive oil and sear the roast well on all sides. Deglaze the pot with the stock.
3. Close and lock the lid. Select "BEANS/CHILI" and cook at HIGH pressure for 45-50 minutes (depending on the thickness of your roast).
4. When time is up, open the Crock Pot Express™ using a quick release method.
5. Add the potatoes and place the whole carrots on top of the roast - do this quickly.
6. Close and lock the lid. Select "BEANS/CHILI" and cook at HIGH pressure for 10 minutes.
7. When time is up, open the Crock Pot Express™ using quick release.
8. Remove the carrots and transfer them to a serving plate, slicing them. Remove the potatoes with a slotted spoon and transfer to the serving plate.
9. Take out the roast and set it on a plate tented with aluminum foil to rest. While the roast is resting, make the au jus sauce.
10. Filter the cooking liquid through a fine sieve and put it back in the Crock Pot Express™. Add the wine and butter and reduce the liquid in the pressure cooker at high heat, without the pressure cooking lid, to about half. Add salt and pepper to taste. On the "Brown/Sauté" function, reduce the cooking liquid to about half its volume.
11. Slice up the roast and serve on a platter with the carrots and potatoes. Drizzle with the reduced cooking liquid and sprinkle with fresh thyme and nuts. Enjoy!

69. Lamb with Mexican Sauce

Prep: 10 minutes • pressure: 45 minutes • total: 55 minutes • pressure level: high • release: normal • Serves 3-4

Ingredients

3 lamb shoulder

1 Spanish onion
3 garlic cloves, minced
1 19 oz. can Old El Paso Enchilada sauce
2 Tbsp. oil
Salt to taste
Cilantro, chopped without the stems
Corn tortillas (3-4 per person)
Limes cut into 8ths
Black beans or refried beans
Chipotle style rice

Directions
1. **Preparing the Ingredients** Marinate lamb overnight in Old El Paso Enchilada sauce (mild, medium or hot).
   Turn on the Crock-Pot Multi-Cooker® to "sauté" mode.
   Add oil. Put in the onions and cook until soft, add garlic and cook for 1 minute.
   Add the lamb and marinade wait until boil.
2. **High pressure for 45 minutes**. Lock the lid on the Crock-Pot Multi-Cooker® and then cook for 45 minutes. To get 45-minutes cook time, press "meat/stew" button and use the TIME ADJUSTMENT button to adjust the cook time to 45 minutes.
3. **Pressure Release** Let the pressure to come down naturally for at least 15 minutes, then quick release any pressure left in the pot.
4. **Finish the dish**. Cut the limes, heat the beans, put the hot rice into a serving bowl.
   Set the Lamb aside. Ladle generous amount of sauce over it.
   Heat up 3-4 corn tortillas.
   Put the lamb mixture onto a soft warm corn tortilla, sprinkle on cilantro, then squeeze on lime juice.
5. Serve and Enjoy!

70. Korean Beef

Preparation + Cook Time: 75 minutes | Servings: 6

Ingredients:
4 pounds bottom roast, cut into cubes
1 apple, Granny Smith or pear, peeled and then chopped
2 tablespoons olive oil
½ cup soy sauce
1 tablespoon ginger, fresh grated
1 large orange OR
2 small orange, juice only
1 cup beef broth

5 cloves garlic, minced
Salt and pepper

Directions:
1. Season the roast cubes generously with pepper and salt. Press the "BROWN/SAUTÉ" key of the Crock Pot Express™.
2. When the pot is hot, coat with the olive oil. In batches, cook the meat until all sides are browned –transfer the browned meat into a plate while cooking.
3. When all the meat is browned, pour the beef broth in the pot and deglaze the pot – scrape the browned bits off from the bottom of the pot.
4. Pour the soy sauce in the pot and stir to mix. Return all the browned meat into the pot.
5. Add the ginger, garlic, and pear /apple on top of the meat. Lightly stir to combine slightly.
6. Add the orange juice.
7. Press the CANCEL key to stop the "Brown/Sauté" function. Cover and lock the lid. Press the "BEANS/CHILI" key, set the pressure to HIGH, and set the timer for 45 minutes.
8. When the Crock Pot Express™ timer beeps, turn the steam valve to Venting to quick release the pressure. Unlock and carefully open the lid.
9. Serve over rice or cauliflower rice.

71. Mongolian Beef

Preparation + Cook Time: 25 minutes | Servings: 4

Ingredients:
1½ pound Flank steak
1 carrot, shredded
1 garlic clove, minced
1 green onion, sliced, for garnish
1 tbsp olive oil
½ cup brown sugar
½ tsp fresh ginger, minced
¼ cup water
¾ cup soy sauce
To thicken the sauce:
3 tbsp water
3 tbsp cornstarch

Directions:
1. Slice the flank into the strips. In a bowl, combine the soy sauce with the oil, garlic, ginger, sugar, and water.
2. Pour the sauce in the Crock Pot Express™.

3. Add the shredded carrot and beef strips, and mix until the beef is coated with the sauce. Cover and lock the lid.
4. Press the "BEANS/CHILI" key, set the pressure to HIGH, and set the timer for 8 minutes.
5. When the Crock Pot Express™ timer beeps, press the CANCEL key and unplug the Crock Pot Express™.
6. Let the pressure release naturally for 10-15 minutes or until the valve drops. Turn the steam valve to release remaining pressure. Unlock and carefully open the lid.
7. In a small-sized bowl, combine the cornstarch with the water until there are no more lumps.
8. Press the "BROWN/SAUTÉ" key and pour cornstarch mixture into the pot. Boil for about 1 to 2 minutes or until the sauce is thick.
9. Serve on a platter and garnish with chopped green onions.

Main Dishes – Poultry

72. Enchilada-Braised Chicken Breasts

Prep: 5 minutes • pressure: 15 minutes • total: 19 minutes • pressure level: high • release: quick • Serves 4

Ingredients
1 teaspoon packed dark brown sugar
1 teaspoon ground cumin
1 teaspoon smoked paprika
½ teaspoon salt
½ teaspoon ground black pepper
½ teaspoon onion powder
¼ teaspoon garlic powder
Four 6- to 8-ounce boneless skinless chicken breasts
2 tablespoons olive oil
One 8-ounce can tomato sauce (1 cup)
½ cup light-colored beer, preferably a Pilsner or an IPA
2 tablespoons chili powder
2 tablespoons fresh lime juice

Directions
1. Preparing the Ingredients. Mix the brown sugar, cumin, smoked paprika, salt, pepper, onion powder, and garlic powder in a medium bowl. Massage the spice rub onto the chicken breasts.
   Heat the oil in the Crock-Pot Multi-Cooker® using the "Sauté" function. Set the breasts in the cooker and brown well, turning once, about 6 minutes.
   Mix the tomato sauce, beer, chili powder, and lime juice in the bowl the spices were in; pour the sauce over the breasts.
2. High pressure for 15 minutes Close the lid and Cook for 15 minutes. To get 15-minutes cook time, press the "Poultry" button.
3. Pressure Release Use the quick-release method to bring the pot's pressure back to normal.
4. Unlock and open the cooker. Serve the chicken with the sauce ladled on top.

73. Honey-Chipotle Chicken Wings

Prep: 5 minutes • pressure: 10 minutes • total: 15 minutes • pressure level: high • release: quick • Serves 2

Ingredients
1 cup water, for steaming

3 tablespoons Mexican hot sauce (such as Valentina brand)

2 tablespoons honey

1 teaspoon minced canned chipotle in adobo sauce

Directions
1. Preparing the Ingredients. If using whole wings, cut off the tips and discard. Cut the wings at the joint into two pieces each, the "drumette" and the "flat."
   Add the water and insert the steamer basket or trivet. Place the wings on the steamer insert.
2. High pressure for 10 minutes. Close the lid and the pressure valve and then cook for 10 minutes. To get 10-minutes cook time, press "Steam" button.
3. Pressure Release Use the quick-release method.
4. Finish the dish. While the wings are cooking, make the sauce. In a large bowl, whisk together the hot sauce, honey, and minced chipotle. Preheat the broiler, and place an oven rack in the top or second position.
   Unlock and remove the lid. Using tongs, carefully transfer the wing segments to the bowl with the sauce. Toss gently to coat. Transfer the wing segments to a baking rack placed over a sheet pan, or to a baking sheet lined with nonstick aluminum foil.
   Place the baking sheet under the broiler for 4 to 5 minutes, or until the wings start to brown, and serve.

PER SERVING: CALORIES: 434; FAT: 27G; SODIUM: 1,152MG; CARBOHYDRATES: 19G; FIBER: 1G; PROTEIN: 31G

74. One Pot Pressure Cooker Chicken And Rice

Prep: 10 minutes • pressure: 10 minutes • total: 20 minutes • pressure level: high • release: natural - Serves 2-4

Ingredients
6 dried shiitake mushrooms, marinated

6 - 8 chicken drumsticks, marinated

2 rice measuring cups (360 ml) Jasmine rice, rinse

1 teaspoon Salt

1½ cup (375 ml) water

1 tablespoon ginger, shredded

Green onions for garnish

Marinade:

1 tablespoon light soy sauce

1 teaspoon dark soy sauce

½ teaspoon sugar

½ teaspoon corn starch
1 teaspoon Shaoxing rice wine
A dash of white pepper powder
1 tablespoon ginger, shredded
1 teaspoon five spice powder

Directions

1. Preparing the Ingredients. Place the dried shiitake mushrooms in a small bowl. Rehydrate them with cold water for 20 minutes.

   Chop the drumsticks into 2 pieces. Then, marinate the chicken and mushrooms with the marinade sauce for 20 minutes.

   Rinse rice under cold water by gently scrubbing the rice with your fingertips in a circling motion. Pour out the milky water, and continue to rinse until the water is clear. Then, drain the water.

   Add the rice, 1 teaspoon of salt, and marinated chicken and mushrooms, and 1½ cup of water in the Crock-Pot Multi-Cooker®.

2. High pressure for 10 minutes. Lock the lid on the Crock-Pot Multi-Cooker® and then cook for 10 minutes. To get 10-minutes cook time, press "Multigrain" button.

3. Pressure Release Let the pressure to come down naturally for at least 15 minutes, then quick release any pressure left in the pot.

4. Serve immediately.

75. Lemon and Olive Ligurian Chicken

Prep: 10 minutes • pressure: 15 minutes • total: 25 minutes • pressure level: high • release: normal • Serves 6-8

Ingredients
  2 garlic cloves, chopped
  3 sprigs of Fresh Rosemary (two for chopping, one for garnish)
  2 sprigs of Fresh Sage
  ½ bunch of Parsley Leaves and stems
  3 lemons, juiced (about ¾ cup or 180ml)
  4 tablespoons extra virgin olive oil
  1 teaspoon sea salt
  ¼ teaspoon pepper
  1 whole chicken, cut into parts or package of bone-in chicken pieces, skin removed (or not) ½ cup (125ml) dry white wine
  3.5oz (100g) Black Gourmet Salt-Cured Olives (Taggiesche , French, or Kalamata)
  1 fresh lemon, for garnish (optional)

Directions

1. **Preparing the Ingredients.** Prepare the marinade by finely chopping together the garlic, rosemary, sage, and parsley. Place them in a container and add the lemon juice, olive oil, salt and pepper. Mix well and set aside.

   Remove the skin from the chicken (save it for a chicken stock).

   In the preheated Crock-Pot Multi-Cooker®, with the lid off, add a swirl of olive oil and brown the chicken pieces on all sides for about 5 minutes.

   De-glaze cooker with the white wine until it has almost all evaporated (about 3 minutes).

   Add the chicken pieces back in - this time being careful with the order. Put all dark-meat (wings, legs, thighs) first, and then the chicken breasts on top so that they do not touch the bottom of the Crock-Pot Multi-Cooker ®.

   Pour the remaining marinade on top. Don't worry if this does not seem like enough liquid, the chicken will also release its juices into the cooker, too.

2. **High pressure for 10 minutes.** Lock the lid on the Crock-Pot Multi-Cooker® and then cook for 10 minutes. To get 10-minutes cook time, press "Multigrain" button.

3. **Pressure Release.** When time is up, open the cooker by releasing the pressure using the Quick-Release Method.

4. **Finish the dish.** Take the chicken pieces out of the cooker and place on a serving platter tightly covered with foil.

   Reduce the cooking liquid in the Crock-Pot Multi-Cooker ®, with the lid off to ¼ of its amount, or until it becomes thick and syrupy.

   Put all of the chicken pieces back into the Crock-Pot Multi-Cooker® to warm up. Mix and spoon the thick glaze onto the chicken pieces and simmer it in the glaze for a few minutes before serving.

   Sprinkle with fresh rosemary, olives and lemon slices. When serving, caution your guests that the olives still have their pits!

   Per Serving Calories: 204.8; Fat: 12.2g; Carbohydrates: 3.1g; Sugar: 0.7g; Fiber: 0.3g; Protein: 17.8g; Sodium: 449.5mg; Cholesterol: 61.6mg

76. Chicken with Artichoke Hearts and Mushrooms

Prep: 5 Minutes • Pressure: 12 Minutes • Total: 17 Minutes • Pressure Level: High • Release: Natural • SERVES 4-6

Ingredients
   ½ teaspoon kosher salt
   2 (8-ounce) or 4 (4-ounce) bone-in, skin-on chicken thighs
   1 tablespoon olive oil
   ¼ cup sliced onion
   4 ounces white button or cremini mushrooms, trimmed and quartered
   ½ cup dry white wine
   1 bay leaf
   ¼ teaspoon dried thyme
   ½ cup frozen artichoke hearts, thawed
   ⅓ cup low-sodium chicken broth

Freshly ground black pepper

Directions

1. **Preparing the Ingredients.** Using ½ teaspoon of kosher salt, sprinkle the chicken thighs on both sides.

   In the Crock-Pot Multi-Cooker® set to "browning", heat the olive oil until it shimmers and flows like water. Add the chicken thighs, skin-side down, and cook, undisturbed, for about 6 minutes, or until the skin is dark golden brown and most of the fat under the skin has rendered. Turn the thighs to the other side, and cook for about 3 minutes more, or until that side is light golden brown. Remove the thighs.

   Carefully pour off almost all the fat, leaving just enough (about 1 tablespoon) to cover the bottom of the Crock-Pot Multi-Cooker ® with a thick coat. Add the onion and mushrooms, and cook for about 5 minutes, or until softened. Add the white wine, and cook for 3 to 5 minutes, or until reduced by half. Add the bay leaf, thyme, artichokes, and chicken broth, and bring to a simmer. Return the chicken to the pot, skin-side up.

2. **High pressure for 12 minutes**. Lock the lid on the Crock-Pot Multi-Cooker® and then cook for 12 minutes. To get 12-minutes cook time, press "Soup" Button and use the TIME ADJUSTMENT button to adjust the cook time to 12 minutes.

3. **Pressure Release.** After cooking, use the natural method to release pressure.

4. **Finish the dish.** Unlock and remove the lid. Remove the chicken thighs from the pan, and set aside. Remove the bay leaf. Strain the sauce into a fat separator, and let it rest until the fat rises to the surface. If you don't have a fat separator, let the sauce sit for a few minutes; then spoon or blot off any excess fat from the top and discard. Pour the defatted sauce back into the cooker, and add the chicken thighs and the solids from the sauce. If you prefer a thicker sauce, turn the Crock-Pot Multi-Cooker ® to the "Sauté" function, and simmer the sauce for several minutes until it's reduced to the consistency you like.

   Adjust the seasoning, adding more salt if necessary and several grinds of pepper, and serve.

PER SERVING: CALORIES: 612; FAT: 38G; SODIUM: 1,269MG; CARBOHYDRATES: 19G; FIBER: 3G; PROTEIN: 37G

77. Chicken Breasts With White Wine And Orange Juice

Prep: 5 minutes • pressure: 18 minutes • total: 25 minutes • pressure level: high • release: quick • Serves 4

Ingredients

3 tablespoons unsalted butter

Four 12-ounce bone-in, skin-on chicken breasts

½ teaspoon salt

½ teaspoon ground black pepper
½ cup fresh orange juice
½ cup dry but light white wine, such as Sauvignon Blanc
One 4-inch fresh rosemary sprig
1 tablespoon honey
½ tablespoon potato starch or cornstarch

Directions

1. **Preparing the Ingredients.** Melt the butter in a Crock-Pot Multi-Cooker®, turned to the browning function. Season the chicken with the salt and pepper, then add two breasts skin side down to the cooker. Brown well, turning once, about 5 minutes; transfer to a large bowl. Brown the remaining breasts, and leave them in the cooker.

   Return the first two breasts to the cooker, arranging them so that all are skin up but overlapping only as necessary, thinner parts over thick. Pour the orange juice and wine over the chicken. Tuck in the rosemary and drizzle everything with honey.

2. **High pressure for 18 minutes.** Lock the lid on the Crock-Pot Multi-Cooker® and then cook for 18 minutes. To get 18-minutes cook time, press Rice/Risotto button and use the TIME ADJUSTMENT button to adjust the cook time to 18 minutes.

3. **Pressure Release** Use the quick-release method to bring the pot's pressure back to normal.

4. **Finish the dish.** Unlock and open the pot. Discard the rosemary sprig. Use kitchen tongs to transfer the chicken breasts to individual serving plates or a serving platter.

   Dissolve the potato starch or cornstarch with ½ tablespoon water in a small bowl. Turn the electric cooker to its browning function, bring the sauce to a simmer. Add this slurry and cook, stirring all the time, until thickened, about 20 seconds. Ladle the sauce over the chicken to serve.

78. Chicken Congee
Preparation + Cook Time: 65 minutes | Servings: 7)

Ingredients:
6 chicken drumsticks
7 cups water
1 cup Jasmine rice
1 tbsp fresh ginger
Salt to taste

Directions:
1. Rinse rice under cool water for a few minutes.
2. Pour rice, water, ginger, and drumsticks into Crock Pot Express™. Seal the lid.
3. Select "BEANS/CHILI" and cook at HIGH pressure for 30 minutes.
4. When time is up, press CANCEL and wait for a natural pressure release.
5. When safe, open the lid and press "BROWN/SAUTÉ".

6. Keep stirring while the congee thickens.
7. Season with salt.
8. Pull off the chicken with tongs, and throw away the bones.
9. Serve right away!

79. Lemongrass Chicken

Preparation time: **10 minutes** - Cooking time: **20 minutes** - Servings: **5**

Ingredients:
1 bunch lemongrass, bottom removed and trimmed
1-inch piece ginger root, peeled and chopped
4 garlic cloves, peeled and crushed
2 tablespoons fish sauce
3 tablespoons coconut aminos
1 teaspoon Chinese five spice powder
10 chicken drumsticks
1 cup coconut milk
Salt and ground black pepper, to taste
1 teaspoon butter
¼ cup cilantro, diced
1 yellow onion, peeled and chopped
1 tablespoon lime juice

Directions:
1. In a food processor, mix the lemongrass with the ginger, garlic, aminos, fish sauce, and five spice powder, and pulse well. Add the coconut milk and pulse again. Set the Crock pot Express™ on "Brown/Sauté" mode, add the butter and melt it. Add the onion, stir, and cook for 5 minutes. Add the chicken, salt, and pepper, stir, and cook for 1 minute. Add the coconut milk and lemongrass mix, stir,
2. Cover, set on "Poultry" mode, and cook for 15 minutes. Release the pressure, uncover, add more salt and pepper and lime juice, stir, divide among plates, and serve with cilantro sprinkled on top.

80. Salsa Chicken

Preparation time: **10 minutes** - Cooking time: **25 minutes** - Servings: **5**

Ingredients:
1 pound chicken breast, skinless and boneless

¾ teaspoon cumin
Salt and ground black pepper, to taste
Dried oregano
1 cup chunky salsa

Directions:
1. Season the chicken with salt and pepper to taste and add it to the Crock pot Express™. Add the oregano, cumin, and the salsa, stir,
2. Cover, set the Crock pot Express™ on "Poultry" mode and cook for 25 minutes. Release the pressure, transfer the chicken and salsa to a bowl, shred meat with a fork, and serve with some tortillas on the side.

81. Chicken Korma

Preparation + Cook Time: 25 minutes | Servings: 6

Ingredients:
1 pound chicken breasts and/or legs, boneless and skinless or with bones, as you prefer
For the Sauce:
1 ounce cashews raw, or substitute with almonds if you prefer
1 small onion chopped
½ cup tomatoes diced
½ green Serrano pepper Jalapeño, or Thai chili pepper
5 cloves garlic
1 tsp Ginger minced
1 tsp turmeric
1 tsp salt
1 tsp garam masala
1 tsp cumin-coriander powder
½ tsp cayenne pepper adjust to your preference
½ cup water (use this to slosh about in the blender jar and then pour it into the pressure cooker)
For Finishing:
1 tsp garam masala
½ cup coconut milk full fat, add more if you'd like
¼ cup cilantro chopped

Directions:
1. Blend together all ingredients listed under "For the Sauce" (all ingredients excluding chicken, garam masala, coconut milk and cilantro).
2. Pour the sauce into the Crock Pot Express™. Place the chicken on top. If your chicken is frozen, just push it down into the sauce a little

3. Cook on the "Beans/Chili" Setting at HIGH pressure for 10 minutes. When time is up, wait 15 minutes for a natural pressure release.
4. Open the lid and carefully take out the chicken and cut into bite size pieces. Add coconut milk and garam masala into the pot and stir.
5. Put the chicken back in, serve and garnish with cilantro if you'd like. Enjoy!

82. hicken Sandwiches

Preparation time: **10 minutes** - Cooking time: **15 minutes -** Servings: **8**

Ingredients:
6 chicken breasts, skinless and boneless
12 ounces orange juice
2 tablespoons lemon juice
15 ounces canned peaches with juice
1 teaspoon soy sauce
20 ounces canned pineapple with juice, chopped
1 tablespoon cornstarch
¼ cup brown sugar
8 hamburger buns
8 grilled pineapple slices, for serving

Directions:
1. In a bowl, mix the orange juice with the soy sauce, lemon juice, canned pineapple, peaches, and sugar and stir well. Pour half of this mixture into the Crock pot Express™, add the chicken and pour the rest of the sauce over meat.
2. Cover the Crock pot Express™ and cook on the "Poultry" setting for 15 minutes. Release the pressure, take out the chicken and put it on a cutting board. Shred the meat and set the dish aside. In a bowl, mix the cornstarch with 1 tablespoon cooking juice and stir well. Transfer the sauce to a pot, add the cornstarch mix and chicken, stir, and cook for a few minutes. Divide this chicken mix onto hamburger buns, top with grilled pineapple pieces, and serve.

83. Chicken BBQ

Preparation + Cook Time: 30 minutes | Servings: 6

Ingredients:
4-5 pound chicken thighs, bone-in or boneless, skinless, fat trimmed off
2 garlic cloves, chopped
1/8 tsp pepper, or more to taste
¼ tsp salt, or more to taste
½ cup PLUS 1½ tbsp water, divided

½ cup barbecue sauce (use your favorite)
1 tbsp olive oil
1 onion, medium-sized, chopped
1½ tbsp cornstarch

Directions:
1. Press the "BROWN/SAUTÉ" key of the Crock Pot Express™. Add the oil and heat.
2. Add the garlic and onion and sauté for about 1 to 2 minutes or until soft.
3. Stir in the 1/2 cup of water and barbecue sauce.
4. With the meaty side faced up, add the chicken in the pot. Press the CANCEL key to stop the "Brown/Sauté" function. Cover and lock the lid.
5. Press the "BEANS/CHILI" key, set the pressure to HIGH, and set the timer for 10 minutes.
6. When the Crock Pot Express™ timer beeps, let the pressure release naturally. Turn the steam valve to release remaining pressure.
7. Unlock and carefully open the lid. Preheat the broiler. Grease a broiler pan and transfer the chicken into the greased pan.
8. Generously season both sides with salt and pepper. Arrange the chicken in the pan with the meaty side faced down. Set aside.
9. Press the "BROWN/SAUTÉ" key of the Crock Pot Express™. Bring the cooking liquid in pot to a boil. In a small-sized bowl, combine the cornstarch with 1 ½ tablespoon of water until smooth.
10. When the cooking liquid is boiling, add about ½ of the cornstarch mix into the pot, stir until the sauce is thick.
11. Add more cornstarch mix, if needed. Simmer the sauce until thick. Taste the sauce and, if needed, season with salt and pepper to taste.
12. Turn off the Crock Pot Express™. Brush the top of the chicken with the sauce.
13. Turn the oven setting to broil, and preheat the broiler 10 to 15 minutes before cooking.
14. Place the pan 6 inches from the heat source and broil for about 2-3 minutes or until the chicken is glazed.
15. Remove the pan from the oven, flip the chicken, and brush the other side with the sauce.
16. Return the pan to the oven and broil for 2-3 minutes more or until the other side is glazed. Serve the chicken barbecue while it's still hot.
17. Serve the remaining sauce on the side.

84. Moroccan Chicken

Preparation time: **10 minutes** - Cooking time: **25 minutes** - Servings: **4**

Ingredients:

6 chicken thighs

2 tablespoons extra virgin olive oil
10 cardamom pods
2 bay leaves
½ teaspoon coriander
1 teaspoon cloves
½ teaspoon cumin
½ teaspoon ground ginger
½ teaspoon turmeric
½ teaspoon ground cinnamon
1 teaspoon paprika
2 yellow onions, peeled and chopped
2 tablespoons tomato paste
5 garlic cloves, peeled and chopped
¼ cup white wine
1 cup green olives
1 cup chicken stock
¼ cup dried cranberries
Juice of 1 lemon
½ cup parsley, diced

Directions:
1. In a bowl, mix the bay leaf with the cardamom, cloves, coriander, ginger, cumin, cinnamon, turmeric, and paprika and stir. Set the Crock pot Express™ on "Brown/Sauté" mode, add the oil and heat up. Add the chicken thighs, brown for a few minutes, and transfer to a plate. Add the onion to the Crock pot Express™, stir, and cook for 4 minutes. Add the garlic, stir and cook for 1 minute. Add the wine, tomato paste, spices from the bowl, stock, and chicken. Stir,
2. Cover and cook on the "Poultry" setting for 15 minutes. Release the pressure, discard bay leaf, cardamom, and cloves, add the olives, cranberries, lemon juice, and parsley, stir, divide the chicken mixture among plates, and serve.

85. Chicken Drumsticks BBQ
Preparation + Cook Time: 35 minutes | Servings: 4-6

Ingredients:
4-10 chicken drumsticks
¾ cup water
¼ cup sweet paprika
4½ tsp black pepper freshly ground
1 tbsp salt
1½ tsp celery salt
1½ tsp cayenne pepper
1½ tsp garlic powder

1½ tsp dry mustard
1½ tsp ground cumin

Directions:
1. Add 3/4 cup of water in the Crock Pot Express™. Place the trivet inside.
2. Place the chicken drumsticks on the trivet. Close the lid tightly and close the vent.
3. Press "POULTRY" function on the Crock Pot Express™ and set the time to 20 minutes.
4. Preheat the oven to Broil. Line a cookie sheet with parchment paper.
5. When the timer goes off, release pressure naturally. Open the lid and take out the drumsticks.
6. Coat the drumsticks with the BBQ rub evenly.
7. Place the drumsticks on the lined cookie sheet (or tinfoil). Broil the drumsticks for 2 minutes per side or until the skin is browned. Be careful not to burn them.
8. Serve immediately. Enjoy!

86. Cacciatore Chicken

Preparation time: **10 minutes** - Cooking time: **15 minutes** - Servings: **4**

Ingredients:
1 cup chicken stock
Salt, to taste
8 chicken drumsticks
1 bay leaf
1 teaspoon garlic powder
1 yellow onion, peeled chopped
28 ounces canned crushed tomatoes
1 teaspoon dried oregano
½ cup black olives, pitted and sliced

Directions:
1. Set the Crock pot Express™ on "Brown/Sauté" mode, add the stock, bay leaf, and salt and stir. Add the chicken, garlic powder, onion, oregano, and crushed tomatoes, stir,
2. Cover the Crock pot Express™ and cook on the "Poultry" setting for 15 minutes. Release the pressure naturally, uncover the Crock pot Express™, discard the bay leaf, divide the cacciatore chicken among plates, drizzle cooking liquid on top, sprinkle with the olives, and serve.

87. Chicken Pina Colada

Preparation + Cook Time: 35 minutes | Servings: 4

Ingredients:
1 cup pineapple chunks, frozen or fresh
2 pounds chicken thighs, organic, cut into 1-inch chunks
1/8 tsp salt
½ cup green onion, chopped, for garnish
½ cup coconut cream, full fat
1 tsp cinnamon
2 tbsp coconut aminos (or soy sauce)
Optional:
1 tsp arrowroot starch
1 tbsp water.

Directions:
1. Except for the green onions, put all of the ingredients in the Crock Pot Express™. Cover and lock the lid.
2. Press the "POULTRY" key and cook on preset HIGH pressure and 15 minutes cooking time.
3. When the Crock Pot Express™ timer beeps, press the CANCEL key and turn off the Crock Pot Express™.
4. Let the pressure release naturally for 10-15 minutes or until the valve drops.
5. Turn the steam valve to Venting to release remaining pressure. Unlock and carefully open the lid. Stir to mix.
6. If you want a thick sauce, stir in 1 teaspoon arrowroot starch with 1 tablespoon water.
7. Press the "BROWN/SAUTÉ" key of the Crock Pot Express™.
8. Add the arrowroot starch mixture into the pot and cook until thick to preferred thickness.
9. Turn the Crock Pot Express™ off.
10. Serve garnished with green onions.

Notes: To make your own coconut cream, simply place a can of full fat coconut milk in the fridge overnight. When ready to use, open can from bottom and drain out coconut water (you can drink it or discard it). You will be left with pure coconut cream in the can.

88. Honey Barbecue Chicken Wings

Preparation time: **10 minutes** - Cooking time: **25 minutes** - Servings: **4**

Ingredients:
2 pounds chicken wings
Salt and ground black pepper, to taste

¾ cup honey barbecue sauce
Cayenne pepper
½ cup apple juice
1 teaspoon red pepper flakes
2 teaspoons paprika
½ cup water
½ teaspoon dried basil
½ cup brown sugar

Directions:
1. Put the chicken wings into the Crock pot Express™. Add the barbecue sauce, apple juice, salt, pepper, red pepper, paprika, basil, sugar, and water. Stir,
2. Cover, and cook on the "Poultry" setting for 10 minutes. Release the pressure, uncover the Crock pot Express™, transfer chicken to a baking sheet, add the sauce all over, place under a preheated broiler, broil for 7 minutes, turn the chicken wings, broil for 7 minutes, divide among plates, and serve.

89. Chicken Alfredo Pasta
Preparation + Cook Time: 5 minutes | Servings: 3

Ingredients:
8-ounces fettuccine
One 15-ounce jar of Alfredo sauce
2 cups water
1 cup cooked + diced chicken
2 tsp chicken seasoning

Directions:
1. Break your pasta in half so it fits in the cooker.
2. Add pasta, water, and chicken seasoning to Crock Pot Express™.
3. Seal the lid. Select STEAM and cook at HIGH pressure for 3 minutes.
4. When the timer beeps, press CANCEL and use a quick release.
5. Drain the pasta and add to serving bowl.
6. Mix in Alfredo sauce and chicken. Serve!

90. Sweet and Tangy Chicken

Preparation time: **10 minutes** - Cooking time: **10 minutes** - Servings: **4**

Ingredients:
2 pounds chicken thighs, boneless and skinless

½ cup fish sauce

1 cup lime juice

2 tablespoons coconut nectar

¼ cup extra virgin olive oil

1 teaspoon ginger, grated

2 teaspoons cilantro, diced

1 teaspoon fresh mint, chopped

Directions:

1. Put chicken thighs into the Crock pot Express™. In a bowl, mix the lime juice with the fish sauce, olive oil, coconut nectar, ginger, mint, and cilantro and whisk well. Pour this over the chicken, cover the Crock pot Express™.

2. Cook on the Benas/Chili setting for 10 minutes. Release the pressure, divide the chicken among plates, and serve.

91. Chicken with Cherries & Pumpkin Seed Wild Rice

Preparation + Cook Time: 55 minutes | Servings: 4-8

Ingredients:

1 cup balsamic vinegar

½ cup evaporated palm sugar

1 tbsp molasses

¼ cup butter melted

1 orange peeled and quartered

1 onion julienned

12 chicken thighs

¼ tsp sea salt

4 sprigs rosemary

2 cups Bing Cherries pitted and halved fresh

4 cups vegetable stock low sodium

1 1/3 cups wild rice rinsed

¼ cup butter

1 onion minced

2 plum tomatoes diced

½ cup pumpkin seeds toasted

Sea salt to taste

Directions:

1. In the inner pot of the Crock Pot Express™ add the balsamic vinegar, evaporated palm sugar, molasses, butter, orange and onion. Mix well.

2. Add the chicken, salt and rosemary. Stir to coat.

3. Add 1½ cups of cherries. Place the lid on the pressure cooker and lock into place. Press the "MEAT/STEW" button; adjust pressure cooking time to 25 minutes.
4. When done and pressure has naturally released, remove the lid.
5. While the chicken is cooking: Bring veggie stock to boil in a medium saucepan on the stove top. Add rinsed wild rice. Cover and simmer for 50 minutes.
6. In a large sauté pan, heat the butter. Sauté onion until caramelized.
7. Add tomato and sauté for 3 to 4 minutes. Add onions and tomato to the rice.
8. Add 1/2 cup of cherries to the sauté pan and sauté for 3 to 4 minutes until soft and juicy.
9. Add cherries and toasted pumpkin seeds to the rice. Stir to incorporate. Add salt if needed.
10. Place wild rice on a serving platter and top with chicken. Pour juices from the chicken over the entire platter and garnish with rosemary. Enjoy!

92. Turkey Chili

Preparation time: **10 minutes** - Cooking time: **10 minutes** - Servings: **4**

Ingredients:
1 pound turkey meat, ground
Salt and ground black pepper, to taste
5 ounces water
15 ounces chickpeas, already cooked
1 yellow onion, peeled and chopped
1 yellow bell pepper, seeded and chopped
3 garlic cloves, peeled and chopped
2½ tablespoons chili powder
1½ teaspoons cumin
Cayenne pepper
12 ounces vegetable stock

Directions:
1. Put the turkey meat into the Crock pot Express™. Add the water, stir, cover and cook on the "Poultry" setting for 5 minutes. Release the pressure, uncover the Crock pot Express™ and add the chickpeas, bell pepper, onion, garlic, chili powder, cumin, salt, pepper, cayenne pepper, and stock. Stir,
2. Cover the Crock pot Express™, and cook on the "Beans/Chili" setting for 5 minutes. Release the pressure for 10 minutes, uncover the Crock pot Express™ again, stir the chili, divide it among plates, and serve.

94. Chicken Romano

Ingredients:

6 chicken thighs, boneless and skinless and cut into medium chunks
Salt and ground black pepper, to taste
½ cup white flour
2 tablespoons vegetable oil
10 ounces tomato sauce
1 teaspoon white wine vinegar
4 ounces mushrooms, sliced
1 tablespoon sugar
1 tablespoon dried oregano
1 teaspoon garlic, minced
1 teaspoon dried basil
1 teaspoon chicken bouillon granules
1 yellow onion, peeled and chopped
1 cup Romano cheese, grated

Directions:
1. Set the Crock pot Express™ on "Brown/Sauté" mode, add the oil and heat it up. Add the chicken pieces, stir, and brown them for 2 minutes. Add the onion and garlic, stir, and cook for 3 minutes. Add the salt, pepper, flour, and stir well. Add the tomato sauce, vinegar, mushrooms, sugar, oregano, basil and bouillon granules, stir,
2. Cover, and cook on the "Beans/Chili" setting for 10 minutes. Release the pressure for 10 minutes, uncover the Crock pot Express™, add the cheese, stir, divide among plates, and serve.

93. One Pot Chinese Chicken and Rice

Preparation + Cook Time: 60 minutes | Servings: 4

Ingredients:

6 shiitake mushrooms dried, marinated
6 - 8 chicken drumsticks, marinated
3 cups jasmine rice rinsed
1 tsp salt
1½ cups water
Ginger shredded, for garnish
Green onions sliced, for garnish
Marinade:
1 tbsp light soy sauce
1 tsp dark soy sauce
½ tsp sugar
½ tsp corn starch

1 tsp Shaoxing rice wine
Dash white pepper powder
1 tbsp Ginger shredded
1 tsp five spice powder

Directions:
1. Place the dried shiitake mushrooms in a small bowl. Rehydrate them with cold water for 20 minutes.
2. Chop the drumsticks into 2 pieces. Then, marinate the chicken and mushrooms with the marinade sauce for 20 minutes.
3. Rinse rice under cold water by gently scrubbing the rice with your fingertips in a circling motion. Pour out the milky water, and continue to rinse until the water is clear. Then, drain the water.
4. Add the rice, 1 teaspoon of salt, marinated chicken and mushrooms, and 1½ cups of water in the Crock Pot Express™.
5. Close the lid. Select "BEANS/CHILI" and cook at HIGH pressure for 9 minutes.
6. When time is up, use natural pressure release for 15 minutes. Serve immediately.

94. Filipino Chicken

Preparation time: **10 minutes** - Cooking time: **15 minutes** - Servings: **4**

Ingredients:
- 5 pounds chicken thighs
- Salt and ground black pepper, to taste
- ½ cup white vinegar
- 1 teaspoon black peppercorns, crushed
- 4 garlic cloves, minced
- 3 bay leaves
- ½ cup soy sauce

Directions:
1. Set the Crock pot Express™ on "Poultry" mode, add the chicken, vinegar, soy sauce, salt, pepper, garlic, peppercorns, and bay leaves, stir,
2. Cover, and cook on the "Beans/Chili" setting for 15 Minutes. Release the pressure for 10 minutes, uncover the Crock pot Express™, discard the bay leaves, stir, divide the chicken between plates, and serve.

95. Filipino Chicken Adobo

Preparation + Cook Time: 55 minutes | Servings: 4

Ingredients:

6 chicken drumsticks or two pounds of chicken

1 tbsp oil

Green onions chopped for garnish

Sauce:

¼ cup Filipino soy sauce

½ cup light soy sauce

¼ cup Filipino vinegar

1 tbsp fish sauce

1 tbsp sugar

Spice:

10 cloves garlic crushed

1 small onion minced

1 tsp black peppercorn ground

1 red chili dried

4 bay leaves dried

1 tsp cornstarch mixed with 1 tbsp water, optional

Directions:

1. Combine Filipino soy sauce, light soy sauce, Filipino vinegar, fish sauce and sugar in a medium mixing bowl.
2. Press the "Brown/Sauté" function. Add oil to the Crock Pot Express™ and brown the chicken for 1 to 2 minutes with the skin side down first. Then, remove the chicken from the pot.
3. Sauté garlic and onion in the pot until fragrant and golden in color. Then, add ground black peppercorn, red chili, and bay leaves to the pot and sauté for 30 seconds.
4. Add the Sauce mixture and deglaze the pot.
5. Cook on the "Beans/Chili" Setting at HIGH pressure for 9 minutes, then use a natural release.
6. Optional: remove the chicken from the pot. Simmer the sauce using the "Brown/Sauté" function and add cornstarch mixture until the sauce is reduced.
7. Optional: Brown the chicken underneath a broiler with the skin side up for 5 minutes.
8. Place the chicken on serving plate, pour in the Sauce mixture, add chopped green onions for garnish.
9. Serve and enjoy!

96. Chicken in Tomatillo Sauce

Preparation time: **10 minutes** - Cooking time: **15 minutes** - Servings: **6**

Ingredients:
1 pound chicken thighs, skinless and boneless
2 tablespoons extra virgin olive oil
1 yellow onion, peeled and sliced thinly
1 garlic clove, peeled and crushed
4 ounces canned chopped green chilies
½ cup cilantro, diced
Salt and ground black pepper, to taste
15 ounces canned tomatillos, chopped
5 ounces canned garbanzo beans, drained
15 ounces rice, already cooked
5 ounces tomatoes, cored and chopped
15 ounces cheddar cheese, grated
4 ounces black olives, pitted and chopped

Directions:
1. Set the Crock pot Express™ on "Brown/Sauté" mode, add the oil, and heat it up. Add the onions, stir, and cook for 5 minutes. Add the garlic, stir, and cook for 15 seconds. Add the chicken, chilies, salt, pepper, cilantro, and tomatillos, stir,
2. Cover the Crock pot Express™, and cook on "Beans/Chili" mode for 8 minutes. Release the pressure, uncover the Crock pot Express™, take the chicken out and shred it. Return the chicken to pot, add rice, beans, set the Crock pot Express™ on "Brown/Sauté" mode, and cook for 1 minute. Add the cheese, tomatoes, and olives, stir, cook for 2 minutes, divide among plates, and serve.

97. Cordon Blue Chicken Casserole
Preparation + Cook Time: 50 minutes | Servings: 8

Ingredients:
1 cup panko bread crumbs
1 pound chicken breast, boneless, skinless, sliced into thin strips
1 pound ham, cubed
1 tbsp spicy mustard
16 ounces Rotini pasta
16 ounces Swiss cheese
2 cups chicken broth
2 tbsp butter
8 ounces Gouda cheese
8 ounces heavy cream

Directions:
1. Put the uncooked pasta in the Crock Pot Express™. Cover the pasta with 2 cups of chicken broth.

2. Put the chicken strips and ham cubes on top. Cover and lock the lid.
3. Press the "BEANS/CHILI" key, set the pressure to HIGH, and set the timer for 25 minutes.
4. When the Crock Pot Express™ timer beeps, press the CANCEL key and unplug the Crock Pot Express™. Turn the steam valve to quick release the pressure. Unlock and carefully open the lid.
5. Pour the mustard and heavy cream in the pot. Add both the cheeses in the pot and stir until smooth and creamy. In a small-sized pan, add the butter and melt.
6. When the butter is melted, add the bread crumbs and stir for about 2 to 3 minutes or until golden and toasty.
7. Serve the pasta mixture sprinkled with the toasted bread on top.

98. Braised Duck and Potatoes

Preparation time: **10 minutes** - Cooking time: **20 minutes** - Servings: **4**

Ingredients:
2 duck breasts, boneless, skinless, and cut into small chunks
Ground black pepper, to taste
1 potato, cut into cubes
1-inch ginger root, peeled and sliced
4 garlic cloves, peeled and minced
4 tablespoons sugar
4 tablespoons soy sauce
2 green onions, roughly chopped
4 tablespoons sherry wine
Salt, to taste
¼ cup water

Directions:
1. Set the Crock pot Express™ on "Brown/Sauté" mode, add the duck, stir, and brown it for a few minutes. Add the garlic, ginger, green onions, soy sauce, sugar, wine, water, and a pinch of salt and black pepper, stir,
2. Cover, set the Crock pot Express™ to "Poultry" mode, and cook for 18 minutes. Release the pressure, uncover the Crock pot Express™, add the potatoes, stir,
3. Cover, and cook on the "Steam" setting for 5 minutes. Release the pressure, divide the braised duck among plates, and serve.

99. Salt Baked Chicken
Preparation + Cook Time: 50 minutes | Servings: 8

Ingredients:
2 tsp sand ginger dried, Kaempferia Galanga or Zeodary Powder
1¼ tsp kosher salt
¼ tsp five spice powder
Dash white pepper optional, ground

Directions:
1. Season the chicken legs by placing the chicken legs in a large mixing bowl. Pour in 2 teaspoons of dried sand ginger, 1¼ teaspoon of kosher salt, and 1/4 teaspoon of five spice powder. Mix well.
2. Place the seasoned chicken legs on a large piece of parchment paper (Do NOT use aluminum foil). Wrap it up tightly and place it on a shallow dish with the opening side facing upwards. Do not stack more than 2 levels of chicken legs.
3. Place a steamer rack in the pressure cooker and pour in 1 cup of water. Carefully place the chicken legs dish onto the rack.
4. Close the lid and cook on the "Beans/Chili" Setting at HIGH Pressure for 18 – 26 minutes, then natural release for 20 minutes (turn off the heat and do NOT touch it). Open the lid carefully. Remove the dish from the pressure cooker and unwrap the parchment paper carefully
5. Optional Step: Pour out all the juice on a small bowl (don't throw it away!), then place the chicken legs on a wire rack on top of an oven tray. Put it under the broiler until the skin is browned but not dried out.
6. Serve immediately. The remaining meat juice can be used as a dipping sauce for the chicken. Taste and add more dried sand ginger to your liking. Enjoy!

100. Duck and Vegetables

Preparation time: **10 minutes** - Cooking time: **40 minutes** - Servings: **8**

Ingredients:
1 duck, chopped into eight pieces
1 cucumber, chopped
1 tablespoon wine
2 carrots, peeled and chopped
2 cups water
Salt and ground black pepper, to taste
1-inch ginger piece, peeled and chopped

Directions:
1. Put the duck pieces into the Crock pot Express™. Add the cucumber, carrots, wine, water, ginger, salt, and pepper, stir,

2. Cover, and cook on "Poultry" mode for 40 minutes. Use the Natural Release Method, divide the mix among plates, and serve.

101. Crack Chicken

Preparation + Cook Time: 40 minutes | Servings: 4

Ingredients:
8 ounces cream cheese
6-8 bacon slices, cooked
4 ounces cheddar cheese
3 tbsp cornstarch
2 pounds chicken breast, boneless
1 packet ranch seasoning
1 cup water

Directions:
1. Put the chicken breasts and cream cheese in the Crock Pot Express™. Sprinkle the top of the chicken and cream cheese with the ranch seasoning.
2. Pour in 1 cup of water. Cover and lock the lid.
3. Press the "BEANS/CHILI" key, set the pressure to HIGH, and set the timer for 25 minutes.
4. When the Crock Pot Express™ timer beeps, turn the steam valve to Venting to quick release the pressure.
5. Carefully open the lid. Transfer the chicken into a large plate and shred the meat.
6. Press the "BROWN/SAUTÉ" key of the Crock Pot Express™ and select LESS. Whisk in the cornstarch.
7. Add the cheese and the shredded chicken into the pot. Stir in the bacon. Serve.

102. Turkey Meatballs

Preparation time: **10 minutes** - Cooking time: **40 minutes** - Servings: **8**

Ingredients:
1 pound turkey meat, ground
1 yellow onion, peeled and minced
¼ cup Parmesan cheese, grated
½ cup panko bread crumbs
4 garlic cloves, peeled and minced
¼ cup parsley, chopped
Salt and ground black pepper, to taste
1 teaspoon dried oregano

1 egg, whisked

¼ cup milk

2 teaspoons soy sauce

1 teaspoon fish sauce

12 cremini mushrooms, chopped

3 dried shiitake mushrooms, soaked in water, drained, and chopped

1 cup chicken stock

2 tablespoons extra virgin olive oil

2 tablespoons butter

Sherry

2 tablespoons cornstarch mixed with 2 tablespoons water

Directions:

1. In a bowl, mix the turkey meat with Parmesan cheese, salt, pepper, onion, garlic, bread crumbs, parsley, oregano, egg, milk, fish sauce, and 1 teaspoon soy sauce, stir well, and shape 16 meatballs. Heat up a pan with 1 tablespoon oil over medium-high heat, add the meatballs, brown them for 1 minutes on each side, and transfer them to a plate. Pour the chicken stock into the pan, stir, and take off heat.

2. Set the Crock pot Express™ on "Brown/Sauté" mode, add 1 tablespoon oil, 2 tablespoons butter, and heat them up. Add the cremini mushrooms, salt, and pepper, stir, and cook for 10 minutes. Add the dried mushrooms, sherry, and the rest of the soy sauce and stir well.

3. Add the meatballs, cover the Crock pot Express™ and cook on the "Beans/Chili" setting for 6 minutes. Release the pressure, uncover the Crock pot Express™, add the cornstarch slurry, stir well, divide everything between plates, and serve.

103. Shredded Chicken Breast

Preparation + Cook Time: 30 minutes | Servings: 4

Ingredients:

1.5-2 lbs boneless chicken breasts

½ tsp salt

½ tsp garlic salt

⅛ tsp pepper

½ cup chicken broth

Directions:

1. Place chicken in your Crock Pot Express™

2. Season both sides of chicken with garlic salt and pepper.

3. Pour the chicken broth.

4. Seal Crock Pot Express™, making sure your valve is set to sealing. Press "POULTRY" button. Once done, wait for Crock Pot Express™ to depressurize on it's own, known as natural release.
5. **Note:** If you are wanting to use the quick release method, I suggest adding 5 extra minutes to the Crock Pot Express™ cooking timer.
6. Place chicken on a cutting board and shred with 2 forks, OR slice chicken breast.

104. Turkey Mix and Mashed Potatoes

Preparation time: **10 minutes** - Cooking time: **50 minutes** - Servings: **3**

Ingredients:
2 turkey quarters
1 yellow onion, peeled and chopped
1 carrot, peeled and chopped
3 garlic cloves, peeled and minced
1 celery stalk, chopped
1 cup chicken stock
Salt and ground black pepper, to taste
White wine
2 tablespoons extra virgin olive oil
Dried rosemary
2 bay leaves
Dried sage
Dried thyme
3 tablespoons cornstarch mixed with 2 tablespoons water
5 Yukon gold potatoes, cut into halves
2 tablespoons Parmesan cheese, grated
3.5 ounces cream
2 tablespoons butter

Directions:
1. Season the turkey with salt and pepper. Put 1 tablespoon oil into the Crock pot Express™, set the Crock pot Express™ on "Brown/Sauté" mode, and heat it up. Add the turkey, brown the pieces for 4 minutes, transfer them to a plate set aside. Add ½ cup stock to the Crock pot Express™ and stir well. Add the 1 tablespoon oil and heat it up. Add the onion, stir, and cook for 1 minute. Add the garlic, stir, and cook for 20 seconds. Add the salt and pepper, carrot and celery, stir and cook for 7 minutes.
2. Add the bay leaves, thyme, sage, and rosemary, stir and cook everything 1 minute. Add the wine, turkey and the rest of the stock. Put the potatoes in the steamer basket and also introduce it in the Crock pot Express™,

3. Cover and cook for 20 minutes on "Steam" mode. Release the pressure for 10 minutes, uncover the Crock pot Express™, transfer the potatoes to a bowl and mash them. Add the salt, pepper, butter, Parmesan cheese, and cream and stir well. Divide the turkey quarters to plates and set the Crock pot Express™ on "Brown/Sauté" mode. Add the cornstarch mixture to pot, stir well, and cook for 2-3 minutes. Drizzle the sauce over the turkey, add the mashed potatoes on the side, and serve.

105. Lemon and Garlic Chicken
Preparation + Cook Time: 25 minutes | Servings: 4

Ingredients:
1 lemon, large-sized, juiced, or more to taste
1 onion, diced
1 tbsp avocado oil, OR ghee, OR lard
1 tsp dried parsley
1 tsp sea salt
½ cup chicken broth, organic or homemade
¼ cup white cooking wine
¼ tsp paprika
1-2 pounds chicken, thighs or breasts
3-4 tsp arrowroot flour, or more
5 garlic cloves, minced

Directions:
1. Press the "BROWN/SAUTÉ" key of the Crock Pot Express™. Put the cooking fat and the diced onion into the pot.
2. Cook for about 5 minutes or until the onions are softened, or you can cook until they begin to brown.
3. Except for the arrowroot flour, add the rest of the ingredients into the pot. Cover and lock the lid.
4. Press the "POULTRY" key let cook on preset cooking time.
5. When the Crock Pot Express™ timer beeps, press the CANCEL key and unplug the Crock Pot Express™.
6. Turn the steam valve to quick release the pressure. Unlock and carefully open the lid.
7. If you want a thick sauce, remove about 1/4 cup of the sauce, add the arrowroot flour in the cup and stir to make slurry.
8. Pour the slurry back into the pot. Stir until thicken. Serve immediately.

106. Stuffed Chicken Breasts

Ingredients:
2 chicken breasts, skinless, boneless, and butterflied
1 piece ham, cut in half and cooked
6 asparagus spears
16 bacon strips
4 mozzarella cheese slices
Salt and ground black pepper, to taste
2 cup water

Directions:
1. In a bowl, mix the chicken breasts with salt and 1 cup water, stir, cover, and keep in the refrigerator for 30 minutes. Pat chicken breasts dry and place them on a working surface. Add 2 slices of mozzarella, 1 piece ham, and 3 asparagus pieces onto each. Add salt and pepper and roll up each chicken breast.
2. Place 8 bacon strips on a working surface, add the chicken and wrap them in bacon. Repeat this with the rest of the bacon strips and the other chicken breast. Put rolls in the steamer basket of the Crock pot Express™, add 1 cup water to the Crock pot Express™,
3. Cover and cook on the "Beans/Chili" setting for 10 minutes. Release the pressure, pat dry rolls with paper towels and leave them on a plate. Set the Crock pot Express™ on "Brown/Sauté" mode, add the chicken rolls and brown them for a few minutes. Divide among plates, and serve.

107. 8-Ingredient Chicken Dinner
Preparation + Cook Time: 45 minutes | Servings: 4

Ingredients:
2 pounds boneless chicken thighs
¼ cup coconut oil
¼ cup coconut aminos (or soy sauce)
¼ cup honey
3 tbsp organic ketchup
2 tsp garlic powder
1 ½ tsp sea salt
½ tsp black pepper

Directions:
1. Put everything in your Crock Pot Express™. Stir, so the chicken becomes completely coated. Close and seal the lid.
2. Press "BEANS/CHILI" and adjust time to 18 minutes. For frozen chicken, 40 minutes.
3. When time is up, hit CANCEL and quick-release.

4. Take out the chicken and hit "BROWN/SAUTÉ".
5. Simmer for 5 minutes until the sauce has thickened nicely.
6. Serve with a vegetable side dish!

108. Simple Chicken Salad

Preparation time: **55 minutes** - Cooking time: **10 minutes** - Servings: **2**

Ingredients:
1 chicken breast, skinless and boneless
3 cups water
Salt and ground black pepper, to taste
1 tablespoon mustard
3 garlic cloves, peeled and minced
1 tablespoon balsamic vinegar
1 tablespoon honey
3 tablespoons extra virgin olive oil
Mixed salad greens
A handful cherry tomatoes, cut into halves

Directions:
1. In a bowl, mix 2 cups water with a pinch of salt. Add the chicken to the mixture, stir, and keep in the refrigerator for 45 minutes. Add the remaining water to the Crock pot Express™, place the chicken breast in the steamer basket of the Crock pot Express™,
2. Cover and cook on the "Beans/Chili" setting for 5 minutes. Release the pressure naturally, set the chicken breast aside to rest, then cut into thin strips. In a bowl, mix the garlic with salt and pepper, mustard, honey, vinegar, and olive oil and whisk well. In a salad bowl, mix chicken strips with the salad greens and tomatoes. Drizzle the vinaigrette on top, and serve.

109. Chipotle Chicken, Rice, and Black Beans
Preparation + Cook Time: 30 minutes | Servings: 6

Ingredients:
1 onion, small-sized, chopped
1 can black beans, organic, drained and rinsed
1 cup Jasmine Rice, uncooked
1 pound chicken thighs or breasts, boneless, skinless, cut into bite sized pieces
1 tbsp chipotle peppers, in adobo sauce
½ cup water, filtered
½ lime, juiced

½ tsp black pepper, finely ground

2 tbsp butter, ghee, or coconut oil

2 tsp real salt, OR sea salt

4 cups diced tomatoes in juice

Directions:

1. Put the chicken, butter, pepper, salt, rice, lime juice, water, chipotle peppers, tomatoes with its juices, and onion in the Crock Pot Express™, stir and combine. Cover and lock the lid.
2. Press the "BEANS/CHILI" key, set the pressure to HIGH, and set the timer for 6 minutes.
3. When the Crock Pot Express™ timer beeps, press the CANCEL key and unplug the Crock Pot Express™. Turn the steam valve to quick release the pressure.
4. Unlock and carefully open the lid.
5. Add the black beans into the pot and stir to combine.
6. Taste and, if needed, season with pepper and salt to taste.
7. Divide between serving bowls and garnish each serving with sour cream, shredded cheese, and guacamole.

110. Chicken and Potatoes

Preparation time: **15 minutes** - Cooking time: **15 minutes** - Servings: **4**

Ingredients:

2 tablespoons extra virgin olive oil

2 pounds chicken thighs, skinless and boneless

¾ cup chicken stock

¼ cup lemon juice

2 pounds red potatoes, peeled, and cut into quarters

3 tablespoons Dijon mustard

2 tablespoons Italian seasoning

Salt and ground black pepper, to taste

Directions:

1. Set the Crock pot Express™ on "Brown/Sauté" mode, add the oil, and heat it up. Add the chicken thighs, salt, and pepper, stir, and brown for 2 minutes. In a bowl, mix the stock with mustard, Italian seasoning, and lemon juice, and stir well. Pour this over the chicken, add the potatoes, stir,
2. Cover the Crock pot Express™ and cook on the "Poultry" setting for 15 minutes. Release the pressure, uncover the Crock pot Express™, stir the chicken, divide among plates, and serve.

111. Fall Off The Bone Chicken Half An Hour

Preparation + Cook Time: 45 minutes | Servings: 10)

Ingredients:
1 whole chicken, about
4 pounds, preferably organic
1½ cups chicken bone broth
1 tbsp coconut oil, organic virgin
1 tsp dried thyme
1 tsp paprika
½ tsp sea salt
¼ tsp black pepper, fresh ground
2 tbsp fresh squeezed lemon juice
6 cloves garlic, peeled

Directions:
1. In a small-sized bowl, combine the pepper, salt, thyme, and paprika. Rub the outside of the chicken with the spice mix.
2. Press the "BROWN/SAUTÉ" key of the Crock Pot Express™. Put the oil in the pot and heat until shimmering.
3. With the breast side faced down, put the chicken in the pot and cook for 6-7 minutes. Rotate the chicken.
4. Add the broth, garlic cloves, and lemon juice. Cover and lock the lid.
5. Press the "BEANS/CHILI" key, set the pressure to HIGH, and set the timer for 25 minutes.
6. When the timer beeps, let the pressure release naturally. Turn the steam valve to Venting to release any remaining pressure. Carefully open the lid.
7. Transfer the chicken into a large plate and let stand for 5 minutes. Carve and serve.

112. Chicken Rogan Josh Curry

Preparation + Cook Time: 60 minutes | Servings: 8

Ingredients:
5-pounds boneless, skinless chicken thighs
1/3 pound curry paste
1½ cups Greek Yogurt
1 tbsp vegetable oil
1 onion – cut into wedges
2 coarsely chopped large tomatoes
4 ounces baby spinach leaves

4 ounces coriander leaves

Directions:
1. First, combine the yogurt and the curry paste in a large bowl.
2. Add the chicken and pour over with the mixture.
3. The chicken should be completely coated in the yogurt and curry mixture.
4. Leave the chicken in the bowl and cover with plastic wrap. Place the bowl in your refrigerator for about 30 minutes.
5. Press "BROWN/SAUTÉ" mode and heat the vegetable oil in your Crock Pot Express™.
6. Add the onion and cook until it is golden brown. This should take about 8 to 10 minutes.
7. Add the onion and the diced tomatoes to the marinated chicken.
8. Combine the ingredients and then pour into the Crock Pot Express™.
9. Close the lid. Press the "BEANS/CHILI" key, set the pressure to HIGH, and set the timer for 15 minutes.
10. When the Crock Pot Express™ timer beeps. Allow the pressure to release naturally and then serve over rice or steamed vegetables.

113. Cacciatore

Preparation + Cook Time: 40 minutes | Servings: 8

Ingredients:
1 can pitted black olives
1 green bell pepper, seeded and diced
1 package (8-10 ounces) mushrooms, sliced
½ cup chicken broth, OR vegetable broth
2 cans crushed tomatoes, organic
2 tbsp organic tomato paste
3 shallots, chopped
4 garlic cloves, crushed
5-6 chicken breasts, boneless, skinless
Extra-virgin olive oil
Fresh parsley
Red pepper, to taste
Sea salt and black pepper, to taste

Directions:
1. Put the oil in a 4-quart or larger Crock Pot Express™. Press the "BROWN/SAUTÉ" key and heat the oil. When the oil is hot, add the bell pepper and shallots into the pot and cook for about 2 minutes, frequently stirring, until the shallots are slightly softened.
2. Stir in the broth and let simmer for about 2-3 minutes, scraping up any browned off from the bottom of the pot. Stir in the garlic and mushrooms.

3. Put the chicken on top and cover the chicken layer with the chopped tomatoes –do not stir. Put the tomato paste on top of the crushed tomatoes.
4. Press the CANCEL key to stop the "Brown/Sauté" function. Cover and lock the lid. Turn the steam valve to Sealing.
5. Press the "BEANS/CHILI" key, set the pressure to HIGH, and set the timer for 8 minutes.
6. When the Crock Pot Express™ timer beeps, press the CANCEL key and unplug the Crock Pot Express™.
7. Let the pressure release naturally for 10-15 minutes or until the valve drops. Turn the steam valve to release remaining pressure.
8. Unlock and carefully open the lid. Stir in the olives, red pepper flakes, pepper, and salt.
9. Divide the cacciatore between serving bowls. If desired, serve heaping over shredded cabbage.

114. Garlic-Ginger Drumsticks

Preparation + Cook Time: 45 minutes | Servings: 4

Ingredients:
6-8 chicken drumsticks, skin on
For the sauce:
2 tbsp rice wine vinegar
2 tbsp honey
2 tbsp brown sugar
2 cloves garlic, minced
¼ cup water
½ onion, chopped
½ cup soy sauce
1 tsp fresh ginger, minced

Directions:
1. In a bowl, mix all of the sauce ingredients until well combined. Pour the sauce in the Crock Pot Express™.
2. Add the chicken in the pot and push them down to submerge them in the sauce – they do not have to be covered completely with sauce. Cover and lock the lid.
3. Press the "BEANS/CHILI" key, set the pressure to HIGH, and set the timer for 15 minutes.
4. When the Crock Pot Express™ timer beeps, let the pressure release naturally for 15 minutes. Turn the steam valve to release remaining pressure. Unlock and carefully open the lid.
5. Press the "BROWN/SAUTÉ" key and boil until the sauce is reduced.
6. Remove the drumsticks and transfer them into a parchment paper lined cookie sheet.
7. Turn the oven setting to broil, and preheat the broiler 10 to 15 minutes before cooking. Broil each side of the chicken for 2 minutes.

8. Meanwhile, let the sauce cook in the Crock Pot Express™ until reduced more.
9. Remove the chicken from the oven and put on a serving platter.
10. Pour the sauce over the chicken. Serve and enjoy!

115. Braised Chicken with Capers and Parsley
Preparation + Cook Time: 45 minutes | Servings: 4

Ingredients:
4 chicken breasts, skinless, bone-in
1 can (14.5 ounces) chicken broth
1 onion, large-sized, minced
1 tbsp cornstarch
1 tbsp water
½ cup flat-leaf parsley, minced, plus more for garnish
1/3 cup salted capers, soaked well in several changes of water
1/3 cup white wine vinegar
2 tbsp olive oil, divided
Freshly ground black pepper
Salt to taste

Directions:
1. Season the chicken with salt and pepper generously.
2. Press the "BROWN/SAUTÉ" key of the Crock Pot Express™. Put 1 tablespoon olive oil in the pot and heat.
3. Cooking in 2 batches, cook the chicken in the pot until both sides are browned. Transfer the browned chicken onto a platter.
4. Put the remaining 1 tablespoon olive oil in the pot.
5. When hot, add the onion; cook, stirring, for about 5 minutes or until soft.
6. Add the capers and parsley and cook for 1 minute. Stir in the broth.
7. Add the vinegar. Return the chicken, along with any accumulated juices, into the pot. Cover and lock the lid.
8. Press the "BEANS/CHILI" key, set the pressure to HIGH, and set the timer for 13 minutes.
9. When the Crock Pot Express™ timer beeps, turn the steam valve to Venting to quick release the pressure. Unlock and carefully open the lid.
10. Transfer the chicken onto a platter using tongs. Cover the platter with foil to keep warm. In a small-sized bowl, mix the cornstarch with the water.
11. Press the "BROWN/SAUTÉ" key. Bring the broth in the pot to a boil.
12. Add the cornstarch mix, constantly stirring until the sauce is thick. Turn off the Crock Pot Express™.
13. Season the salt and pepper to taste. Spoon the sauce over the cooked chicken.

14. Garnish with parsley and serve.

116. Melted Mozzarella Marinara Chicken

Preparation + Cook Time: 35 minutes | Servings: 4

Ingredients:

4 large chicken breasts, boneless, skinless
1 can (14 ounces) crushed tomatoes in puree
1 cup low-fat Mozzarella, grated
1 cup water
1 tbsp olive oil
1 tsp dried basil
¼ tsp red pepper flakes
¼ tsp salt
2 cloves garlic, crushed or pressed

Directions:

1. Season the chicken breast with salt and pepper.
2. Add the oil into the Crock Pot Express™, press the "BROWN/SAUTÉ" key, and heat the oil.
3. Cooking in 2 batches, cook the chicken breast until browned. Transfer onto a plate. If needed, add more oil in the pot.
4. Add the garlic; sauté for 1 minute. Add the water, tomatoes, red pepper flakes, basil, or salt. Stir until combined.
5. Return the chicken into the Crock Pot Express™. Cover and lock the lid.
6. Press the "BEANS/CHILI" key, set the pressure to HIGH, and set the timer for 5 minutes.
7. When the Crock Pot Express™ timer beeps, turn the steam valve to Venting to quick release the pressure. Unlock and carefully open the lid.
8. Check the chicken to make sure the meat is cooked and the middle is no longer pink. Preheat the broiler.
9. Grease a small-sized glass casserole with nonstick cooking spray.
10. Put the chicken in the dish. Press the "BROWN/SAUTÉ" key of the Crock Pot Express™. Bring the sauce in the pot to a simmer and cook until thick to your preferred consistency.
11. Pour the thickened sauce over the chicken in the dish. Sprinkle grated mozzarella cheese over the chicken.
12. Put the dish in the broiler and broil until the cheese starts to brown lightly and melted.
13. Watch carefully because the cheese can brown quickly.

117. Asian Inspired Chicken

Preparation + Cook Time: 20 minutes | Servings: 6

Ingredients:
6 chicken thighs, boneless, skinless
5 garlic cloves, minced
3 tbsp scallions, chopped
1/3 cup white wine
½ cup soy sauce
1 tsp sesame seeds
1 tbsp Sriracha Hot Chili Sauce
1 tbsp olive oil
1 ½ tsp fresh ginger, grated
1 ½ tbsp honey
1½ cups water

Directions:
1. Season both sides of the chicken thighs with garlic powder and pepper. Press the "BROWN/SAUTÉ" key and select the More option. Add the olive oil and heat.
2. When the oil is hot, add the chicken and cook until both sides are browned – do not overcrowd the Crock Pot Express™. You will need to cook in batches.
3. While the chicken is browning, mix the Sriracha with the water, honey, soy sauce, wine, ginger, and garlic in a bowl.
4. When the last batch of the chicken is browned, return all the browned chicken in the pot. Pour the Sriracha mixture in the pot.
5. Press the CANCEL key to stop the "Brown/Sauté" function. Cover and lock the lid.
6. Press the "BEANS/CHILI" key, set the pressure to HIGH, and set the timer for 5 minutes.
7. When the Crock Pot Express™ timer beeps, turn the steam valve to quick release the pressure. Unlock and carefully open the lid.
8. Transfer the chicken into a serving platter and tent with foil to keep warm.
9. Press the "BROWN/SAUTÉ" key and select the More option. Boil the sauce for 10 minutes. Pour the sauce over the chicken and top with scallions and sesame seeds.
10. Serve with broccoli and cauliflower rice.
11. You can pour some of the sauce over the broccoli and the cauliflower rice.

118. Slow Cook Chicken Paprikash
Preparation + Cook Time: 3 hours 25 minutes | Servings: 6

Ingredients:

6 chicken thighs skinless and boneless, trimmed, about 1 3/4 pounds
½ tsp salt
½ tsp black pepper freshly ground
3 tbsp white rice flour
1 tbsp canola oil
2 cups onion chopped
1 cup red bell pepper chopped
½ cup carrots matchstick-cut
3 cloves garlic minced
Cooking Spray
1 package mushrooms pre-sliced, 8 ounces
1¼ cups chicken broth fat-free, lower-sodium
2 tbsp Hungarian sweet paprika
½ cup sour cream reduced-fat
1 tbsp parsley chopped fresh

Directions:
1. Sprinkle chicken with 1/4 teaspoon of the salt and 1/4 teaspoon of the black pepper. Place flour in a shallow dish; dredge chicken in flour, reserving any remaining flour.
2. Heat a large well-seasoned cast-iron skillet over medium-high heat. Add oil to pan; swirl to coat. Add chicken to pan; cook 3 minutes on each side or until golden brown. Transfer chicken to a 6-quart Crock Pot Express™.
3. Add onion, red bell pepper, carrots, and garlic to pan; coat vegetables with cooking spray. Cook, stirring constantly, 6 minutes or just until tender. Transfer onion mixture to cooker.
4. Coat mushrooms with cooking spray, and add to pan. Cook, stirring constantly, 5 minutes or until browned. Transfer mushrooms to cooker.
5. Combine reserved flour, remaining 1/4 teaspoon salt, remaining 1/4 teaspoon black pepper, broth, and paprika in a bowl; stir with a whisk.
6. Add broth mixture to cooker. Close and lock the lid of the Crock Pot Express™. Turn the steam release handle to Venting position. Press SLOW COOK, and adjust 3 hours cook time.
7. Remove chicken from cooker, and place on a serving platter. Skim fat from surface of cooking liquid.
8. Stir sour cream into cooking liquid. Serve sauce with chicken, and sprinkle with parsley.

119. The Whole Chicken

Preparation + Cook Time: 30 minutes | Servings: 8

Ingredients:

1 medium-sized, whole chicken

1 minced green onion

2 tbsp sugar

2-3 cups water or chicken broth

1 tbsp cooking wine

1 minced piece of ginger

2 tsp soy sauce

2 tsp salt

Directions:

1. Season the chicken thoroughly with salt and sugar.
2. Sprinkle 1 teaspoon of salt into the bottom of the Crock Pot Express™.
3. Pour the wine, water or broth and soy sauce into the cooker, and add the chicken.
4. Choose "POULTRY" and cook on HIGH pressure for 15 minutes.
5. When time is up, flip the chicken, and push "POULTRY" again.
6. Let the pressure come down naturally before opening the cooker.
7. Serve chicken pieces with green onion on top and any side dishes you'd like.

Main Dishes – Pork

120. Pork Shoulder Chops With Soy Sauce, Maple Syrup, And Carrots

Prep: 5 minutes • pressure: 40 minutes • total: 45 minutes • pressure level: high • release: natural • Serves 6

Ingredients
1 tablespoon bacon fat
3 pounds bone-in pork shoulder chops, each ½ to ¾ inch thick
6 medium carrots
3 medium garlic cloves
⅓ cup soy sauce
⅓ cup maple syrup
⅓ cup chicken broth
½ teaspoon ground black pepper

Directions
1. **Preparing the Ingredients.** Melt the bacon fat in a Crock-Pot Multi-Cooker®, turned to the browning function. Add about half the chops and brown well, turning once, about 5 minutes. Transfer these to a large bowl and brown the remaining chops.

    Stir the carrots and garlic into the pot; cook for 1 minute, stirring constantly. Pour in the soy sauce, maple syrup, and broth, stirring to dissolve the maple syrup and to get up any browned bits on the bottom of the pot. Stir in the pepper. Return the shoulder chops and their juices to the pot. Stir to coat them in the sauce.

2. **High pressure for 40 minutes**. Lock the lid on the Crock-Pot Multi-Cooker® and then cook for 40 minutes. To get 40-minutes cook time, press "meat/stew" button and use the TIME ADJUSTMENT button to adjust the cook time to 40 minutes.

3. **Pressure Release** Let the pressure to come down naturally for at least 14 to 16 minutes, then quick release any pressure left in the pot.

4. **Finish the dish** Unlock and open the pot. Transfer the chops, carrots, and garlic cloves to a large serving bowl. Skim the fat off the sauce and ladle it over the servings.

121. Pulled BBQ Pork

Preparation + Cook Time: 1 hour 45 minutes | Servings: 4

Ingredients:
2.6 pounds pork roast
2 cups chicken stock OR water
¼ cup vegetable oil
Any of your preferred spices (Worcestershire sauce, pepper, salt)
BBQ sauce, optional

Directions:
1. Slice the roast into halves to make it easier to handle and fit in the pot.
2. Season and spice the roast with your choice of spices or seasoning or marinade; let sit for about 20 minutes, if desired.
3. Press the "BROWN/SAUTÉ" key. Put the vegetable oil in the pot and heat. When the oil is hot, add the pork and sear each side for 3 minutes.
4. Add 2 cups of liquid – stock or water – into the pot. Press the CANCEL key to stop the "Brown/Sauté" function. Cover and lock the lid.
5. Press the "MEAT/STEW" key and set the timer for 90 minutes
6. When the Crock Pot Express™ timer beeps, release the pressure naturally for 10 minutes.
7. Turn the steam valve to release remaining pressure. Unlock and carefully open the lid. Transfer the pork into a plate and shred.
8. At this point, you can eat this dish as is or continue to the BBQ option. Make sure that there is 1/2 cup water in the pot.
9. Add your preferred BBQ sauce into the pot. Return the shredded pork into the pot. Stir to mix. Cover and lock the lid.
10. Press the "BEANS/CHILI" key, set the pressure to HIGH, and set the timer for 5 minutes.
11. When the Crock Pot Express™ timer beeps, turn the steam valve to Venting to quick release the pressure. Unlock and carefully open the lid.
12. Serve with your favorite bread.

122. Pork Chops and Smashed Potatoes

Preparation time: **15 minutes** - Cooking time: **20 minutes** - Servings: **6**

Ingredients:
6 pork chops, boneless
2 pounds potatoes, cut into chunks
2 cups chicken stock
3 garlic cloves, peeled and chopped

1 yellow onion, peeled and cut into chunks
1 bunch mixed rosemary, sage, oregano, and thyme
Salt and ground black pepper, to taste
2 tablespoons butter
1 teaspoon smoked paprika
2 tablespoons white flour

Directions:
1. Put the potatoes into the Crock pot Express™. Add the garlic and half of the onion. Add the herbs and stock. Place the pork chops on top, add salt, pepper, and paprika.
2. Cover and cook on the "meat/stew" setting for 15 minutes. Meanwhile, heat up a pan over medium heat, add butter, and heat it up. Add the flour, stir well, cook for 2 minutes, and take off heat. Release the pressure, transfer the pork to a platter and discard the herbs. Transfer the potatoes to a bowl, add some of the cooking liquid, add the salt and pepper, and stir using a hand mixer. Set the Crock pot Express™ on "Beans/Chili" mode, and cook the cooking liquid for 2 minutes. Add the butter mix and stir until it thickens. Divide the pork chops on plates, add the mashed potatoes on the side, and drizzle the gravy from the Crock pot Express™ all over.

123. Pulled Pork

Prep: 5 minutes • pressure: 80 minutes • total: 85 minutes • pressure level: high • release: natural - • Serves 8

Ingredients
2 tablespoons smoked paprika
2 tablespoons packed dark brown sugar
1 tablespoon ground cumin
2 teaspoons ground black pepper
½ tablespoon dry mustard
1 teaspoon ground coriander
1 teaspoon dried thyme
1 teaspoon onion powder
1 teaspoon salt
½ teaspoon garlic powder
½ teaspoon ground cloves
½ teaspoon ground cinnamon
One 4- to 4½-pound bone-in skinless pork shoulder, preferably pork butt
Up to 1½ cups light-colored beer, preferably a pale ale or amber lager

Directions

1. **Preparing the Ingredients.** Mix the smoked paprika, brown sugar, cumin, pepper, mustard, coriander, thyme, onion powder, salt, garlic powder, cloves, and cinnamon in a small bowl. Massage the mixture all over the pork.
   Set the pork in the Crock-Pot Multi-Cooker®. Pour 1 cup beer into the electric cooker without knocking the spices off the meat.
2. **High pressure for 80 minutes**. Lock the lid on the Crock-Pot Multi-Cooker® and then cook for 80 minutes. To get 80-minutes cook time, press "meat/stew" button and use the TIME ADJUSTMENT button to adjust the cook time to 80 minutes.
3. **Pressure Release** Let its pressure fall to normal naturally, 25 to 35 minutes.
4. **Finish the dish** Transfer the meat to a large cutting board. Let stand for 5 minutes. Use a spoon to skim as much fat off the sauce in the pot as possible.
   Set the "browning "function. Bring the sauce to a simmer, stirring occasionally; continue boiling the sauce, stirring often, until reduced by half, 7 to 10 minutes.
   Use two forks to shred the meat off the bones; discard the bones and any attached cartilage. Pull any large chunks of meat apart with the forks and stir the meat back into the simmering sauce to reheat.
5. Serve and Enjoy!

124. Pulled Pork Chipotle Salad Bowl

Preparation + Cook Time: 2 hours | Servings: 6

Ingredients:
4 pounds pork shoulder butt OR 7 pound shoulder on the bone
2 tsp sea salt
2 cups chicken stock
1 tsp smoked paprika powder, optional
1 tsp garlic powder
1 tsp black pepper
1 pinch dried oregano leaves
4 tbsp coconut oil OR other GAPS approved fat (like chicken grease or bacon fat)
6 cloves garlic

Directions:
1. Remove the rind from the pork and then cut the meat from the bone, slicing them into large-sized chunks.
2. Trim the fat off the meat – do not worry too much about this since the fat will dissolve while cooking.
3. Press the "BROWN/SAUTÉ" key of the Crock Pot Express™. Put the oil in the pot and let heat.
4. When the oil is hot, layer the chunks of meat in the bottom of the pot and sauté for a couple of minutes until nicely browned in spots – this will take about 30 minutes, about how long the "Brown/Sauté" function will last.

5. While the meat is browning, peel the garlic cloves and cut into small-sized chunks.
6. When the meat is browned, transfer into a large-sized bowl. Pour in a few tablespoons of chicken stock in the pot to deglaze.
7. Scrape the browned bits off from the bottom of the using a wooden spoon.
8. Transfer the browned bits into the bowl with the browned meat and continue cooking the rest of the meat chunks.
9. If not all the meat chunks are browned after 30 minutes, simply press the "BROWN/SAUTÉ" key again and continue cooking.
10. When all the meat is browned and transferred into the bowl, put the garlic, oregano leaves, smoked paprika, garlic powder, black pepper, and sea salt to the bowl with the meat.
11. Put all the chicken stock in the pot to deglaze the pot, scraping the browned bits off from the bottom and bring to a simmer.
12. When simmering, return the browned meat and browned bits into the pot.
13. Stir to combine. Press the CANCEL key to stop the "Brown/Sauté" function. Cover and lock the lid. Turn the steam valve to Sealing.
14. Press the MEAT key, set the pressure to HIGH, and set the timer for 42 minutes.
15. When the Crock Pot Express™ timer beeps, quick release the pressure.
16. Unlock and carefully open the lid. Remove the meat from the pot and shred using 2 forks.
17. Put the meat in a bowl. Pour the cooking liquid separator or simply skim the fat off from the top of the cooking liquid.
18. Pour in some of the de-fatted broth in the bowl with the shredded meat.
19. Save the leftover broth and use it to add to stews or soup.
20. Top each serving with lime guacamole and salsa over salad greens.

125. Country-style Ribs

Preparation time: **2 hours** - Cooking time: **20 minutes** - Servings: **8**

Ingredients:

5 pounds country style ribs, boneless
For the brine:
½ cup brown sugar
½ cup salt
4 cups water
2 tablespoons liquid smoke
3 garlic cloves, peeled and crushed
For the ribs:
2 tablespoons butter
½ tablespoons water
1 cup onion, peeled and chopped
1 pound apples, cored, peeled and sliced
½ teaspoon ground cinnamon
1 teaspoon chili powder
Cayenne pepper
For the sauce:
1 tablespoons liquid smoke
2 tablespoons yellow mustard
2 tablespoons Dijon mustard
2 tablespoons brown sugar
1 teaspoon hot sauce
1 tablespoon Worcestershire sauce
1 tablespoon soy sauce
¼ cup honey
2 tablespoons water
2 tablespoons cornstarch

Directions:
1. In a bowl, mix the 4 cups water with ½ cup salt, ½ cup sugar, 2 tablespoons liquid smoke, and garlic. Stir, add the pork ribs and keep in the refrigerator for 2 hours. Set the Crock pot Express™ on "Brown/Sauté" mode, add 2 tablespoons butter and melt it. Add the ribs, brown them on all sides, and transfer to a plate. Add the onions½ tablespoon water, stir, and cook for 2 minutes. Add the cinnamon, cayenne, chili powder, and apples. Return the ribs,
2. Cover the Crock pot Express™, and cook on the "meat/stew" setting for 15 minutes. Release the pressure, transfer the ribs to a plate and set aside. Puree the onions and apples using a food processor, and set the Crock pot Express™ on "Brown/Sauté" mode

again. Add the yellow mustard, Dijon mustard, 1 tablespoon liquid smoke, 2 tablespoons sugar, Worcestershire sauce, hot sauce, soy sauce, and honey and stir well. Add the cornstarch mixed with 2 tablespoons water, stir, and cook for 2 minutes. Divide the ribs on plates, drizzle the gravy all over, and serve.

126. Pork Carnitas

Prep: 15 minutes • pressure: 50 minutes • total: 65 minutes • pressure level: high • release: natural • Serves 11

Ingredients
2 1/2 pounds trimmed, boneless pork shoulder blade roast
2 teaspoons kosher salt
black pepper, to taste
6 cloves garlic, cut into sliver
1 1/2 teaspoons cumin
1/2 teaspoon sazon
1/4 teaspoon dry oregano
3/4 cup reduced sodium chicken broth
2-3 chipotle peppers in adobo sauce (to taste)
2 bay leaves
1/4 teaspoon dry adobo seasoning
1/2 teaspoon garlic powder

Directions
1. **Preparing the Ingredients.** Season pork with salt and pepper. Bring the cooker to high pressure by pressing the Brown/ Sauté button, and brown pork on all sides on high heat for about 5 minutes. Remove from heat and allow to cool.
   Using a sharp knife, insert blade into pork about 1-inch deep, and insert the garlic slivers, you'll want to do this all over. Season pork with cumin, sazon, oregano, adobo and garlic powder all over.
   Pour chicken broth, add chipotle peppers and stir, add bay leaves and place pork in the Crock-Pot Multi-Cooker®.
6. **High pressure for 50 minutes.** Lock the lid on the Crock-Pot Multi-Cooker® and then cook for 50 minutes. To get 50-minutes cook time, press "meat/stew" button and use the TIME ADJUSTMENT button to adjust the cook time to 50 minutes.
2. **Pressure Release.** Use natural-release method.
3. Serve and Enjoy!

Per Serving **Calories: 160; Fat: 7g; Sat Fat: 3g; Carb: 1g; Fiber: 0g; Protein: 20g; Sugar: 0g; Sodium: 397 mg; Cholesterol: 69mg.**

127. Cranberry BBQ Pulled Pork

Preparation + Cook Time: 55 minutes | Servings: 10)

Ingredients:
3-4 pounds pork shoulder or roast, boneless, fat trimmed off
For the sauce:
3 tbsp liquid smoke
2 tbsp tomato paste
2 cups fresh cranberries
¼ cup buffalo hot sauce
1/3 cup blackstrap molasses
½ cup water
½ cup apple cider vinegar
1 tsp salt, or more to taste
1 tbsp adobo sauce
1 cup tomato puree
1 chipotle pepper in adobo sauce, diced

Directions:
1. Cut the pork against the grain in halves or thirds and set aside.
2. Press the "BROWN/SAUTÉ" key of the Crock Pot Express™.
3. When the pot is hot, add the cranberries and the water.
4. Let simmer for about 4 to 5 minutes or until the cranberries start to pop. Add the remaining sauce ingredients in the pot and continue simmering for 5 minutes more.
5. Add the pork in the pot. Press the CANCEL key to stop the "Brown/Sauté" function. Cover and lock the lid.
6. Select "BEANS/CHILI" and cook at HIGH pressure for 40 minutes.
7. When the Crock Pot Express™ timer beeps, turn the steam valve to Venting to quick release the pressure. Unlock and carefully open the lid.
8. With a fork, pull the pork apart into shreds.
9. Serve the pork with plenty of sauce on rolls or bread or over your favorite greens.

128. Ribs and Coleslaw

Preparation time: **15 minutes** - Cooking time: **35 minutes** - Servings: **4**

Ingredients:
2½ pounds pork baby back ribs
Salt and ground black pepper, to taste
1 teaspoon onion powder

½ teaspoon paprika
½ teaspoon dry mustard
½ teaspoon chili powder
½ teaspoon garlic powder

For the sauce:

1 small yellow onion, peeled and chopped
2 bacon slices, chopped
6 ounces tomato paste
¾ cup tomato sauce
2 garlic cloves, peeled and minced
Salt and ground black pepper, to taste
¼ cup coconut aminos
½ teaspoon smoked paprika
Cayenne pepper
⅓ cup apple cider vinegar
1 tablespoon vegetable oil
½ cup apple juice

For the coleslaw:

1 cup red cabbage, shredded
3 cups green cabbage, shredded
1 cup raisins
2½ teaspoons caraway seeds
¼ cup apple cider vinegar
¾ cup mayonnaise
Salt and ground black pepper, to taste
2 carrots, peeled and grated
2 green onions, chopped

Directions:

1. In a salad bowl, mix the cabbage with the green onions, carrots, and raisins. In a small bowl, mix the caraway seeds with the mayonnaise, salt, pepper¼ cup vinegar, and stir well. Pour this over the coleslaw, toss to coat and keep in the refrigerator until ready to serve. In a bowl, mix the onion powder with paprika, salt, pepper, dry mustard, garlic powder, and chili powder. Rub the ribs with this mixture and place them into the Crock pot Express™.

2. Add some water, cover the Crock pot Express™ and cook on the "meat/stew" setting for 15 minutes. Heat up a pan with the oil over medium heat, add the bacon and cook for 2 minutes. Add the onion and garlic, stir, and cook for 5 minutes. Add the tomato sauce and tomato paste, apple juice, coconut aminos, ⅓ cup vinegar, paprika, and a pinch of cayenne pepper, salt, and pepper, stir, and cook for 10 minutes. Release the pressure from the Crock pot Express™, uncover, and transfer the ribs to a plate. Add some of the sauce to the bottom of the Crock pot Express™ , add a layer of ribs, then a layer of sauce, then another layer of ribs until all of the ribs are in the Crock pot Express™. Cover the Crock pot Express™ and cook on the "Beans/Chili"

setting for 10 minutes. Release the pressure again, divide the ribs and sauce among plates, and serve with the coleslaw.

129. Easy Pork Chops

Prep: 15 minutes • pressure: 5 minutes • total: 20 minutes • pressure level: low • release: natural - Serves 6

Ingredients
3-4 Pork Chops – ½ to ¾ inch thick
One egg – beaten
Flour
Salt and Pepper
Bread Crumbs
Onions – chopped – as much as you like – ½ cup maybe
2 – 4 Garlic cloves – squashed and chopped
Butter- 1 tbsp.
Oil 1-2 tbsp. or orange/ginger coconut oil

Directions
1. **Preparing the Ingredients.** Turn on the Crock-Pot Multi-Cooker® to the Sauté setting, then wait for it to boil. Heat the oil and butter to very hot.
   Make sure your pork chops are at room temperature. Dredge them in flour, dip into beaten egg, dredge them in bread crumbs. Brown them lots on both sides in the hot Crock-Pot Multi-Cooker®. When well browned on both sides, remove and put on plate. Throw in the onions, swish them around for a minute until softer looking, then throw in the garlic and swish around.
   Leave the onions, garlic and drippings in the pot. Add about two to three tablespoons of water. Put steamer in pot, place browned pork chops on steamer above the water and drippings.
2. **High pressure for 5 minutes.** Lock the lid on the Crock-Pot Multi-Cooker® and then cook for 5 minutes. To get 5-minutes cook time, press "Steam" button and use the TIME ADJUSTMENT button to adjust the cook time to 5 minutes.
3. **Pressure Release** Let the pressure to come down naturally for at least 15 minutes, then quick release any pressure left in the pot.
4. **Finish the dish.** Remove from the pot. Perfect, juicy pork chops you may use the 'juice' in the pot to pour over the pork chops or you can add a little polenta (or flour) and water, Sauté and make it like a gravy.
5. Serve and enjoy!

130. Mexican Pulled-Pork Lettuce Wraps

Preparation + Cook Time: 1 hour 40 minutes | Servings: 6

Ingredients:
4 pounds pork roast
1 head washed and dried butter lettuce
2 grated carrots
2 tbsp oil
2 lime wedges
1 chopped onion
1 tbsp salt
2-3 cups water
<u>Spice Mix:</u>
1 tbsp unsweetened cocoa powder
2 tsp oregano
1 tsp red pepper flakes
1 tsp garlic powder
1 tsp white pepper
1 tsp cumin
⅛ tsp cayenne
⅛ tsp coriander

Directions:
1. Marinate the pork the night before by mixing all the ingredients in the second list and rubbing into the pork. Store in the fridge.
2. The next day, turn your Crock Pot Express™ to "BROWN/SAUTÉ". When warm, brown roast all over.
3. Pour in 2-3 cups water, so the roast is almost totally submerged. Close and seal the lid.
4. Select "BEANS/CHILI" and cook at HIGH pressure for 55 minutes.
5. When time is up, press CANCEL and let the pressure release naturally.
6. When ready, take out the meat and pull with two forks.
7. Turn the cooker back to "BROWN/SAUTÉ" and reduce the liquid by half.
8. Strain and skim off any excess fat. If you want crispy pork, fry in a pan with some oil until it becomes light brown.
9. Mix pork with the cooking liquid before serving in the lettuce with grated carrots, a squirt of lime, and any other toppings.

131. Asian Short Ribs

Preparation time: **10 minutes** - Cooking time: **60 minutes** - Servings: **4**

Ingredients:

2 green onions, chopped
1 teaspoon vegetable oil
3 garlic cloves, peeled and minced
3 ginger slices
4 pounds short ribs
½ cup water
½ cup soy sauce
¼ cup rice wine
¼ cup pear juice
2 teaspoons sesame oil

Directions:

1. Set the Crock pot Express™ on "Brown/Sauté" mode, add the oil, and heat it up. Add the green onions, ginger, and garlic, stir, and cook for 1 minute. Add the ribs, water, wine, soy sauce, sesame oil, and pear juice, stir, and cook for 2-3 minutes.

2. Cover the Crock pot Express™ and cook on the "meat/stew" setting for 45 minutes. Release the pressure naturally for 15 minutes, uncover the Crock pot Express™, and transfer the ribs to a plate. Strain the liquid from the Crock pot Express™, divide the ribs among plates and drizzle the sauce all over.

132. Pork Chops With Applesauce

Prep: 10 minutes • pressure: 10 minutes • total: 20 minutes • pressure level: high • release: natural • Serves 2-4

Ingredients

2 – 4 pork loin chops (we used center cut, bone-on)
1 tablespoon grapeseed oil or olive oil
1 small onion, sliced
3 cloves garlic, roughly minced
2 gala apples, thinly sliced
2 pieces whole cloves (optional)
1 teaspoon cinnamon powder
1 tablespoon honey
½ cup unsalted homemade chicken stock or water
2 tablespoons light soy sauce
1 tablespoon butter
Kosher salt and ground black pepper to taste
1 ½ tablespoon cornstarch mixed with 2 tablespoons water (optional)

Directions

1. **Preparing the Ingredients.** Make a few small cut around the sides of the pork chops so they will stay flat and brown evenly.

   Season the pork chops with generous amount of kosher salt and ground black pepper.

   Heat up your Crock-Pot Multi-Cooker®. Add grapeseed oil into the pot. Add the seasoned pork chops into the pot, then let it brown for roughly 2 – 3 minutes on each side. Remove and set aside.

   Add in the sliced onions and stir. Add a pinch of kosher salt and ground black pepper to season if you like. Cook the onions for roughly 1 minute until soften. Then, add garlic and stir for 30 seconds until fragrance.

   Add in the thinly sliced gala apples, whole cloves (optional) and cinnamon powder, then give it a quick stir. Add the honey and partially deglaze the bottom of the pot with a wooden spoon.

   Add chicken stock and light soy sauce, then fully deglaze the bottom of the pot with a wooden spoon. Taste the seasoning and add more salt and pepper if desired.

   Place the pork chops back with all the meat juice into the pot.

2. **High pressure for 10 minutes.** Lock the lid on the Crock-Pot Multi-Cooker® and then cook for 10 minutes. To get 10-minutes cook time, press "Soup" Button and use the TIME ADJUSTMENT button to adjust the cook time to 10 minutes.

3. **Pressure Release.** Let it fully natural release (roughly 10 minutes). Open the lid carefully.

4. **Finish the dish.** Remove the pork chops and set aside. Turn the pressure cooker to the Sauté setting. Remove the cloves and taste the seasoning one more time. Add more salt and pepper if desired. Add butter and stir until it has fully dissolved into the sauce.

   Mix the cornstarch with water and mix it into the applesauce one third at a time until desired thickness.

   Drizzle the applesauce over the pork chops and serve immediately with side dishes!

133. Pulled Pork Tacos

Preparation + Cook Time: 70 minutes | Servings: 8

Ingredients:

For the pork:

1 ½ tsp sea salt

1 cup chicken broth, OR beef broth

1 piece (4 pounds) pork shoulder (a.k.a pork butt, bone out or in)

1 tsp freshly ground pepper

1 yellow onion, large-sized, peeled and thinly sliced

½ tsp chipotle chili powder

½ tsp cumin

½ tsp garlic powder
Your favorite or preferred tortillas
Garnish:
Purple cabbage, sliced
Cilantro, chopped
Lime

Directions:

1. In a bowl, combine all of the spices until well mixed.
2. Put the onion in the Crock Pot Express™ and pour in the broth.
3. Rub all the sides of the pork with the spice mixture and then put the spice-rubbed pork into the pot. Cover and lock the lid.
4. Press the MEAT key and set the timer for 60 minutes.
5. When the Crock Pot Express™ timer beeps, press the CANCEL key and unplug the Crock Pot Express™. Turn the steam valve to quick release the pressure. Unlock and carefully open the lid.
6. Transfer the meat into a cutting board, discard the onion and the cooking liquid.
7. With 2 forks, shred the meat, discarding the fat in the process.
8. If you want crispy, browned edges, you can sear the shredded meat in a hot pan or broil in the oven for a couple of minutes.
9. Use the shredded meat to make tacos, garnishing with sliced purple cabbage and chopped cilantro.
10. Top with your favorite guacamole and salsa.

134. Short Ribs and Beer

Preparation time: **15 minutes** - Cooking time: **60 minutes** - Servings: **6**

Ingredients:
4 pounds short ribs, cut into small pieces
1 teaspoon vegetable oil
1 yellow onion, peeled and chopped
Salt and ground black pepper, to taste
¼ cup tomato paste
1 cup dark beer
1 cup chicken stock
1 thyme sprig
1 bay leaf
6 thyme sprigs
1 Portobello mushroom, dried

Directions:

1. Set the Crock pot Express™ on "Brown/Sauté" mode, add the oil, and heat it up. Add the ribs, salt, and pepper, brown for 3 minutes on each side, and transfer to a bowl. Add the tomato paste and onion to the Crock pot Express™, stir, and cook for 5 minutes. Add the stock and beer, stir, and cook 30 seconds. Add the mushroom, bay leaves, thyme, and ribs, stir,
2. Cover the Crock pot Express™ and cook on the "meat/stew" setting for 35 minutes. Release the pressure naturally for 15 minutes, uncover the Crock pot Express™, discard the thyme, mushroom, and bay leaves and strain the sauce. Divide the ribs among plates, and serve with beer sauce drizzled all over.

135. Spare Ribs With Wine

Prep: 5 minutes • pressure: 15 minutes • total: 20 minutes • pressure level: high • release: natural • Serves 2-4

Ingredients
1 pound pork spare ribs, cut into pieces
1 tablespoon oil
1 tablespoon corn starch
1 – 2 teaspoon water
Green onions as garnish
1 teaspoon fish sauce (optional)
Black Bean Marinade:
1 tablespoon black bean sauce
1 tablespoon light soy sauce
1 tablespoon Shaoxing wine
1 tablespoon ginger, grated
3 cloves garlic, minced
1 teaspoon sesame oil
1 teaspoon sugar
A pinch of white pepper

Directions
1. **Preparing the Ingredients.** Marinate the pork spare ribs with Black Bean Marinade in an oven-safe bowl. Then, sit it in the fridge for 25 minutes.
   First, mix 1 tablespoon of oil into the marinated spare ribs. Then, add 1 tablespoon of corn starch and mix well. Finally, add 1 – 2 teaspoon of water into the spare ribs and mix well.
   Add 1 cup of water into the Crock-Pot Multi-Cooker®. Place steam rack in the Crock-Pot Multi-Cooker®. Then, put the bowl of spare ribs on the rack.
2. **High pressure for 15 minutes.** Lock the lid on the Crock-Pot Multi-Cooker® and then cook for 15 minutes. To get 15-minutes cook time, press "Poultry" button.

3. **Pressure Release** Let the pressure to come down naturally for at least 15 minutes, then quick release any pressure left in the pot.
4. **Finish the dish**. Taste and add one teaspoon of fish sauce and green onions as garnish if you like.
5. Serve immediately.

136. Cilantro Pork Tacos
Preparation + Cook Time: 45 minutes | Servings: 6

Ingredients:
1 tbsp cilantro
10 oz ground pork
1 tbsp tomato paste
1 red onion
1 tsp salt
1 tsp basil
1 tbsp butter
1 cup lettuce
7 oz corn tortilla
1 tsp paprika

Directions:
1. Combine the ground pork, salt, cilantro, paprika, and basil together in the mixing bowl.
2. Add butter and tomato paste. Stir the mixture well.
3. After this, place the ground pork mixture in the Crock Pot Express™ and close the lid.
4. Cook the dish at the MEAT mode for 27 minutes.
5. Meanwhile, chop the lettuce and peel the onion. Slice the onion.
6. When the meat is cooked – remove it from the Crock Pot Express™ and transfer in the corn tortillas.
7. Then add chopped lettuce and sliced onion. Wrap the tacos.
8. Serve the dish immediately.

137. Pork Carnitas

Preparation time: **10 minutes** - Cooking time: 1 hour and 10 minutes - Servings: **8**

Ingredients:
2 tablespoons extra virgin olive oil
3 pounds pork shoulder, chopped
Salt and ground black pepper, to taste

1 jalapeño pepper, chopped
1 poblano pepper, seeded and chopped
1 green bell pepper, seeded and chopped
3 garlic cloves, peeled and minced
1 yellow onion, peeled and chopped
1 pound tomatillos, cut into quarters
1 teaspoon dried oregano
1 teaspoon cumin
2 cups chicken stock
2 bay leaves
Flour tortillas, for serving
1 red onion, chopped, for serving
Shredded cheddar cheese, for serving

Directions:
1. Set the Crock pot Express™ on "Brown/Sauté" mode, add the oil and heat it up. Add the pork, salt, and pepper and brown them for 3 minutes. Add the bell pepper, jalapeño pepper, poblano pepper, tomatillos, onion, garlic, oregano, cumin, bay leaves, and stock. Stir,
2. Cover, and cook on the "meat/stew" setting for 55 minutes. Release the pressure naturally for 10 minutes, uncover and transfer meat to a cutting board. Puree the mix from the Crock pot Express™ using an immersion blender. Shred the meat with a fork and mix with the puree. Divide the pork mixture onto flour tortillas, add the onion and cheese, and serve.

138. Sausage and Cheesy Mashed Potatoes

Preparation + Cook Time: 35 minutes | Servings: 2

Ingredients:
For the potatoes:
4 floury potatoes, large-sized, peeled and then cut into 1½ -inch sized cubes
½ cup milk
1 tsp mustard powder OR 2 tsp whole-grain or Dijon mustard
1 knob butter
2 oz double Gloucester or mature cheddar cheese, grated, use more, if desired
Salt and pepper to taste
For the sausages:
6 pork sausages, thick pieces (prick each sausage with a sharp knife once)
2 tsp olive oil
1½ cup water
½ cup red wine

½ cup sticky onions (about 6 rounded tablespoon), see notes
1 tbsp corn flour mixed with 1 tbsp cold water
Salt and black pepper to taste

Directions:
1. Put the potatoes in the Crock Pot Express™ and pour in 1 cup of water. Cover and lock the lid.
2. Press the "BEANS/CHILI" key, set the pressure to HIGH, and set the timer for 4 minutes.
3. When the Crock Pot Express™ timer beeps, turn the steam valve to quick release the pressure.
4. Unlock and carefully open the lid. Drain the potatoes in a colander. Let sit for a couple of minutes.
5. Discard the cooking water. Dry the inner pot and return to the housing.
6. Press the "BROWN/SAUTÉ" key and press the More option. Put the oil in the pot and let heat.
7. Add the sausages and cook, stirring occasionally, until all the sides of the sausage are nicely colored.
8. When the sausages are browned, add the onion. Immediately follow with the wine and then ½ cup of water.
9. Press the CANCEL key to stop the "Brown/Sauté" function. Cover and lock the lid.
10. Press the "BEANS/CHILI" key, set the pressure to HIGH, and set the timer for 8 minutes.
11. Meanwhile, heat the milk in a saucepan until hot. Stir in the butter, mustard, and seasoning.
12. Mash the potatoes and mix in the milk mixture into the mashed potatoes until desired texture is achieved.
13. Stir in the cheese and tightly cover with a foil.
14. When the Crock Pot Express™ timer beeps, turn the steam valve to Venting to quick release the pressure.
15. Unlock and carefully open the lid. Press the "BROWN/SAUTÉ" key. While stirring the contents of the pot, pour the corn flour mix in the pot.
16. Bring to a bubble for a few minutes until the sauce is thick to desired consistency.
17. Season to taste and serve over the mash.

Notes: To make sticky onions, cook finely sliced onions in a knob of butter and a little oil until translucent and soft in very low heat for about 30 minutes in a saucepan with the lid on. After 30 minutes, take the lid off, sprinkle the onion with a bit of brown sugar and balsamic vinegar, and then generously season with pepper and salt. Cook until the liquid has evaporated and the onions are nice and sticky.

139. Pork with Orange and Honey

Preparation time: **10 minutes** - Cooking time: **1 hour** - Servings: **4**

Ingredients:

1½ pounds pork shoulder, chopped
3 garlic cloves, peeled and minced
1 cinnamon stick
Juice from 1 orange
Salt and ground black pepper, to taste
1 yellow onion, peeled and sliced
1 tablespoon ginger, sliced
2 cloves
½ cup water
1 teaspoon dried rosemary
1 tablespoon maple syrup
2 tablespoons soy sauce
1 tablespoon vegetable oil
1 tablespoon honey
1 tablespoon water
1½ tablespoons cornstarch

Directions:

1. Set the Crock pot Express™ on "Brown/Sauté" mode, add the oil, and heat it up. Add the pork, salt and pepper, stir, brown for 5 minutes on each side, and transfer to a plate. Add the onions, ginger, salt, and pepper to the Crock pot Express™, stir, and cook for 1 minute. Add the garlic and cook for 30 seconds. Add the orange juice, water, soy sauce, honey, maple syrup, cinnamon, cloves, rosemary, and pork pieces.
2. Cover the Crock pot Express™, cook on the "meat/stew" setting for 50 minutes and release the pressure naturally. Uncover the Crock pot Express™, discard the cinnamon and cloves, add the cornstarch mixed with water, stir, set the Crock pot Express™ on "Brown/Sauté" mode, and cook until the sauce thickens. Divide the pork and sauce among plates, and serve.

140. First Timer's Pork Belly

Preparation + Cook Time: 1 hour 10 minutes | Servings: 4

Ingredients:

1 pound pork belly
½ - 1 cup white wine
1 garlic clove
1 tbsp olive oil to coat the bottom
Rosemary sprig
Salt to taste
Black pepper to taste

Directions:

1. Put oil in your Crock Pot Express™ and turn to the "BROWN/SAUTÉ" setting.
2. When hot, add pork and sear 2-3 minutes on each side until golden and crispy.
3. Pour in wine, about a quarter inch. Season pork with salt, pepper, and garlic.
4. Add garlic clove. Turn on the cooker to "BROWN/SAUTÉ" to boil the liquid.
5. When boiling, lock the lid. Select "BEANS/CHILI" and cook at HIGH pressure for 40 minutes.
6. If you want the pork to be more like steak, cook for 30 minutes.
7. When time is up, hit CANCEL and wait for the pressure to go down on its own.
8. When the pork is room-temperature, slice and season to taste with more salt.

141. Pork Tamales

Preparation time: **10 minutes** - **Cooking time:** 1 hour and 35 minutes - Servings: **24 pieces**

Ingredients:

8 ounces dried corn husks, soaked for 1 day and drained
4 cups water
3 pounds pork shoulder, boneless and chopped
1 yellow onion, peeled and chopped
2 garlic cloves, peeled and crushed
3 tablespoons chili powder
Salt and ground black pepper, to taste
1 teaspoon cumin
4 cups masa
¼ cup corn oil
¼ cup shortening
1 teaspoon baking powder

Directions:

1. In the Crock pot Express™, mix 2 cups of the water with the salt, pepper, onion, garlic, chili powder, and cumin. Add the pork, stir,
2. Cover the Crock pot Express™, and cook on the "meat/stew" setting for 75 minutes. Release the pressure naturally for 10 minutes, uncover the Crock pot Express™, transfer meat to a cutting board, and shred it with 2 forks. Put the pork in a bowl, add 1 tablespoon of the cooking liquid and more salt and pepper, stir and set aside. In a bowl, mix the masa with salt, pepper, baking powder, shortening, and oil and combine using a hand mixer. Add the cooking liquid from the Crock pot Express™ and blend again well. Add 2 cups of water to the Crock pot Express™ and place the steamer basket inside.
3. Unfold 2 of the corn husks, place them on a work surface, add ¼ cup of the masa mixture near the top of the husk, press into a square and leaves 2 inches at the bottom.

Add 1 tablespoon pork in the center of the masa, wrap the husk around the dough and place standing up in the steamer basket. Repeat with the rest of the husks, cover the Crock pot Express™ and cook on the "Steam" setting for 20 minutes. Release the pressure for 15 minutes, uncover the Crock pot Express™, transfer the tamales to plates, and serve.

142. Red Cooked Pork

Preparation + Cook Time: 50 minutes | Servings: 4

Ingredients:
2 pounds fatty pork belly, cut into 1 ½-inch cubes
1/3 cup water OR bone broth
1 tsp sea salt
1 tbsp blackstrap molasses
1 piece (1-inch) ginger, peeled and then smashed
2 tbsp coconut aminos (or soy sauce)
2 tbsp maple syrup
3 tbsp sherry
A couple sprigs coriander OR cilantro leaves, to garnish

Directions:
1. Put the pork cubes in the pot and pour in enough water to cover the pork cubes.
2. Select "BROWN/SAUTÉ" mode and press the More option.
3. Bring to a boil and boil the pork cubes for 3 minutes.
4. When boiled, press the CANCEL setting. Drain the pork cubes and rinse off any impurities of scum off the meat.
5. Put the pork cubes in a colander and set aside in the sink to drain.
6. Clean and dry the inner pot of the Crock Pot Express™.
7. Pour the maple syrup in the pot and press the "BROWN/SAUTÉ" key and heat.
8. Add the pork cubes and brown the meat for about 10 minutes. Add the rest of the ingredients in the pot.
9. Bring to a boil and then press the CANCEL key to stop the "Brown/Sauté" function. Cover and lock the lid.
10. Select "BEANS/CHILI" and cook at HIGH pressure for 25 minutes.
11. When the Crock Pot Express™ timer beeps, release the pressure naturally for 10-15 minutes or until the valve drops. Turn the steam valve to Venting to release remaining pressure. Unlock and carefully open the lid.
12. Press the "BROWN/SAUTÉ" key and bring the contents to a simmer.
13. Cook until the sauce is reduced and thick to your liking.
14. Serve with cilantro or coriander leaves to garnish.
15. Serve the pork cubes with Boston lettuce leaves to wrap them with.

143. Pork Tostadas

Preparation time: **10 minutes** - Cooking time: **30 minutes** - Servings: **4**

Ingredients:
4 pounds pork shoulder, boneless and cubed
Salt and ground black pepper, to taste
2 cups cola
⅓ cup brown sugar
½ cup picante sauce
2 teaspoons chili powder
2 tablespoons tomato paste
¼ teaspoon cumin
1 cup enchilada sauce
Corn tortillas, for serving
Mexican cheese, shredded for serving
Shredded lettuce, for serving
Salsa, for serving
Guacamole, for serving

Directions:
1. In the Crock pot Express™, mix 1 cup of the cola with picante sauce, salsa, sugar, tomato paste, chili powder, and cumin and stir. Add the pork, stir,
2. Cover, and cook on "meat/stew" mode for 25 minutes. Release the pressure for 15 minutes, uncover the Crock pot Express™, drain juice from the Crock pot Express™, transfer the meat to a cutting board and shred it. Return the meat to Crock pot Express™, add the rest of the cola and enchilada sauce, stir, set the Crock pot Express™ on "Brown/Sauté" mode and heat thoroughly. Brown tortillas in the oven at 350ºF for 5 minutes and place them on a working surface. Add the lettuce leaves, cheese and guacamole, fold, and serve.

144. Spare Ribs and Black Bean Sauce

Preparation + Cook Time: 5 minutes | Servings: 4

Ingredients:
1 pound pork spareribs, cut into pieces
1 tbsp corn starch
1 tbsp oil

1 tsp fish sauce, optional
1 cup water plus 1-2 tsp water
Green onions as garnish
For the black bean marinade:
1 tbsp black bean sauce
1 tbsp ginger, grated
1 tbsp light soy sauce
1 tbsp Shaoxing wine
1 tsp sesame oil
1 tsp sugar
3 cloves garlic, minced
A pinch white pepper

Directions:
1. In an oven-safe bowl, combine all the marinade ingredients. Add the pork and marinate for 25 minutes in the refrigerator.
2. When marinated, mix 1 tablespoon oil into the pork and then add the corn starch. Mix well. Add 1 to 2 teaspoon of water and mix well.
3. Pour 1 cup of water into the Crock Pot Express™.
4. Put a steamer rack in the pot and put the bow with the marinated spare ribs on the rack.
5. Press the CANCEL key to stop the "Brown/Sauté" function. Cover and lock the lid. Turn the steam valve to Sealing. Press the "BEANS/CHILI" key, set the pressure to HIGH, and set the timer for 15 minutes.
6. When the Crock Pot Express™ timer beeps, release the pressure naturally for 10-15 minutes or until the valve drops.
7. Turn the steam valve to release remaining pressure. Unlock and carefully open the lid.
8. Taste and, if desired, add 1 teaspoon fish sauce and garnish with green onions.

145. Pork with Hominy

Preparation time: **10 minutes** - Cooking time: **30 minutes** - Servings: **6**

Ingredients:
1¼ pounds pork shoulder, boneless and cut into medium pieces
2 tablespoons vegetable oil
Salt and ground black pepper, to taste
2 tablespoons chili powder
1 white onion, peeled and chopped
4 garlic cloves, peeled and minced
30 ounces canned hominy, drained
4 cups chicken stock

Avocado slices, for serving
Lime wedges, for serving
¼ cup water
2 tablespoons cornstarch

Directions:
Set the Crock pot Express™ on "Brown/Sauté" mode, add 1 tablespoon oil and heat it up. Add the pork, salt, and pepper, brown on all sides, and transfer to a bowl. Add the rest of the oil to the Crock pot Express™ and heat it up. Add the garlic, onion, and chili powder, stir, and sauté for 4 minutes. Add half of the stock, stir, and cook for 1 minute. Add the rest of the stock and return pork to pot, stir,
Cover, and cook on the "Beans/Chili" setting for 30 minutes. Release the pressure naturally for 10 minutes, transfer the pork to a cutting board, and shred with 2 forks. Add the cornstarch mixed with water to the Crock pot Express™ and set on "Brown/Sauté" mode. Add the hominy, more salt and pepper, and shredded pork, stir, and cook for 2 minutes. Divide among bowls, and serve with avocado slices on top and lime wedges on the side.

146. Pork-and-Egg Fried Rice

Preparation + Cook Time: 40 minutes | Servings: 4

Ingredients:
3 cups + 2 tbsp water
2 cups long-grain white rice
1 beaten egg
1 finely-chopped onion
1 peeled and finely-chopped carrot
½ cup frozen peas
8-ounces sliced pork loin chop (½-inch pieces)
3 tbsp soy sauce
3 tbsp veggie oil
Salt and pepper to taste

Directions:
1. Preheat the cooker to "BROWN/SAUTÉ" function and add 1 tablespoon of oil. Stir the onion and carrot for about 2 minutes.
2. Add pork after seasoning with salt and pepper. Cook for 5 minutes or until the meat is cooked all the way through.
3. Press CANCEL and take out the onion, carrot, and pork. Pour in water and deglaze, scraping up any bits.
4. Pour in rice, salt, and seal the lid. Select RICE/RISOTTO and cook for default time.

5. When time is up, press CANCEL and wait 10 minutes for a natural release. Then quick-release any leftover steam.
6. Create a hole in the rice, and pour in the rest of the olive oil before hitting "BROWN/SAUTÉ". Add egg and scramble.
7. When the egg is just about ready, add the peas, onion, carrot, and pork.
8. Keep stirring for a few minutes until everything is mixed in well.
9. Serve with soy sauce!

147. Pork Chops and Brown Rice

Preparation time: **10 minutes** - Cooking time: **25 minutes** - Servings: **6**

Ingredients:
2 cups water
⅓ cup brown sugar
⅓ cup salt
2 cups ice
2 hot peppers, minced
1 tablespoon peppercorns, crushed
4 garlic cloves, peeled and crushed
2 bay leaves
2 pounds pork chops
2 cups brown rice
1 cup onion, peeled and chopped
3 tablespoons butter
2½ cups beef stock
Salt and ground black pepper, to taste

Directions:
1. Heat up a pan over medium-high heat with the water. Add the salt and brown sugar, stir until it dissolves, take off heat, and add the ice. Add the hot peppers, garlic, peppercorns, and bay leaves and stir. Add the pork chops, toss to coat, cover, and keep in the refrigerator for 4 hours. Rinse the pork chops and pat them dry with paper towels. Set the Crock pot Express™ on "Brown/Sauté" mode, add the butter and melt it. Add the pork chops, brown them on all sides, transfer to a plate and set the dish aside. Add the onion to the Crock pot Express™ and cook for 2 minutes. Add the rice, stir, and cook for 1 minute. Add the stock, pork chops,
2. Cover the Crock pot Express™ and cook on the "meat/stew" setting for 22 minutes. Release the pressure naturally for 10 minutes, uncover the Crock pot Express™, add salt and pepper, divide the pork chops and rice among plates, and serve.

148. Kalua Pork

Preparation time: **10 minutes** - Cooking time: **90 minutes** - Servings: **5**

Ingredients:
4 pounds pork shoulder, cut into half
½ cup water
2 tablespoons vegetable oil
Salt and ground black pepper, to taste
1 tablespoon liquid smoke
Steamed green beans, for serving

Directions:
1. Set the Crock pot Express™ on "Brown/Sauté" mode, add the oil, and heat it up. Add the pork, salt, and pepper, brown for 3 minutes on each side, and transfer to a plate. Add the water and liquid smoke to the Crock pot Express™ and stir. Return the meat, stir,
2. Cover the Crock pot Express™ and cook on the "meat/stew" setting for 90 minutes. Release the pressure for 15 minutes, transfer the meat to a cutting board and shred it with 2 forks. Divide the pork on plates, add some of the sauce on top, and serve with steamed green beans on the side.

Main Dishes – Soups

149. Cheddar Broccoli and Potato Soup

Preparation + Cook Time: 25 minutes | Servings: 4

Ingredients:
1 broccoli head, medium-sized, broken into large florets
1 cup cheddar cheese, shredded
1 cup half and half
2 cloves garlic, crushed
2 pounds Yukon Gold Potatoes, peeled and then cut into small chunks
2 tbsp butter
4 cups vegetable broth
Chives or green onion, chopped, for garnish
Salt and pepper to taste

Directions:
1. Press the "BROWN/SAUTÉ" key. When the pot is hot, add the butter and the garlic, and sauté for 1 minute or until the garlic starts to brown.
2. Add the potatoes, broccoli, broth, and season with a bit of salt and pepper. Lock the lid and close the steam valve. Cook on the "Steam" setting for 5 minutes at HIGH pressure.
3. When the timer beeps, press CANCEL and let the pressure release naturally for 10 minutes. Open the steam valve to release remaining pressure.
4. Add the half-and-half and ½ cup cheddar cheese. Using an immersion blender, blend until smooth.
5. Alternatively, you can blend in batches in a large-sized blender. If you want a thinner soup, just add more broth.
6. Season with salt and pepper to taste.
7. Serve hot with remaining cheddar.

150. Cream of Asparagus Soup

Prep: 10 Minutes • Pressure: High • Time Under Pressure: 5 Minutes • Release: Natural • SERVES: 4-6

Ingredients

    1 tablespoon olive oil

    3 green onions, sliced crosswise into ¼-inch pieces

    1 pound asparagus, tough ends removed, cut into 1-inch pieces

    4 cups salt-free Chicken Stock

    1 tablespoon unsalted butter

    1 tablespoon all-purpose flour

    2 teaspoons salt

    1 teaspoon ground white pepper, plus more as needed

    ½ cup heavy cream

Directions

1. **Preparing the Ingredients.** Heat the Crock-Pot Multi-Cooker® using the "Sauté" function, add the oil, green onions, and a pinch of salt. Sauté the green onions for a few minutes, then add the asparagus and stock.
2. **High pressure for 5 minutes**. Lock the lid on the Crock-Pot Multi-Cooker® and then cook for 5 minutes. To get 5-minutes cook time, press "Soup" Button and use the TIME ADJUSTMENT button to adjust the cook time to 5 minutes.

   Meanwhile, make a blond roux: In a small saucepan over low heat, mix together the butter and flour and cook, stirring constantly, until the butter has melted and the mixture foams and begins to turn golden beige. Remove from the heat.
3. **Pressure Release.** When the time is up, open the cooker with the Natural Release method.
4. **Finish the dish.** Add the roux, salt, and pepper to the soup and puree with an immersion blender until smooth. Taste and season with more pepper if you wish. Swirl in the cream just before serving.
5. Serve and Enjoy!

151. Chicken Soup

Preparation time: **10 minutes** - Cooking time: **17 minutes** - Servings: **4**

Ingredients:

4 chicken breasts, skinless and boneless

2 tablespoons extra virgin olive oil

1 onion, peeled and chopped

3 garlic cloves, peeled and minced

16 ounces chunky salsa

29 ounces canned diced tomatoes

29 ounces chicken stock

Salt and ground black pepper, to taste

2 tablespoons dried parsley

1 teaspoon garlic powder

1 tablespoon onion powder

1 tablespoon chili powder
15 ounces frozen corn
32 ounces canned black beans, drained

Directions:
1. Set the Crock pot Express™ on "Brown/Sauté" mode, add the oil, and heat it up. Add the onion, stir, and cook 5 minutes. Add the garlic, stir, and cook for 1 minute. Add the chicken breasts, salsa, tomatoes, stock, salt, pepper, parsley, garlic powder, onion powder, and chili powder, stir,
2. Cover, and cook on the "Soup" Setting for 8 minutes. Release the pressure for 10 minutes, uncover the Crock pot Express™, transfer the chicken breasts to a cutting board, shred with 2 forks, and return to pot. Add the beans and corn, set the Crock pot Express™ on "Steam" mode and cook for 2-3 minutes. Divide into soup bowls, and serve.

152. Potato Soup with Leek and Cheddar
Preparation + Cook Time: 25 minutes | Servings: 8

Ingredients:
4 medium gold potatoes, peeled and diced, I used Yukon
1½ cups cream or half and half
1/3 cup cheddar cheese, grated
3 tbsp leeks, cleaned and thinly sliced, white and light green (reserve 2 for serving)
1½ tsp dried oregano
1 tsp kosher salt
2 bay leaves
2 tbsp unsalted butter
¾ cup white wine
4 cloves garlic, crushed
4 sprigs fresh thyme
5 cups vegetable broth
Leeks, and cheese, for topping

Directions:
1. Set the Crock Pot Express™ to "BROWN/SAUTÉ".
2. Put the butter in the pot and melt. When melted, add the leek and season with salt and sauté until soft.
3. Add the garlic and sauté for 30 seconds. Press CANCEL. Reserve a few portion of the leek and set aside for serving.
4. Add the thyme, bay leaves, oregano, broth, white wine, and potatoes into the pot. Stir to mix.
5. Close and lock the lid. Cook on the "Beans/Chili" setting for 10 minutes Set the pressure to HIGH .

6. When the timer beeps, quick release the pressure. Carefully open the pot.
7. Add the cream and with an immersion blender, puree the soup until desired consistency. Press the "KEEP WARM" button and heat the soup through.
8. When the soup is hot, sprinkle with the sautéed leeks, and sprinkle with cheese.

153. Chicken Soup

Prep: 10 minutes • pressure: 35 minutes • total: 45 minutes • pressure level: high • release: natural • Serves 8

Ingredients
2 frozen boneless skinless chicken breasts
4 washed medium size diced potatoes (I did not peel you can if you want)
3 peeled carrots chopped into similar size as potatoes for even cooking time
1/2 large onion diced
4 cups of water and chicken concentrate/bullion of your choice to equal 32 ounces – or if you have it, use chicken stock
Salt and pepper to taste (flavors will intensify while under pressure)

Directions

1. **Preparing the Ingredients** Mix the broth, chicken, potatoes, onion, carrots, salt, and pepper in the Crock-Pot Multi-Cooker®.
2. **High pressure for 35 minutes.** Lock the lid on the Crock-Pot Multi-Cooker® and then cook for 35 minutes. To get 35-minutes cook time, press "Soup" Button and use the TIME ADJUSTMENT button to adjust the cook time to 35 minutes.
3. **Pressure Release** Let the pressure to come down naturally for at least 15 minutes, then quick release any pressure left in the pot.
4. Open when all pressure is released stir and enjoy.

154. Corn Soup

Preparation time: **10 minutes** - Cooking time: **15 minutes** - Servings: **4**

Ingredients:
2 leeks, chopped
2 tablespoons butter
2 garlic cloves, peeled and minced
6 ears of corn, kernels cut off, cobs reserved
2 bay leaves
4 tarragon sprigs, chopped

1-quart chicken stock
Salt and ground black pepper, to taste
Extra virgin olive oil
1 tablespoon fresh chives, chopped

Directions:
1. Set the Crock pot Express™ on "Brown/Sauté" mode, add the butter and melt it. Add the garlic and leeks, stir, and cook for 4 minutes. Add the corn, corn cobs, bay leaves, tarragon, and stock to cover everything,
2. Cover the Crock pot Express™ and cook on the "Soup" Setting for 15 minutes. Release the pressure, uncover the Crock pot Express™, discard the bay leaves and corn cobs, and transfer everything to a blender. Pulse well to obtain a smooth soup, add the rest of the stock and blend again. Add the salt and pepper, stir well, divide into soup bowls, and serve cold with chives and olive oil on top.

155. Bean Soup

Preparation + Cook Time: 65 minutes | Servings: 6

Ingredients:
1 cup cannellini beans
7 cups water
1 cup dill
4 tbsp salsa
1 jalapeno pepper
1/3 cup cream
2 tsp salt
1 tsp white pepper
1 white onions
1 sweet red pepper
1-pound chicken fillet
1 tsp soy sauce

Directions:
1. Place the cannellini beans in the Crock Pot Express™.
2. Chop the chicken fillet and add it in the Crock Pot Express™ too.
3. Add water and cook the beans at the "Beans/Chili" mode on HIGH PRESSURE for 35 minutes.
4. Meanwhile, chop the dill and jalapeno peppers. Slice the onions and chop the sweet red peppers.
5. Add the vegetables to bean mixture and close the lid. Press "Soup" Mode and cook the dish for 15 minutes more.

6. Then sprinkle the soup with the cream, salsa, white pepper, and soy sauce. Stir the soup carefully and cook it for 5 minutes more.
7. Remove the soup from the Crock Pot Express™ and let it a little chill.
8. Ladle the soup into the serving bowls. Enjoy!

156. Chicken Stock

Prep: 10 minutes • pressure: 60 minutes • total: 70 minutes • pressure level: high • release: natural • Serves 10 cups

Ingredients
2 ½ pounds chicken carcasses
2 onions (keep the outer layers too), diced
2 celery stalks, diced
2 carrots, diced
2 bay leaves
4 garlic cloves, crushed
1 teaspoon whole peppercorn
10 cups water
Your favorite fresh herbs
1 tablespoon apple cider vinegar (optional)

Directions
1. **Preparing the Ingredients.** Optional step: Brown the chicken carcasses in your Crock-Pot Multi-Cooker® with 1 tablespoon of oil. This will slightly elevate the flavors and result in a brown stock. Then, add water to deglaze the pot with 100 ml of water.
   Add all ingredients in the Crock-Pot Multi-Cooker®
2. **High pressure for 60 minutes**. Lock the lid on the Crock-Pot Multi-Cooker® and then cook for 60 minutes. To get 60-minutes cook time, press "Soup" Button and use the TIME ADJUSTMEN button to adjust the cook time to 60 minutes.
3. **Pressure Release.** When the time is up, open the cooker with the Natural Release method
4. **Finish the dish** Open the lid. Strain the stock through a colander discarding the solids, and set aside to cool. Let the stock sit in the fridge until the fat rises to the top and form a layer of gel. Then, skim off the fat on the surface.
   You can use the stock immediately, keep it in the fridge, or freeze it for future use.
   Storage: -Silicone Mold – We love freezing our chicken stock with this mold!! After they freeze in the mold, we pop them out and store them in Ziploc freezer bags. It's a great portion for many recipes, thaws quickly, and super convenient.

157. Butternut Squash Soup

Preparation time: **10 minutes** - Cooking time: **16 minutes** - Servings: **6**

Ingredients:
1½ pounds butternut squash, baked, peeled and cubed
½ cup green onions, chopped
3 tablespoons butter
½ cup carrots, peeled and chopped
½ cup celery, chopped
29 ounces chicken stock
1 garlic clove, peeled and minced
½ teaspoon Italian seasoning
15 ounces canned diced tomatoes
Salt and ground black pepper, to taste
1/8 teaspoon red pepper flakes
1 cup orzo, already cooked
1/8 teaspoon nutmeg, grated
1½ cup half and half
1 cup chicken meat, already cooked and shredded
Green onions, chopped, for serving

Directions:
1. Set the Crock pot Express™ on "Brown/Sauté" mode, add the butter and melt it. Add the celery, carrots, and onions, stir, and cook for 3 minutes. Add the garlic, stir, and cook for 1 minute. Add the squash, tomatoes, stock, Italian seasoning, salt, pepper, pepper flakes, and nutmeg. Stir,
2. Cover the Crock pot Express™, and cook on the "Soup" Setting for 10 minutes. Release the pressure, uncover, and puree everything with an immersion blender. Set the Crock pot Express™ on "Steam" mode, add the half and half, orzo, and chicken, stir, and cook for 3 minutes. Divide the soup into bowls, sprinkle green onions on top, and serve.

157. Mushroom Barley Soup

Preparation + Cook Time: 35 minutes | Servings: 8

Ingredients:
1 onion, medium-sized, diced
1 pound baby Bella mushrooms, sliced
1 sage sprig
1 tsp salt
¼ tsp freshly ground pepper
¼ tsp garlic powder

2 carrots, diced

2 stalks celery, diced

¾ cup pearl barley (do not use instant)

4 garlic cloves, chopped

4 thyme sprigs

8 cups beef broth or stock

Directions:

1. Pour all of the ingredients in the Crock Pot Express™ and stir to mix. Cover and lock the lid.
2. Press the "BEANS/CHILI" key, set the pressure to HIGH, and set the timer for 20 minutes.
3. When the Crock Pot Express™ timer beeps, press the CANCEL key and unplug the Crock Pot Express™. Let the pressure release naturally for 10 minutes. Turn the steam valve to release remaining pressure.
4. Unlock and carefully open the lid. Serve and enjoy!

158. French Onion Soup

Prep: 5 minutes • pressure: 35 minutes • total: 40 minutes • pressure level: high • release: natural • Serves 2-4

Ingredients

2 tablespoons unsalted butter, divided

4 cups thinly sliced white or yellow onions, divided

½ teaspoon kosher salt, plus additional for seasoning

¼ cup dry sherry

2 cups low-sodium chicken broth

½ cup Beef Stock, Mushroom Stock, or low-sodium broth

½ teaspoon Worcestershire sauce

¼ teaspoon dried thyme

1 teaspoon sherry vinegar or red wine vinegar, plus additional as needed

1 ounce Gruyère or other Swiss-style cheese, coarsely grated (about ⅓ cup)

2 thin slices French or Italian bread

Directions

1. **Preparing the Ingredients.** Set the Crock-Pot Multi-Cooker® to "brown," heat 1 tablespoon of butter until it stops foaming, and then add 1 cup of onions. Sprinkle with a pinch or two of kosher salt, and stir to coat with the butter. Cook the onions in a single layer for about 4 minutes, or until browned. Resist the urge to stir them until you see them browning. Stir them to expose the other side to the heat, and cook for 4 minutes

more. The onions should be quite browned but still slightly firm. Remove the onions from the pan, and set aside.

Pour the sherry into the pot, and stir to scrape up the browned bits from the bottom. When the sherry has mostly evaporated, add the remaining 1 tablespoon of butter, and let it melt. Stir in the remaining 3 cups of onions, and sprinkle with ½ teaspoon of kosher salt.

2. **High pressure for 25 minutes.** Lock the lid on the Crock-Pot Multi-Cooker® and then cook for 25 minutes. To get 25-minutes cook time, press "Soup" Button and use the TIME ADJUSTMENT button to adjust the cook time to 25 minutes.
3. **Pressure Release** Use the quick-release method.

   Unlock and remove the lid.

   The onions should be pale and very soft, with a lot of liquid in the pot. Add the chicken broth, Beef Stock, Worcestershire sauce, and thyme.
4. **High pressure for 10 minutes**. Lock the lid on the Crock-Pot Multi-Cooker® and then cook for 10 minutes. To get 10-minutes cook time, press "Soup" Button and use the TIME ADJUSTMENT button to adjust the cook time to 10 minutes.
5. **Pressure Release** Use the quick-release method.
6. **Finish the dish.** Unlock and remove the lid. Stir in the sherry vinegar, and taste. The soup should be balanced between the sweetness of the onions, the savory stock, and the acid from the vinegar. If it seems bland, add a pinch or two of kosher salt or a little more vinegar. Stir in the reserved cup of onions, and keep warm while you prepare the cheese toasts.
7. Preheat the broiler. Reserve 2 tablespoons of the cheese, and sprinkle the remaining cheese evenly over the 2 bread slices. Place the bread slices on a sheet pan under the broiler for 2 to 3 minutes, or until the cheese melts.

   Place 1 tablespoon of the reserved cheese in each of 2 bowls. Ladle the soup into the bowls, float a toast slice on top of each, and serve.

PER SERVING: CALORIES: 366; FAT: 17G; SODIUM: 1,122MG; CARBOHYDRATES: 40G; FIBER: 6G; PROTEIN: 14G

159. Potato and Cheese Soup

Preparation time: **10 minutes** - Cooking time: **10 minutes** - Servings: **6**

Ingredients:
6 cups potatoes, cubed
2 tablespoons butter
½ cup yellow onion, chopped
28 ounces chicken stock
Salt and ground black pepper, to taste
2 tablespoons dried parsley
1/8 teaspoon red pepper flakes

2 tablespoons cornstarch
2 tablespoons water
3 ounces cream cheese, cubed
2 cups half and half
1 cup cheddar cheese, shredded
1 cup corn
6 bacon slices, cooked and crumbled

Directions:
1. Set the Crock pot Express™ on "Brown/Sauté" mode, add the butter and melt it. Add the onion, stir, and cook 5 minutes. Add half of the stock, salt, pepper, pepper flakes, and parsley and stir. Put the potatoes in the steamer basket,
2. Cover the Crock pot Express™ and cook on the "Steam" setting for 4 minutes. Release the pressure: Quick Method, uncover the Crock pot Express™, and transfer the potatoes to a bowl. In another bowl, mix the cornstarch with water and stir well. Set the Crock pot Express™ to "Brown/Sauté" mode, add the cornstarch slurry, cream cheese, and shredded cheese and stir well. Add the rest of the stock, corn, bacon, potatoes, half and half. Stir, bring to a simmer, ladle into bowls, and serve.

160. Cream of Asparagus Soup

Preparation + Cook Time: 25 minutes | Servings: 4

Ingredients:
8 ounces organic sour cream
5 cups bone broth, homemade or store-bought
3 tbsp ghee, grass-fed butter or healthy fat of choice
2 pounds fresh asparagus, woody ends removed and then cut into 1-inch pieces
2 garlic cloves, smashed or chopped
½ tsp dried thyme
1 yellow onion, chopped
1 tsp sea salt to taste
1 lemon, organic, zested and juiced

Directions:
1. Press the "BROWN/SAUTÉ" key of the Crock Pot Express™. Add your healthy fat of choice.
2. When the fat is melted, add the garlic and onion, and cook for 5 minutes, occasionally stirring, just until the garlic and onions are fragrant and start to caramelize.
3. Add the dried thyme and cook, stirring, for 1 minute. Add the broth.
4. With a wooden spoon, scrape any caramelized bits in the bottom of the pot.
5. Add the asparagus, lemon juice, lemon zest, and salt. Press the CANCEL key to stop the "Brown/Sauté" function. Lock the lid and close the steam valve.

6. Press the "BEANS/CHILI", set the pressure to HIGH, and set the timer to 5 minutes.
7. When the timer beeps, press CANCEL and unplug the pot. Let the pressure release naturally. Open the steam valve and carefully open the lid.
8. With an immersion blender, puree the soup or blend in small batches using a blender until soft.
9. Add the sour cream during blending. Return into the Crock Pot Express™, if using a blender and reheat if needed. Alternatively, you can reheat in a stockpot.
10. Season to taste, as needed.
11. Top each serving with extra sour cream, extra-virgin olive oil, or lemon juice.

Notes: If you want a dairy-free soup, use plain or full-fat coconut milk instead of sour cream. This will change the taste of the soup a bit. You can also use bacon fat or avocado oil instead of ghee. You can store this soup in the refrigerator for 2 days.

161. Roasted Tomato Soup

Prep: 5 minutes • pressure: high • time under pressure: 10 minutes • release: quick • Serves: 2

Ingredients.
3 tablespoons olive oil
½ cup sliced onion
Kosher salt
1 medium garlic clove, sliced or minced
¼ cup dry or medium-dry sherry
1 (14.5-ounce) can fire-roasted tomatoes
1 small roasted red bell pepper, cut into chunks (about ¼ cup)
¾ cup Chicken Stock or low-sodium broth
⅛ teaspoon ground cumin
⅛ teaspoon freshly ground black pepper
1 tablespoon heavy (whipping) cream (optional)

Directions
1. **Preparing the Ingredients.** Set the Crock-Pot Multi-Cooker ® to brown, heat the olive oil until it shimmers and flows like water. Add the onions, and sprinkle with a pinch or two of kosher salt. Cook for about 5 minutes, stirring, until the onions just begin to brown. Add the garlic, and cook for 1 to 2 minutes more, or until fragrant.
   Pour in the sherry, and simmer for 1 to 2 minutes, or until the sherry is reduced by half, scraping up any browned bits from the bottom of the pan. Add the tomatoes, roasted red bell pepper, and Chicken Stock to the Crock-Pot Multi-Cooker®
2. **High pressure for 10 minutes.** Lock the lid on the Crock-Pot Multi-Cooker® and then cook for 10 minutes. To get 10-minutes cook time, press "Soup" Button and use the TIME ADJUSTMENT button to adjust the cook time to 10 minutes.

3. **Pressure Release** Use the quick-release method.
4. **Finish the dish** For a smooth soup, blend using an immersion or standard blender. Add the cumin and pepper, and adjust the salt, if necessary. If you like a creamier soup, stir in the heavy cream.

   If using a standard blender, be careful. Steam can build up and blow the lid off if the soup is very hot. Hold the lid on with a towel, and blend in batches, if necessary; don't fill the jar more than halfway full.

PER SERVING: CALORIES: 287; FAT: 24G; SODIUM: 641MG; CARBOHYDRATES: 16G; FIBER: 4G; PROTEIN: 4G

162. Split Pea Soup

Preparation time: **10 minutes** - Cooking time: **20 minutes** - Servings: **6**

Ingredients:
2 tablespoons butter
1 pound chicken sausage, ground
1 yellow onion, peeled and chopped
½ cup carrots, peeled and chopped
½ cup celery, chopped
2 garlic cloves, peeled and minced
29 ounces chicken stock
Salt and ground black pepper, to taste
2 cups water
16 ounces split peas, rinsed
½ cup half and half
¼ teaspoon red pepper flakes

Directions:
1. Set the Crock pot Express™ on "Brown/Sauté" mode, add the sausage, brown it on all sides and transfer to a plate. Add the butter to the Crock pot Express™ and melt it. Add the celery, onions, and carrots, stir, and cook 4 minutes. Add the garlic, stir and cook for 1 minute. Add the water, stock, peas and pepper flakes, stir,
2. Cover and cook on the "Soup" Setting for 10 minutes. Release the pressure, puree the mix using an immersion blender and set the Crock pot Express™ on "Brown/Sauté" mode. Add the sausage, salt, pepper, and half and half, stir, bring to a simmer, and ladle into soup bowls.

163. Butternut Squash Soup with Chicken Orzo

Prep: 5 minutes • pressure: high • time under pressure: 20 minutes • release: quick • Serves: 6

Ingredients
1 ½ pounds of fresh baked butternut squash, peeled and cubed
1 tomato diced
3 tablespoons butter
1 onion, diced
1 garlic clove, minced
½ cup celery, diced
½ cup carrots, diced
2 cans chicken broth
2 tablespoon red pepper flakes
2 tablespoon dried parsley flakes
¼ teaspoon freshly ground black pepper
1 cup orzo, cooked
1 cup chicken breast, seasoned, cooked and diced

Directions
1. **Preparing the Ingredients.** Set the Crock-Pot Multi-Cooker ® to brown, and melt butter to sauté the onion, garlic clove, celery and carrots.
   Then add the chicken broth, red pepper flakes, dried parsley flakes, black pepper, baked butternut squash and tomato diced to the Crock-Pot Multi-Cooker®
2. **High pressure for 15 minutes.** Lock the lid on the Crock-Pot Multi-Cooker® and then cook for 15 minutes. To get 15-minutes cook time, press "Poultry" button.
3. **Pressure Release** Use the quick-release method.
   Blend/puree until mixture is smooth.
4. **High pressure for 5 minutes.** Then add it back to your Crock-Pot Multi-Cooker® along with the chicken breast and orzo and cook for another 5 minutes. To get 5-minutes cook time, press "Soup" Button.
5. **Pressure Release** Use the quick-release method.
6. Serve with fresh dinner rolls and butter on the side

164. BEEF STOCK

Prep: 5 minutes • pressure: high • time under pressure: 90 minutes • release: quick • Serves: 10

Ingredients
2 lb (907 g) beef soup bones
3 large carrots
1 large onion, quartered, skin on
1 bay leaf

3 celery sticks
Handful fresh parsley
2 tsp (5 g) ground pepper
1 tsp (5 g) ground Himalayan salt
2 tbsp (19 g) garlic, minced
3 tbsp (45 ml) apple cider vinegar
Water

Directions

1. **Preparing the Ingredients.** Ideally, baking the bones at 375°F (190°C) for 30 minutes prior to pressure cooking them helps draw out the marrow, but if you only have access to your pressure cooker, it will still get the job done. To start the stock, place the bones, veggies and seasonings into the Crock-Pot Multi-Cooker®. Pour in the apple cider vinegar and cover with water. The amount of water will vary based on the size and quantities of your vegetables. You can add in extra greens if you want.
2. **High pressure for 90 minutes.** Lock the lid on the Crock-Pot Multi-Cooker® and then cook for 90 minutes. To get 90-minutes cook time, press "meat/stew" button and use the TIME ADJUSTMENT button to adjust the cook time to 90 minutes.
3. **Pressure Release** Once complete, quick-release the pressure valve, allowing the steam to escape.

165. Butternut Squash Sweet Potato Soup
Preparation + Cook Time: 40 minutes | Servings: 4

Ingredients:
3 cups bone broth or vegetable broth or chicken broth
2 tbsp coconut oil
2 cups sweet potatoes, peeled and cubed
2 cups butternut squash, peeled, seeded, and cubed
2 cloves garlic, crushed
½ tsp turmeric
½ tsp ground nutmeg
1 tsp walnuts, chopped, for garnish, optional
1 tsp or pinch of sea salt
1 tsp fresh parsley, for garnish, optional
1 tsp dried tarragon
1 tsp cinnamon
1 onion, small-medium, cubed
1 inch ginger, peeled
1 ½ tsp curry powder

Directions:
1. Press the "BROWN/SAUTÉ" key of the Crock Pot Express™.

2. When the pot is hot, add the coconut oil, ginger, garlic, onions, and pinch of salt. Sauté until the onion is slightly soft.
3. Add the rest of the ingredients and stir to mix. Lock the lid and close the steam valve. Press "BEANS/CHILI" and cook at HIGH pressure for 10 minutes.
4. When the timer beeps, let the pressure release naturally. Carefully open the lid.
5. With an immersion blender, puree the soup right in the pot.
6. Alternatively, transfer the soup in a blender of a food processor, and puree in batches if needed. Be careful because the soup will be hot.
7. Serve immediately and garnish.

166. Enchilada Soup

Preparation + Cook Time: 35 minutes | Servings: 6

Ingredients:
1 ½ pounds chicken thighs, boneless, skinless
1 bell pepper, thinly sliced
1 can (14.5 ounces) fire-roasted crushed tomatoes
1 onion, thinly sliced
1 tbsp chili powder
1 tbsp cumin
1 tsp oregano
½ cup water
½ tsp ground pepper
½ tsp sea salt
½ tsp smoked paprika
2 cups bone broth
3 cloves garlic, minced
For garnish:
Fresh cilantro
1 avocado

Directions:
1. Except for the garnish ingredients, put all of the ingredients in the pot in the following order: chicken, tomatoes, bell pepper, onion, garlic, broth, water, cumin, chili powder, oregano, paprika, sea salt, pepper. Cover and lock the lid.
2. Press the "BEANS/CHILI" key, set the pressure to HIGH, and set the timer for 20minutes.
3. When the Crock Pot Express™ timer beeps, press the CANCEL key and unplug the Crock Pot Express™. Turn the steam valve to quick release the pressure.
4. Unlock and carefully open the lid. Using 2 forks, shred the chicken right in the Crock Pot Express™.

5. Ladle into servings bowls and top each serving with fresh cilantro and avocado.

167. Simple Chicken Soup

Preparation + Cook Time: 50 minutes | Servings: 4

Ingredients:
2 cups water
2 cups chicken stock
2 frozen, boneless chicken breasts
4 medium-sized potatoes
Three peeled carrots
½ big diced onion
Salt and pepper to taste

Directions:
1. Put everything into the Crock Pot Express™, including salt and pepper.
2. Select "BEANS/CHILI" and cook at HIGH pressure for 35 minutes.
3. When time is up, turn off the cooker and let the pressure release naturally for 15 minutes.
4. Carefully open the cooker, stir, and serve!

168. Beef and Rice Soup

Preparation time: **10 minutes** - Cooking time: **15 minutes** - Servings: **6**

Ingredients:
1 pound ground beef
3 garlic cloves, peeled and minced
1 yellow onion, peeled and chopped
1 tablespoon vegetable oil
1 celery stalk, chopped
28 ounces beef stock
14 ounces canned crushed tomatoes
½ cup white rice
12 ounces spicy tomato juice
15 ounces canned garbanzo beans, rinsed
1 potato, cubed
Salt and ground black pepper, to taste
½ cup frozen peas
2 carrots, peeled and sliced thin

Directions:

1. Set the Crock pot Express™ on "Brown/Sauté" mode, add the beef, stir, cook until it browns, and transfer to a plate. Add the oil to the Crock pot Express™ and heat it up. Add the celery and onion, stir, and cook for 5 minutes. Add the garlic, stir and cook for 1 minute. Add the tomato juice, stock, tomatoes, rice, beans, carrots, potatoes, beef, salt, and pepper, stir,
2. Cover and cook on the "Beans/Chili" setting for 5 minutes. Release the pressure, uncover the Crock pot Express™, and set it on "Brown/Sauté" mode. Add more salt and pepper, if needed, and the peas, stir, bring to a simmer, transfer to bowls, and serve hot.

169. Chicken Noodle Soup

Preparation + Cook Time: 30 minutes | Servings: 6

Ingredients:
3 TB butter
1 medium onion diced
2 large carrots diced
3 celery stalks diced
5 garlic cloves minced
1 tsp dried thyme
1 tsp oregano
1 tsp dried basil
8 cups chicken broth or vegetable broth, Homemade broth is preferable for extra nourishment but use a quality store-bought broth if you need.
2 cups cooked chicken leftovers cubed, You can add more if you like your soup meatier, or leave it out if you wish for it to be a vegetable-based soup.
8 oz spaghetti noodles break them in half
2-3 cups chopped spinach amount depends on your preference.
Salt and black pepper to taste

Directions:

1. Press the "BROWN/SAUTÉ" button and melt the butter in the Crock Pot Express™. Once melted, add the onion, carrot, celery, and a big pinch of salt to bring out their juices. You can cook the veggies for about 5 minutes until they're soft and sweet.
2. Add the garlic, thyme, oregano, and basil. Cook for 1 minute.
3. Add the broth, chicken, and noodles, and turn off the Crock Pot Express™ so the "Brown/Sauté" mode turns off.
4. Close the lid and press the "Soup" Button. Cook for 5 minutes.

5. The Crock Pot Express™ will take about 10 minutes to come to pressure, and then it will count down the 4 minutes. When the 4 minutes is done, quick release the pressure. It will take 1-2 minutes to release all of the pressure.
6. Take the lid off, stir in your chopped spinach to wilt, and more salt and pepper (to your taste). The soup is hot enough to wilt the spinach - no need to add more heat!
7. Taste the soup, and add salt as needed.
8. Serve warm.

170. Chicken Noodle Soup

Preparation time: **10 minutes** - Cooking time: **12 minutes** - Servings: **6**

Ingredients:
1 yellow onion, peeled and chopped
1 tablespoon butter
1 celery stalk, chopped
4 carrots, peeled and sliced
Salt and ground black pepper, to taste
6 cups chicken stock
2 cups chicken, already cooked and shredded
Egg noodles, already cooked

Directions:
1. Set the Crock pot Express™ on "Brown/Sauté" mode, add the butter and heat it up. Add the onion, stir, and cook 2 minutes. Add the celery and carrots, stir, and cook 5 minutes. Add the chicken and stock, stir,
2. Cover the Crock pot Express™ and cook on the "Soup" Setting for 5 minutes. Release the pressure, uncover the Crock pot Express™, add salt and pepper to taste, and stir. Divide the noodles into soup bowls, add the soup over them, and serve.

171. Chicken Cream Cheese

Preparation + Cook Time: 35 minutes | Servings: 6

Ingredients:
1 can black beans, drained and rinsed (15 ounces)
1 can corn, undrained (15.25 ounces)
1 can rotel tomato, undrained (10 ounces)
1 pound chicken breasts, boneless skinless
1 package dry ranch seasoning (1 ounce)

2 tsp cumin, or to taste

2 tsp chili powder, or to taste

8 oz of cream cheese

Directions:
1. Put all the ingredients in the Crock Pot Express™. Lock the lid and close the steam valve.
2. Press the "BEANS/CHILI", set the pressure to HIGH, and set the timer to 20 minutes.
3. When the timer beeps, let the pressure release for 10-15 minutes.
4. Open the steam valve to release any remaining pressure from the pot. Carefully open the lid.
5. Remove the chicken and shred.
6. Break up the cream cheese and stir into the pot. Cover and let the cheese melt.
7. When the cheese is melted, open the lid and return the shredded meat in the pot. Stir everything to mix.

Notes: Serve with tortilla chips or rice.

172. Chicken and Wild Rice Soup

Preparation time: **10 minutes** - Cooking time: **15 minutes** - Servings: **6**

Ingredients:
1 cup yellow onion, peeled and chopped
2 tablespoons butter
1 cup celery, chopped
1 cup carrots, chopped
28 ounces chicken stock
2 chicken breasts, skinless, boneless and chopped
6 ounces wild rice
Red pepper flakes
Salt and ground black pepper, to taste
1 tablespoon dried parsley
2 tablespoons cornstarch mixed with 2 tablespoons water
1 cup milk
1 cup half and half
4 ounces cream cheese, cubed

Directions:
1. Set the Crock pot Express™ on "Brown/Sauté" mode, add the butter and melt it. Add the carrot, onion, and celery, stir and cook for 5 minutes. Add the rice, chicken, stock, parsley, salt, and pepper, stir,

2. Cover, and cook on the "Soup" Setting for 5 minutes. Release the pressure, uncover, add the cornstarch mixed with water, stir, and set the Crock pot Express™ on "Brown/Sauté" mode. Add the cheese, milk, and half and half, stir, heat up, transfer to bowls, and serve.

173. Chicken Tortilla Soup

Preparation + Cook Time: 30 minutes | Servings: 4

Ingredients:
2, 6-inch corn tortillas cut into 1-inch squares
3-4 cups chicken broth
3 chicken breasts
1 big, chopped tomato
1 chopped onion
2 minced garlic cloves
15 ounces of black beans
1 cup frozen corn
2 tbsp chopped cilantro
1 bay leaf
1 tbsp olive oil
2 tsp chili powder
1 tsp ground cumin
¼ tsp ground cayenne pepper

Directions:
1. Turn on the Crock Pot Express™ to "BROWN/SAUTÉ".
2. Pour in the olive oil and cook the onion while stirring until soft.
3. Add the cilantro, garlic, and tortillas. Stir and wait 1 minute.
4. Add the black beans, corn, tomato, 3 cups of broth, chicken, and spices.
5. Turn off the "BROWN/SAUTÉ" function and close the lid.
6. Switch over to "Soup" Mode and adjust the time to just 5 minutes.
7. When time is up, quick-release the pressure.
8. Carefully take out the chicken and shred before returning back to the pot. Stir everything well.
9. Serve with cilantro, cheese, lime juice, and any other toppings you enjoy.

174. Creamy Tomato Soup

Preparation time: **10 minutes** - Cooking time: **6 minutes** - Servings: **8**

Ingredients:
1 yellow onion, peeled and chopped
3 tablespoons butter
1 carrot, peeled and chopped
2 celery stalks, chopped
2 garlic cloves, peeled and minced
29 ounces chicken stock
Salt and ground black pepper, to taste
¼ cup fresh basil, chopped
3 pounds tomatoes, peeled, cored, and cut into quarters
1 tablespoon tomato paste
1 cup half and half
½ cup Parmesan cheese, shredded

Directions:
1. Set the Crock pot Express™ on "Brown/Sauté" mode, add the butter and melt it. Add the onion, carrots, and celery, stir, and cook for 3 minutes. Add the garlic, stir, and cook for 1 minute. Add the tomatoes, tomato paste, stock, basil, salt, and pepper, stir,
2. Cover, and cook on the "Soup" Setting for 5 minutes. Release the pressure, uncover the Crock pot Express™ and puree the soup using and immersion blender. Add the half and half and cheese, stir, set the Crock pot Express™ on "Brown/Sauté" mode and heat everything up. Divide the soup into soup bowls, and serve.

175. Buffalo Chicken Soup

Preparation + Cook Time: 20 minutes | Servings: 4

Ingredients:
3 cups chicken bone-broth
2 tbsp ghee, OR butter
2 cups cheddar cheese, shredded
2 chicken breasts, boneless, skinless, frozen or fresh
¼ cup diced onion
1/3 cup hot sauce
½ cup celery, diced

1 tbsp ranch dressing mix
1 cup heavy cream
1 clove garlic, chopped

Directions:
1. Except for the cheddar cheese and heavy cream, put the rest of the ingredients into the Crock Pot Express™. Cover and lock the lid.
2. Press the "BEANS/CHILI" key, set the pressure to HIGH, and set the timer for 10 minutes.
3. When the Crock Pot Express™ timer beeps, press the CANCEL key and unplug the Crock Pot Express™. Turn the steam valve to quick release the pressure. Unlock and carefully open the lid.
4. Carefully remove the chicken, shred the meat, and then return the shredded meat into the soup.
5. Add the cheese and cream and stir to combine. Ladle into bowls and serve.

176. Chicken and White Bean Chili with Tomatoes

Preparation + Cook Time: 35 minutes | Servings: 8

Ingredients:
4 ounces canned mild green chilies, diced,
3 cups canned great northern beans, drain and rinse
3 ¾ cups chicken, boneless breasts, diced
2 cups chicken broth or stock, reduced fat
14 ounces canned tomatoes, diced
¼ tsp cayenne pepper
½ tsp paprika
½ tsp garlic powder
1 tbsp cumin
1 ¼ cups onion, diced

Directions:
1. Combine all of the ingredients in the Crock Pot Express™. Lock the lid and close the steam valve.
2. Press the "Soup" Button and adjust the time for 10 minutes.
3. When the timer beeps, release the pressure quickly.
4. Serve and enjoy.

177. Fennel Chicken Soup

Preparation + Cook Time: 55 minutes | Servings: 6

Ingredients:
4 green onions, chopped
4 cups water
3 cloves garlic, peeled and chopped
2 cups chicken bone broth
1/8 tsp salt
½ onion, chopped
1 tbsp dried oregano
1 pound chicken thighs or/ and breast, boneless, skinless, cut into chunks
1 cup spinach or kale, chopped
1 bulb fennel, large-sized, chopped
1 bay leaf

Directions:
1. Put all of the ingredients into the Crock Pot Express™. Cover and lock the lid.
2. Press the "Soup" Button and set the timer for 30 minutes.
3. When the Crock Pot Express™ timer beeps, press the CANCEL key and unplug the Crock Pot Express™. Let the pressure release naturally for 10 minutes. Turn the steam valve to release remaining pressure.
4. Unlock and carefully open the lid.
5. Divide between serving bowls and serve.

Notes: This soup can be frozen and reheated.

178. Cheese Tortellini and Chicken Soup

Preparation + Cook Time: 35 minutes | Servings: 6

Ingredients:
2 whole chicken breast, skinless and boneless
2 small bags frozen cheese tortellini
2 cups baby carrots, chopped
½ white onion, chopped

1 cup celery, chopped
2 cartons (32 ounces each) chicken broth
<u>Your choice of spices for chicken (I used the following):</u>
1 tbsp garlic, minced
1 tbsp paprika
1 tbsp parsley
1 tsp pepper
1 tsp salt

Directions:
1. Pour 1 cup of the chicken broth in the Crock Pot Express™. Add the chicken breast. Sprinkle the top of the chicken with the spices. Lock the pot and close the steam valve.
2. Press the "BEANS/CHILI" key, set the pressure to HIGH, and set the timer to 15 minutes.
3. Meanwhile, prepare the vegetables.
4. When the timer beeps, open the steam valve to quick release the pressure.
5. Remove the chicken from the pot and shred using two forks. Return the shredded meat into the pot.
6. Add the vegetables and the tortellini.
7. Add one container of the chicken broth and add 1/2 of the other container in the pot.
8. If desired, add more parsley or spices. Lock the lead and close the steam valve. Press "BEANS/CHILI", set the pressure to HIGH and set the timer for 3 minutes.
9. When the timer beeps, let the pressure release quickly.
10. Ladle into bowls and enjoy!

179. Cream Of Sweet Potato Soup

Prep: 5 minutes • pressure: high • time under pressure: 15 minutes • release: quick •
Serves: 6

Ingredients
8 tablespoons (1 stick) unsalted butter, cut into small pieces
2 pounds sweet potatoes (about 2 large), peeled and cut into 2-inch pieces
1 teaspoon salt
½ teaspoon ground cinnamon
½ teaspoon ground ginger
¼ teaspoon baking soda
2½ cups chicken broth
½ cup heavy cream

Directions
1. **Preparing the Ingredients.** Melt the butter in a Crock-Pot Multi-Cooker® turned to the browning function. Stir in the sweet potatoes, salt, cinnamon, ginger, and baking soda. Pour ½ cup water over everything.
2. **High pressure for 15 minutes.** Lock the lid on the Crock-Pot Multi-Cooker® and then cook for 15 minutes. To get 15-minutes cook time, press "Poultry" button.
3. **Pressure Release** Use the quick-release method to bring the pot's pressure back to normal.
4. **Finish the dish.** Unlock and open the pot. Stir in the broth and cream. Use an immersion blender to puree the soup in the pot; or ladle the soup in batches into a blender, remove the knob from the blender's lid, cover the hole with a clean kitchen towel, and blend until smooth.

Main Dishes – Seafood

180. Farro With Fennel And Smoked Trout

Prep: 5 minutes • pressure: 17 minutes • total: 22 minutes • pressure level: high • release: quick • Serves 4

Ingredients
1 cup semi-perlato farro
1 large fennel bulb, trimmed and shaved into thin strips
½ cup regular or low-fat mayonnaise
¼ cup regular or low-fat sour cream
3 tablespoons lemon juice
2 tablespoons Dijon mustard
1 teaspoon sugar
1 teaspoon ground black pepper
12 ounces smoked trout, skinned and chopped

Directions
1. **Preparing the Ingredients.** Pour the farro into the Crock-Pot Multi-Cooker®; pour in enough water that the grains are submerged by 2 inches.
2. **High pressure for 17 minutes.** Lock the lid on the Crock-Pot Multi-Cooker® and then cook for 17 minutes. To get 17-minutes cook time, press "Poultry" button and use the TIME ADJUSTMENT button to adjust the cook time to 17 minutes.
3. **Pressure Release.** Use the quick-release method to drop the pot's pressure to normal.
4. **Finish the dish.** Unlock and open the cooker. Place the fennel strips in a colander set in the sink and drain the farro into the colander over the fennel. Toss well, then let cool for 30 minutes in the colander.

   Whisk the mayonnaise, sour cream, lemon juice, mustard, sugar, and pepper in a large serving bowl until creamy. Add the farro, fennel, and smoked trout; toss gently to coat well.

181. Shrimp and Tomatillo Casserole

Preparation + Cook Time: 20 minutes | Servings: 4

Ingredients:
1 ½ pounds peeled and cleaned shrimp

1 ½ pounds peeled and chopped tomatillos

1 stemmed, seeded, and minced jalapeno

1 cup shredded cheddar cheese

1 chopped yellow onion

½ cup clam juice

¼ cup chopped cilantro

2 tbsp lime juice

2 tbsp olive oil

2 tsp minced garlic

Directions:
1. Heat the oil in your Crock Pot Express™ on the "BROWN/SAUTÉ" setting.
2. When shiny and hot, add the onion and stir until it becomes clear.
3. Add the garlic and jalapeno. Stir until aromatic; this should only take a minute or so.
4. Add tomatillos, lime juice, and clam juice.
5. Close and seal the lid. Select "BEANS/CHILI" and cook at HIGH pressure for 9 minutes.
6. When the timer beeps, press CANCEL and quick-release. Open the lid and press "BROWN/SAUTÉ" again.
7. Add cilantro and shrimp, and stir for 2 minutes. Add cheese, stir and cover the lid, but don't bring to pressure.
8. Wait 2 minutes for the cheese to melt. Open the lid and stir before serving.

182. Tuna and Capers Tomato Pasts

Preparation + Cook Time: 20 minutes | Servings: 2

Ingredients:
1 can (15 ounces) fire-roasted diced tomatoes

1 can (3.5 ounces) solid tuna packed in vegetable oil

2 cups pasta, your choice (I used Orecchiette)

2 garlic cloves, sliced

2 tbsp olive oil

2 tbsp capers

Grated parmesan

Red wine (just enough to fill 1/2 of the tomato can)

Salt and pepper to taste

Seasonings (I use oregano and dried chilies)

Directions:

1. Set the Crock Pot Express™ to "BROWN/SAUTÉ" and wait until hot. Add the garlic and sauté until fragrant.
2. Add the pasta, seasonings, and tomatoes. Fill the empty can of tomatoes with red wine until 1/2 full and then pour enough water into the can until full.
3. Pour the wine mix in the Crock Pot Express™. Lock the lid and turn the steam valve to Sealing.
4. Select "BEANS/CHILI" and cook at HIGH pressure for 6 minutes. When the timer beeps, turn the steam valve to quick release the pressure.
5. Carefully open the capers and tuna. Gently add into the pot and stir.
6. Divide the pasta into serving bowls.

183. White Fish with Orange Sauce

Preparation time: **10 minutes** • Cooking time: **7 minutes** • Servings: **4**

Ingredients:
4 white fish fillets
4 green onions, chopped
Extra virgin olive oil
2 tablespoons ginger, chopped
Salt and ground black pepper, to taste
Juice from 1 orange
Zest from 1 orange
1 cup fish stock

Directions:
1. Pat the fish fillets dry, season with salt and pepper and rub them with the olive oil. Put the stock, ginger, orange juice, orange zest, and onions into the Crock pot Express™. Put the fish fillets in the steamer basket,
2. Cover the Crock pot Express™ and cook on the **"Steam" setting** for 7 minutes. Release the pressure, divide fish among plates, and drizzle the orange sauce on top.

184. Cheesy Tuna Helper

Preparation + Cook Time: 15 minutes | Servings: 6

Ingredients:
1 can (5 ounces) tuna, drained
1 cup frozen peas
¼ cup bread crumbs (optional)
16 ounces egg noodles
28 ounces canned cream mushroom soup
3 cups water

4 ounces cheddar cheese

Directions:
1. Put the noodles in the Crock Pot Express™. Pour the water to cover the noodles.
2. Add the frozen peas, tuna, and the soup on top of the pasta layer. Cover and lock the lid.
3. Select "BEANS/CHILI" and cook at HIGH pressure for 4 minutes. When the Crock Pot Express™ timer beeps, press the CANCEL key and unplug the Crock Pot Express™. Turn the steam valve to quick release the pressure.
4. Unlock and carefully open the lid. Add the cheese and stir.
5. If desired, you can pour the pasta mixture in a baking dish, sprinkle the top with bread crumbs, and broil for about 2 to 3 minutes. Serve.

185. Pasta with Tuna and Capers

Prep: 2 minutes • pressure: 3 minutes • total: 5 minutes • pressure level: high • release: quick • Serves 2-4

Ingredients
1 tablespoon olive oil
1 garlic clove
3 anchovies
2 cups tomato puree
1½ teaspoons salt
16 oz. (500g) fusilli pasta
2 5.5oz (160g) cans Tuna packed in olive oil water to cover
2 tablespoons capers

Directions
1. **Preparing the Ingredients.** In the pre-heated Crock-Pot Multi-Cooker® on "Sauté" mode, add the oil, garlic and anchovies. Sauté until the anchovies begin to disintegrate and the garlic cloves are just starting to turn golden.
   Add the tomato puree and salt and mix together.
   Pour in the un-cooked pasta, and the contents of one tuna can (5 oz.) mixing to coat the dry pasta evenly.
   Flatten the pasta in an even layer and pour in just enough water to cover.
2. **High pressure for 3 minutes.** Lock the lid on the Crock-Pot Multi-Cooker® and then cook for 3 minutes. To get 3-minutes cook time, press "Steam" button and use the TIME ADJUSTMENT button to adjust the cook time to 3 minutes.
3. **Pressure Release** When time is up, open the cooker by releasing the pressure.
4. **Finish the dish** Mix in the last 5oz of tuna and sprinkle with capers before serving.
5. Enjoy!

186. Tuna and Buttery Crackers Casserole

Preparation + Cook Time: 25 minutes | Servings: 8

Ingredients:
8 ounces fresh tuna
3 tbsp butter
3 tbsp all-purpose flour
3 ½ cups chicken stock
2 tsp salt
2 cups pasta (I used elbow mac)
¼ cup heavy cream
1 cup onion
1 cup frozen peas
1 cup cheddar, shredded
1 cup celery
1 cup buttery crackers, crushed
Fresh ground black pepper

Directions:
1. Press "BROWN/SAUTÉ" to preheat the Crock Pot Express™. When hot, put the celery and onion.
2. Sauté until the onion is translucent. Pour the chicken stock and pasta, and season with salt and pepper.
3. Stir to combine for a bit. Put the fresh tuna on top of the pasta mix. Press CANCEL to stop the "Brown/Sauté" function. Close and lock the lid.
4. Select "BEANS/CHILI" and cook at HIGH pressure for 5 minutes. Meanwhile, heat the sauté pan over medium-high.
5. Put the butter in the pan and melt. Add the flour and stir, cook for 2 minutes. Remove the pan from the heat and set aside.
6. When the timer beeps, turn the steam valve to Venting to quick release the pressure. Transfer the tuna onto a plate and set aside.
7. Pour the butter mix into the Crock Pot Express™. Press the "Brown/Sauté" key. Stir until the mixture is thick. Turn off the Crock Pot Express™. Add the heavy cream, peas, tuna and stir.
8. Cover the mix with the crackers and then with the grated cheese.
9. Cover and let stand for 5 minutes. Serve.

187. Shrimp And Tomatillo Casserole

Prep: 10 minutes • pressure: 9 minutes • total: 20 minutes • pressure level: high • release: quick • Serves 4

Ingredients
2 tablespoons olive oil
1 medium yellow onion, chopped
1 small fresh jalapeño chile, stemmed, seeded, and minced
2 teaspoons minced garlic
1½ pounds fresh tomatillos, husked and chopped
½ cup bottled clam juice
2 tablespoons fresh lime juice
1½ pounds medium shrimp (about 30 per pound), peeled and deveined
¼ cup loosely packed fresh cilantro leaves, chopped
1 cup shredded Monterey jack cheese (about 4 ounces)

Directions
1. **Preparing the Ingredients.** Heat the oil in the Crock-Pot Multi-Cooker® turned to the "Browning" function. Add the onion and cook, stirring often, until translucent, about 3 minutes.
   Add the jalapeño and garlic; cook until aromatic, stirring all the while, less than a minute.
   Stir in the tomatillos, clam juice, and lime juice.
2. **High pressure for 9 minutes.** Lock the lid on the Crock-Pot Multi-Cooker® and then cook for 9 minutes. To get 9-minutes cook time, press "Rice/Risotto" button and use the TIME ADJUSTMENT button to adjust the cook time to 9 minutes.
3. **Pressure Release** Use the quick-release method.
4. **Finish the dish.** Unlock and open the pot. Turn the Crock-Pot Multi-Cooker® to its "browning" or "simmer" function. Stir in the shrimp and cilantro; cook for 2 minutes, stirring frequently. Sprinkle the cheese over the top of the casserole, cover the cooker, and lock the lid in place. Set aside off the heat for 2 minutes to melt the cheese and blend the flavors.
   Use the quick-release method (if necessary) to bring any pressure in the pot back to normal.
5. Unlock and open the pot. Stir gently before serving.

188. Cod Fillets with Almonds and Peas

Preparation + Cook Time: 10 minutes | Servings: 4

Ingredients:
1 pound frozen cod fish fillet
2 halved garlic cloves
10-ounces frozen peas
1 cup chicken broth

½ cup packed parsley

2 tbsp fresh oregano

2 tbsp sliced almonds

½ tsp paprika

Directions:

1. Take the fish out of the freezer.
2. In a food processor stir together garlic, oregano, parsley, paprika, and 1 tablespoon almonds.
3. Turn your Crock Pot Express™ to "BROWN/SAUTÉ" and heat a bit of olive oil.
4. When hot, toast the rest of the almonds until they are fragrant.
5. Take out the almonds and put on a paper towel.
6. Pour the broth in the cooker and add your herb mixture.
7. Cut the fish into 4 pieces and put in the steamer basket.
8. Lower into the cooker and close the lid.
9. Select "BEANS/CHILI" and cook at HIGH pressure for 3 minutes.
10. Press CANCEL and quick release the pressure.
11. The fish is done when it is solid, not translucent.
12. Add the frozen peas and close the lid again.
13. Cook at HIGH pressure for 1 minute. Use a quick release.
14. Serve with the toasted almonds on top.

Notes: If you want a thicker sauce, remove the fish before mixing 1 tablespoon of cornstarch with 1 tablespoon of cold water, and pouring into the cooker. Turn the cooker to "Brown/Sauté" and bring to a simmer until thickened.

189. Lemon and Dill Fish Packets

Prep: 10 minutes • pressure: 5 minutes • total: 15 minutes • pressure level: hig • release: quick • Serves 2

Ingredients

2 tilapia or cod fillets

Salt, pepper, and garlic powder

2 sprigs fresh dill

4 slices lemon

2 tablespoons butter

Directions

1. **Preparing the Ingredients.** Lay out 2 large squares of parchment paper. Place a fillet in the center of each parchment square, and then season with a generous amount of salt, pepper, and garlic powder.

On each fillet, place in order: 1 sprig of dill, 2 lemon slices, and 1 tablespoon of butter.

For best results, place a small metal rack or trivet at the bottom of your Crock-Pot Multi-Cooker®.

Pour 1 cup of water into the cooker to create a water bath.

Close up parchment paper around the fillets, folding to seal, and then place both packets on metal rack inside cooker.

2. **High pressure for 5 minutes**. Lock the lid on the Crock-Pot Multi-Cooker® and then cook for 5 minutes. To get 5-minutes cook time, press "Soup" Button.
3. **Pressure Release** Perform a quick release to release the cooker's pressure. Unwrap packets and serve.

There is no need to remove the fish from the packets before serving. In fact, it makes a really nice presentation.

190. Lemon-Dill Cod with Broccoli

Preparation + Cook Time: 5 minutes | Servings: 4

Ingredients:
1 pound, 1-inch thick frozen cod fillet
2 cups of broccoli
1 cup water
Dill weed
Lemon pepper
Dash of salt

Directions:
1. Cut the fish into four pieces.
2. Season with lemon pepper, salt, and dill weed.
3. Pour 1 cup of water into the Crock Pot Express™ and lower in the steamer basket.
4. Put the fish and broccoli florets in the basket. Close the cooker.
5. Select "BEANS/CHILI" and cook for 2 minutes at LOW pressure. (Press Stop when complete 2 Minute).
6. Quick-release the pressure after time is up, and you've turned off the cooker.
7. Serve right away.

191. Fish Filets

Prep: 5 minutes • pressure: 5 minutes • total: 10 minutes • pressure level: low • release: normal • Serves 2

Ingredients

4 White Fish fillets (any white fish)
1 lb. (500g) Cherry Tomatoes, halved
1 cup Black salt-cured Olives (Taggiesche, French or Kalamata)
2 Tbsp.Pickled Capers
1 bunch of fresh Thyme Olive Oil
1 clove of garlic, pressed
Salt and pepper to taste

Directions

1. **Preparing the Ingredients.** Prepare the base of the Crock-Pot Multi-Cooker® with 1½ to 2 cups of water and trivet or steamer basket.
   Line the bottom of the heat-proof bowl with cherry tomato halves (to keep the fish filet from sticking), add Thyme (reserve a few springs for garnish).
   Place the fish fillets over the cherry tomatoes, sprinkle with remaining tomatoes, crushed garlic, a dash of olive oil and a pinch of salt.
   Insert the dish in the Crock-Pot Multi-Cooker® - if your heat proof dish does not have handles construct them by making a long aluminum sling.
2. **Low pressure for 5 minutes**. Lock the lid on the Crock-Pot Multi-Cooker® and then cook for 5 minutes. To get 5-minutes cook time, press "Soup" Button and use the TIME ADJUSTMENT button to adjust the cook time to 5 minutes
3. **Pressure Release** Perform a quick release to release the cooker's pressure.
   Distribute fish into individual plates, top with cherry tomatoes, and sprinkle with olives, capers, fresh Thyme, a crackle of pepper and a little swirl of fresh olive oil.

Per Serving Calories: 278.2; Fat: 5.8g; Carbohydrates: 18.8g; Sodium: 1056.8mg; Fiber: 2.5g; Protien: 25.6g

192. Wild Alaskan Cod In The Pot

Preparation + Cook Time: 15 minutes | Servings: 2

Ingredients:

1 large filet wild Alaskan cod (the big fillets can feed easily 2-3 people)
1 cup cherry tomatoes
Salt and pepper to taste
Your choice of seasoning
2 tbsp butter
Olive oil

Directions:

1. Choose an ovenproof dish that will fit your Crock Pot Express™.

2. Put the tomatoes in the dish.
3. Cut the large fish fillet into 2-3 serving pieces. Lay them on top of the tomatoes.
4. Season the fish with salt, pepper, and your choice of seasoning.
5. Top each fillet with 1 tablespoon butter and drizzle with a bit of olive oil. Put 1 cup water in the Crock Pot Express™ and set a trivet.
6. Place the dish on the trivet. Lock the lid and close the steam valve.
7. Press "BEANS/CHILI" and set the timer for 5 minutes if using thawed fish or for 9 minutes if using frozen fish.
8. When the timer beeps, let the pressure release naturally. Enjoy!

193. Mediterranean Tuna Noodle Delight

Prep: 6 minutes • pressure: 10 minutes • total: 16 minutes • pressure level: high • release: natural • Serves 2

Ingredients
1 Tablespoon of Oil
½ cup of chopped red onion
8 ounces of dry wide egg noodles (uncooked)
1 can (14 ounces) diced tomatoes with basil, garlic and oregano(undrained) or any kind you have on hand.
1-1/4 cups of water
¼ teaspoon of salt
1/8 teaspoon of pepper
1 can of tuna fish in water, drained
1 jar (7.5 oz.) marinated artichoke hearts, drained with saving the liquid, then chop it up
Crumpled feta cheese
Fresh chopped parsley or dried

Directions
1. **Preparing the Ingredients** Sauté the red onion for about 2 minutes.
   Add the dry noodles, tomatoes, water, salt and pepper .
2. **High pressure for 10 minutes.** Lock the lid on the Crock-Pot Multi-Cooker® and then cook for 10 minutes. To get 10-minutes cook time, press "Steam" button.
3. **Pressure Release.** Release the pressure using natural release method.
   Turn off the warm setting.
   Add tuna, artichokes and your reserved liquid from the artichokes and sauté on normal while stirring for about 4 more minutes till hot.
   Plate, then top with a little feta cheese and parsley to your liking.

Per Serving Calories: 258.3; Fat: 5.8g; Carbohydrates: 15.8g; Sugar: 0.2g; Sodium: 1146.8mg; Fiber: 2.5g; Protien: 29.6g

194. Cod Chowder

Preparation + Cook Time: 40 minutes | Servings: 6

Ingredients:
2 pounds cod
4 cups potatoes, peeled and diced
4 cups chicken broth, organic
2 tbsp butter
½ mushrooms, sliced
½ cup flour
1 tsp old bay seasoning (or more)
1 cup onion, chopped
1 cup half-and-half OR heavy cream OR 1 can evaporated milk
1 cup clam juice
4-6 bacon slices, optional
Salt and pepper to taste

Directions:
1. Pour 1 cup of water into the Crock Pot Express™ and set a trivet. Put the cod on the trivet. Close and lock the lid.
2. Press "BEANS/CHILI", set the pressure to HIGH, and set the timer for 9 minutes. Once cooking is complete, use a quick release.
3. Transfer the cod onto a large-sized plate. With a fork or a knife, cut the fish into large chunks. Set aside.
4. Remove the trivet and pour the liquid out from the inner pot.
5. Press the "BROWN/SAUTÉ" key. Add the butter, onion, and mushrooms; sauté for 2 minutes or until soft.
6. Add the chicken broth and the potatoes.
7. Press the CANCEL key to stop the "Brown/Sauté" function. Close and lock the lid.
8. Select "BEANS/CHILI" and cook at HIGH pressure for 8 minutes.
9. When the timer beeps, turn the steam valve to quick release the pressure.
10. Add and stir the seasoning, pepper, salt, and fish.
11. In a bowl, mix the clam juice with the flour until well blended.
12. Pour the mix into the pot. Turn off the Crock Pot Express™.
13. Add the half-and-half and stir well until blended. Serve with fresh baked buttered rolls.

Notes: If you are using bacon, cook the bacon until crisp and then transfer into a paper towel lined plate. Add the onions and the mushrooms, cooking them in the bacon fat before adding the broth and potatoes.

195. Beer Potato Fish

Prep: 15 minutes • pressure: 40 minutes • total: 55 minutes • pressure level: low • release: natural • Serves 6

Ingredients
1 pound fish fillet
4 medium size potatoes, peeled and diced
1 cup beer
1 red pepper sliced
1 tablespoon oil
1 tablespoon oyster flavored sauce
1 tablespoon rock candy
1 teaspoon salt

Directions
1. **Preparing the Ingredients** .Put all ingredients into your Crock-Pot Multi-Cooker®.
2. **High pressure for 40 minutes.** Lock the lid on the Crock-Pot Multi-Cooker® and then cook for 40 minutes. To get 40-minutes cook time, press "meat/stew" button and use the TIME ADJUSTMENT button to adjust the cook time to 40 minutes.
3. **Pressure Release.** Release the pressure using natural release method
   Then that is it! Simple, fast, delicious, retaining flavour and nutrition, consistent results all the time.
4. Serve and Enjoy!

Per Serving Calories: 250.3; Fat: 4.8g; Sodium: 1146.8mg; Fiber: 2.5g; Protien: 25.6g

196. Coconut Fish Curry

Preparation + Cook Time: 45 minutes | Servings: 4

Ingredients:
1½ pounds white fish fillet rinsed and cut into bite sized pieces
1 heaping cup cherry tomatoes
2 green chilies sliced into stripes
2 medium onions sliced into strips
2 cloves garlic finely chopped
1 tbsp Ginger freshly grated
6 curry leaves, bay leaves, basil or kaffir leaves work too
1 tbsp ground coriander
1 tbsp ground cumin
½ tsp ground turmeric

1 tsp chili powder
½ tsp ground fenugreek
2 cups coconut milk unsweetened, about one small can
1 tsp olive oil
Salt to taste
Lemon juice to taste

Directions:

1. Press "BROWN/SAUTÉ" to pre-heat the Crock Pot Express™. When "Hot" appears on the display, add the oil and the curry leaves.
2. Lightly fry the leaves until golden around the edges (about 1 minute).
3. Add in the onion, garlic, and ginger. Sauté until the onion is soft
4. Add all of the ground spices: coriander, turmeric, chili powder and fenugreek. Sauté them together with the onions until they have released their aroma (about 1 minute).
5. Deglaze the pot with the coconut milk, scraping everything from the bottom of the pot to incorporate it into the sauce.
6. Add the green chilies, tomatoes and fish. Stir to coat.
7. Close and lock the lid. Select "BEANS/CHILI" and cook at HIGH pressure for 3 minutes. When time is up, use a quick release. Open the lid.
8. Add salt and lemon juice to taste before serving. Enjoy!

197. Red Curry Cod With Red Beans

Prep: 5 minutes • pressure: 5 minutes • total: 10 minutes • pressure level: hihg • release: quick • Serves 4

Ingredients

1 can (13 1/2 ounces, or 400 ml) unsweetened coconut milk
2 tablespoons (30 g) red Thai curry paste
1 tablespoon (8 g) finely grated fresh ginger
1 1/2 pounds (680 g) cod or halibut fillet, cut into 2-inch (5 cm) pieces
8 ounces (225 g) green beans
1/2 cup (8 g) fresh cilantro leaves
2 scallions (white and light green parts), thinly sliced
1 lime, quartered

Directions

1. **Preparing the Ingredients** To the Crock-Pot Multi-Cooker®, add the coconut milk, curry paste, and ginger, and whisk together.
   Add the cod. Lay the green beans on top.
2. **High pressure for 5 minutes.** Lock the lid on the Crock-Pot Multi-Cooker® and then cook for 5 minutes. To get 5-minutes cook time, press "Soup" Button and use the TIME ADJUSTMENT button to adjust the cook time to 5 minutes

3. **Pressure Release**. Use the "Quick Release" method to vent the steam, then open the lid.
4. Top the curry with the cilantro and scallions, and serve with the lime quarters for squeezing.

198. Fish in Orange Ginger Sauce

Preparation + Cook Time: 20 minutes | Servings: 4

Ingredients:
4 pieces white fish fillets
3-4 spring onions
1 piece (thumb-sized) ginger, chopped
1 orange for juice and zest
1 tsp orange zest
1 cup white wine or fish stock
Olive oil
Salt and pepper to taste

Directions:
1. Using a paper towel, pat the fish fillets dry. Rub the fillets with the olive oil and then season them lightly.
2. Add the white wine/ fish stock, orange zest, orange juice, ginger, and spring onion into the Crock Pot Express™.
3. Set a steamer basket in the pot and then put the fish in the steamer basket. Close and lock the lid.
4. Press "BEANS/CHILI" and cook at HIGH pressure for 7 minutes.
5. Once cooking is complete, use a quick release. Open the lid.
6. Serve. The sauce will serve as the dressing.

198. Smoked Salmon Chowder

Prep: 5 minutes • pressure: 6 minutes • total: 10 minutes • pressure level: low • release: quick • Serves 6

Ingredients
1 tablespoon unsalted butter
2 large scallions, chopped
½ teaspoon kosher salt, plus additional for seasoning
1 tablespoon all-purpose flour
¼ cup dry white wine, dry vermouth, or dry sherry
2½ cups whole milk

2 small (or 1 medium) red or Yukon gold potatoes (about 5 ounces), peeled and cut into ½-inch cubes
1 (4- or 5-ounce) salmon fillet, skinned
1½ ounces hot-smoked salmon, chopped or flaked into small chunks
3 teaspoons chopped fresh dill, divided
1 teaspoon lemon zest
Freshly ground black pepper

Directions

1. **Preparing the Ingredients.** The Crock-Pot Multi-Cooker® set to "browning," melt the butter. When the butter is foaming, add the scallions and sprinkle with ½ teaspoon of kosher salt. Cook for 1 minute, stirring, until softened. Add the flour, and cook for 2 to 3 minutes, or until it turns a very light tan color. Add the white wine, and cook for about 2 minutes, or until the mixture has thickened. Add the milk, and whisk until the mixture is smooth.
   Add the potatoes.
2. **High pressure for 5 minutes.** Lock the lid on the Crock-Pot Multi-Cooker® and then cook for 5 minutes. To get 5-minutes cook time, press "Soup" Button and use the TIME ADJUSTMENT button to adjust the cook time to 5 minutes
3. **Pressure Release.** Use the quick-release method.
   Unlock and remove the lid. Add the raw salmon fillet, and replace the lid.
4. **High pressure for 1 minutes** Lock the lid in place, bring the cooker to high pressure by pressing the "Steam" button. Allow cooking for 1 minute and press STOP.
5. **Pressure Release.** After cooking, use the natural method to release pressure for 4 minutes, then the quick method to release the remaining pressure.
6. **Finish the dish** Unlock and remove the lid. Using a large slotted spoon or fish spatula, remove the salmon fillet to a plate or cutting board. Use a fork to break it into chunks. Don't worry if the fish is not completely cooked; it will finish cooking later.
   Turn the Crock-Pot Multi-Cooker® to "brown, add the salmon chunks, smoked salmon, 2 teaspoons of dill, and the lemon zest, an sim for 1 to 2 minutes, or until the fish is heated through. Adjust the seasoning with additional kosher salt and pepper. Sprinkle the remaining 1 teaspoon of dill over the soup just before serving.

199. Caramelized Haddock

Preparation + Cook Time: 55 minutes | Servings: 4

Ingredients:
1 pound of haddock
3 garlic cloves, chopped
1 cup of coconut water
1 minced red chili
1 minced spring onion

⅓ cup water

¼ cup white sugar

3 tbsp fish sauce

2 tsp black pepper

Directions:

1. Marinate the fish in garlic, fish sauce, and pepper for at least 30 minutes.
2. Put the sugar and water in the Crock Pot Express™ and heat on "BROWN/SAUTÉ" mode until the sugar has browned into a caramel.
3. Add fish and coconut water to the cooker. Close and seal lid.
4. Select "BEANS/CHILI" and cook at HIGH pressure for 10 minutes.
5. When time is up, press CANCEL and let the pressure release naturally.
6. Serve with chili and onion.

200. Steamed Mussels in Porter Cream Sauce

Prep: 5 minutes • pressure: 1 minutes • total: 6 minutes • pressure level: high • release: quick • Serves 2-4

Ingredients

tablespoon olive oil

2 garlic cloves, minced

2 scallions, minced (about ⅓ cup)

1 (12-ounce) bottle porter or other dark beer

⅛ teaspoon red pepper flakes

2 pounds mussels, scrubbed and debearded

2 tablespoons heavy (whipping) cream

Directions

1. **Preparing the Ingredients.** Set the Crock-Pot Multi-Cooker® to "browning," heat the olive oil until it shimmers and flows like water. Add the garlic and scallions, and cook for about 3 minutes, stirring, until the scallions just begin to brown. Pour in the beer, stirring for 1 minute, or until the foam dissipates. Add the red pepper flakes and mussels, and stir to coat with the liquid.
2. **High pressure for 1 minute.** Bring the cooker to high pressure by pressing the "Steam" button. Allow cooking for 1 minute and press Stop.
3. **Pressure Release** Use the quick-release method.
4. **Finish the dish** Unlock and remove the lid. The mussels should be opened; if not, replace but don't lock the lid, turn the Crock-Pot Multi-Cooker® to "brown", for 1 to 2 minutes more. Discard any mussels that still have not opened. Stir in the heavy cream; then pour the mussels with their sauce into a large serving bowl, and enjoy.

PER SERVING (MAIN COURSE): CALORIES: 584; FAT: 23G; SODIUM: 1,313MG; CARBOHYDRATES: 25G; FIBER: 0G; PROTEIN: 56G

201. Mackerel Salad

Preparation + Cook Time: 25 minutes | Servings: 6

Ingredients:
1 cup lettuce
8 oz mackerel
1 tsp salt
1 tsp paprika
1 tbsp olive oil
½ tsp rosemary
1 garlic clove
½ cup fish stock
1 tsp oregano
7 oz tomatoes
1 big cucumbers
1 red onion

Directions:
1. Wash the lettuce and chop it. Rub the mackerel with the salt, paprika, and rosemary.
2. Place the spiced mackerel in the Crock Pot Express™.
3. Add the fish stock and close the lid. Select "BEANS/CHILI" and cook at HIGH pressure for 10 minutes.
4. Peel the garlic clove and slice it. Peel the red onion and slice it.
5. Combine the sliced red onion with the chopped lettuce. Slice the cucumber and chop tomatoes.
6. Add the vegetables to the lettuce mixture.
7. Once cooking is complete, use a quick release. The mackerel is cooked – remove it from the Crock Pot Express™ and chill it little. Chop the fish roughly.
8. Add the chopped fish in the lettuce mixture.
9. Sprinkle the salad with the olive oil and stir it carefully with the help of the fork, do not damage the fish.
10. Serve the cooked salad immediately. Enjoy!

202. Steamed Fish

Preparation time: **10 minutes** • Cooking time: **10 minutes** • Servings: **4**

Ingredients:
4 white fish fillets
1 cup olives, pitted and chopped
1 pound cherry tomatoes, cut into halves
Thyme, dried
1 garlic clove, peeled and minced
Olive oil
Salt and ground black pepper, to taste
1 cup water

Directions:
1. Put the water into the Crock pot Express™. Put the fish fillets in the steamer basket of the Crock pot Express™. Add the tomatoes and olives on top. Add the garlic, thyme, oil, salt, and pepper.
2. Cover the Crock pot Express™ and cook on **"Steam" mode** for 10 minutes. Release the pressure, uncover the Crock pot Express™, divide fish, olives, and tomatoes mix among plates, and serve.

203. Green Chili Mahi-Mahi Fillets

Preparation + Cook Time: 10 minutes | Servings: 2

Ingredients:
¼ cup green chili enchilada sauce, homemade or store-brought
2 Mahi-Mahi fillets, thawed
2 tbsp butter
Salt and pepper to taste
1 cup water

Directions:
1. Pour 1 cup of water into the Crock Pot Express™ and set a steamer rack.
2. Grease the bottom of each mahi-mahi fillet with 1 tablespoon of butter, spreading the butter from end to end – this will prevent the fish from sticking to the rack.
3. Put the fillets on the rack. Spread 1/4 cup of enchilada sauce between each fillet using a pastry brush – cover them well.
4. Top with more enchilada sauce, if desired. Season fillets with salt and pepper. Lock the lid and close the steam valve. Press "BEANS/CHILI", set the pressure to HIGH, and set the timer for 5 minutes.

5. When the timer beeps, quickly release the pressure and transfer the fillets into serving plates. Serve.

Notes: The cooking time is sufficient to cook the fillets if they are thawed. Test the fish before taking out. If they are not done, close the lid and let cook with the residual heat of the pot for 1 minute.

204. Fish Curry

Preparation time: **10 minutes** • Cooking time: **15 minutes** • Servings: **6**

Ingredients:
6 fish fillets, cut into medium pieces
1 tomato, chopped
14 ounces coconut milk
2 onions, sliced
2 bell peppers, cored and cut into strips
2 garlic cloves, peeled and minced
2 tablespoons curry powder
1 tablespoons coriander
1 tablespoon ginger, grated
½ teaspoon turmeric
2 teaspoons cumin
Salt and ground black pepper, to taste
½ teaspoon fenugreek
1 teaspoon red pepper flakes
2 tablespoons lemon juice

Directions:
1. Set the Crock pot Express™ on "Brown/Sauté" mode, add the oil and curry powder, and fry for 1 minute. Add the ginger, onion, and garlic, stir, and cook for 2 minutes. Add the coriander, turmeric, cumin, fenugreek, and red pepper flakes, stir, and cook 2 minutes. Add the coconut milk, tomatoes, fish, and bell peppers, stir,
2. Cover, and cook on **"Steam" mode** for 5 minutes. Release the pressure naturally, add the salt and pepper, stir, and divide into bowls. Serve with lemon juice on top.

205. Trout-Farro Salad

Preparation + Cook Time: 55 minutes | Servings: 4

Ingredients:

12-ounces skinned and chopped cooked trout
1 cup semi-pearled Farro
1 large, shaved fennel bulb
½ cup low-fat mayonnaise
¼ cup low-fat sour cream
3 tbsp lemon juice
2 tbsp Dijon mustard
1 tsp white sugar
1 tsp ground black pepper
Water as needed

Directions:
1. Put the farro in your Crock Pot Express™ and pour in just enough water so the grain is covered by two inches. Close and seal the lid.
2. Select "BEANS/CHILI" and cook at HIGH pressure for 17 minutes.
3. When time is up, press CANCEL and quick-release the pressure.
4. Shave your fennel and put in a colander. Pour farro right on top of it, draining.
5. Toss fennel and farro together, and set aside for about 30 minutes.
6. When you're just about ready to serve, mix the mayo, sour cream, lemon juice, Dijon, white sugar, and pepper together.
7. Add the farro, fish and fennel. Serve right away.

206. Mediterranean Fish

Preparation time: **10 minutes** • Cooking time: **10 minutes** • Servings: **4**

Ingredients:
4 cod fillets
17 ounces tomatoes, cored and cut into halves
1 garlic clove, peeled and crushed
1 cup olives, pitted and chopped
2 tablespoons capers, drained and chopped
Salt and ground black pepper, to taste
1 tablespoon fresh parsley, chopped
1 tablespoon extra virgin olive oil

Directions:
1. Put the tomatoes on the bottom of a heat-proof bowl. Add the parsley, salt, and pepper and toss to coat. Place the fish fillets on top, add the olive oil, salt, pepper, garlic, olives, and capers.
2. Place the bowl in the steamer basket of the Crock pot Express™, cover and cook on the **"Steam" setting** for 5 minutes. Release the pressure naturally, divide among plates, and serve.

207. Cod and Peas

Preparation time: **15 minutes** • Cooking time: **5** • Servings: **4**

Ingredients:
16 ounces cod fillets
1 tablespoon fresh parsley, chopped
10 ounces peas
9 ounces wine
½ teaspoon dried oregano
½ teaspoon paprika
2 garlic cloves, peeled and chopped
Salt and ground black pepper, to taste

Directions:
1. In a food processor, mix the garlic with the parsley, oregano and paprika and blend well. Add the wine, blend again and set the dish aside. Place the fish fillets in the steamer basket of the Crock pot Express™, add salt and pepper,
2. Cover and cook on the **"Steam" setting** for 2 minutes. Release the pressure and divide fish among plates. Add the peas to the steamer basket, cover the Crock pot Express™ again and cook for 2 minutes. Release the pressure again and arrange peas next to fish fillets and serve.

208. Tasty Cuttlefish

Preparation + Cook Time: 40 minutes | Servings: 6

Ingredients:
1 pound squid
1 tbsp minced garlic
1 tsp onion powder
1 tbsp lemon juice
2 tbsp starch
1 tbsp chives
1 tsp salt
1 tsp white pepper
3 tbsp fish sauce
2 tbsp butter
¼ chili pepper

Directions:
1. Slice the squid.
2. Combine the minced garlic, onion powder, starch, chives, salt, and white pepper together. Stir the mixture.
3. Then chop the chili and add it to the spice mixture.
4. Then combine the sliced squid and spice mixture together. Stir it carefully.
5. After this, sprinkle the seafood mixture with the lemon juice and fish sauce. Stir it. Leave the mixture for 10 minutes.
6. Toss the butter in the Crock Pot Express™ and melt it.
7. Then place the sliced squid mixture in the Crock Pot Express™ and close the lid. Cook the dish for 13 minutes at the "Beans/Chili" mode.
8. When the dish is cooked – remove it from the Crock Pot Express™.
9. Sprinkle the dish with the liquid from the cooked squid. Serve.

Main Dishes – Vegetables

209. Ratatouille

Prep: 5 minutes • pressure: 4 minutes • total: 9 minutes • pressure level: high • release: quick • Serves 4

Ingredients
  Kosher salt, for salting and seasoning
  1 small eggplant, peeled and sliced ½ inch thick
  1 medium zucchini, sliced ½ inch thick
  2 tablespoons olive oil
  1 cup chopped onion
  3 garlic cloves, minced or pressed
  1 small green bell pepper, cut into ½-inch chunks (about 1 cup)
  1 small red bell pepper, cut into ½-inch chunks (about 1 cup)
  1 rib celery, sliced (about 1 cup)
  1 (14.5-ounce) can diced tomatoes, undrained
  ¼ cup water
  ½ teaspoon dried oregano
  ¼ teaspoon freshly ground black pepper
  2 tablespoons minced fresh basil
  ¼ cup pitted green or black olives (optional)

Directions
1. **Preparing the Ingredients.** Place a rack over a baking sheet. With kosher salt, very liberally salt one side of the eggplant and zucchini slices, and place them, salted-side down, on the rack. Salt the other side. Let the slices sit for 15 to 20 minutes, or until they start to exude water (you'll see it beading up on the surface of the slices and dripping into the sheet pan). Rinse the slices, and blot them dry. Cut the zucchini slices into quarters and the eggplant slices into eighths.

   Turn the Crock-Pot Multi-Cooker® to "brown," heat the olive oil until it shimmers and flows like water. Add the onion and garlic, and sprinkle with a pinch or two of kosher salt. Cook for about 3 minutes, stirring, until the onions just begin to brown.

   Add the eggplant, zucchini, green bell pepper, red bell pepper, celery, and tomatoes with their juice, water, and oregano.
2. **High pressure for 4 minutes.** Lock the lid on the Crock-Pot Multi-Cooker® and then cook for 4 minutes. To get 4-minutes cook time, press "Steam" button and use the TIME ADJUSTMENT button to adjust the cook time to 4 minutes.
3. **Pressure Release.** Use the quick-release method.

4. **Finish the dish.** Unlock and remove the lid. Stir in the pepper, basil, and olives (if using). Taste, adjust the seasoning as needed, and serve.
While this vegetable dish is usually served on its own, it's great tossed with cooked pasta or served over polenta.

PER SERVING: CALORIES: 149; FAT: 8G; SODIUM: 55MG; CARBOHYDRATES: 20G; FIBER: 8G; PROTEIN: 4G

210. Brussels Sprouts

Preparation + Cook Time: 5 minutes | Servings: 4

Ingredients:
1 pound Brussels sprouts
¼ cup pine nuts
Salt and pepper to taste
Olive oil
1 cup water

Directions:
1. Pour the water into the Crock Pot Express™. Set the steamer basket.
2. Put the Brussels sprouts into the steamer basket.
3. Close and lock the lid. Press the "BEANS/CHILI" button. Set the pressure to HIGH and set the time to 3 minutes.
4. When the timer beeps, turn the valve to Venting to quick release the pressure.
5. Transfer the Brussels sprouts into a serving plate, season with olive oil, salt, pepper, and sprinkle with the pine nuts.

Notes: To prepare the Brussels sprouts, wash them and remove the outer leaves. If some of them are quite large, cut those in half for uniformity - so that they will cook evenly.

211. CHICKPEA STEW WITH CARROTS, DATES, AND CRISP ARTICHOKES

Prep: 5 minutes • pressure: 12 minutes • total: 17 minutes • pressure level: high • release: quick • Serves 4

Ingredients
1½ cups dried chickpeas
2 cups chicken broth
2 tablespoons all-purpose flour
2½ tablespoons olive oil

1 medium red onion, halved and sliced into thin half-moons
2 teaspoons minced garlic
1 tablespoon sweet paprika
½ teaspoon ground cinnamon
½ teaspoon ground coriander
½ teaspoon ground cumin
½ teaspoon salt
One 14-ounce can diced tomatoes (about 1¾ cups)
1 pound "baby" carrots, cut into 1-inch pieces
6 pitted dates, preferably Medjool, chopped
One 9-ounce box frozen artichoke heart quarters, thawed and squeezed of excess moisture

Directions

1. **Preparing the Ingredients.** Soak the chickpeas in a big bowl of water for at least 12 hours or up to 16 hours.

   Drain the chickpeas in a colander set in the sink. Whisk the broth and flour in a medium bowl until the flour dissolves.

   Heat 1½ tablespoons oil in the Crock-Pot Multi-Cooker® turned to the browning function. Add the onion and cook, stirring often, until softened, about 4 minutes.

   Stir in the garlic, paprika, cinnamon, coriander, cumin, and salt until aromatic, about 30 seconds. Pour in the tomatoes as well as the broth mixture. Stir well, then add the carrots, dates, and drained chickpeas.

2. **High pressure for 12 minutes.** Lock the lid on the Crock-Pot Multi-Cooker® and then cook for 12 minutes. To get 12-minutes cook time, press "Soup" Button and use the TIME ADJUSTMENT button to adjust the cook time to 12 minutes.

3. **Pressure Release** Use the quick-release method to drop the pot's pressure back to normal.

4. **Finish the dish.** Unlock and open the cooker. Heat the remaining tablespoon oil in a large nonstick skillet set over medium-high heat. Add the artichoke heart quarters; fry until brown and crisp, stirring and turning occasionally, about 10 minutes. Dish up the chickpea mixture into big bowls and top with the crisp artichoke bits.

212. Maple Mustard Brussels Sprouts

Preparation + Cook Time: 25 minutes | Servings: 8

Ingredients:

16 Brussels sprouts, medium or large-sized (about 1-2 inch diameter), cut into halves or into quarters to make 3 cups total
1 ½-2 tbsp Dijon mustard
1 tsp olive oil
½ cup onion, diced
½ cup vegetable stock OR water
½-1 tbsp maple syrup
2 tsp pure sesame OR sunflower oil, optional

Salt and freshly ground black pepper

Directions:
1. Set the Crock Pot Express™ to "BROWN/SAUTÉ". Pour the oil in the pot.
2. Add onion and sauté for about 1-2 minutes or until starting to soften.
3. In a glass jar or in a jar, whisk the stock with the mustard. Set aside.
4. Add the Brussels sprouts and then the stock mix in the pot.
5. Stir to coat and then drizzle the maple syrup over the veggies without stirring. Close and lock the lid. Select "BEANS/CHILI" and cook at LOW pressure for 3 minutes.
6. When the timer beeps, turn the steam valve to Venting for quick pressure release. Carefully unlock and open the lid.
7. Transfer the sprouts into a bowl.
8. If desired, season to taste with salt and pepper.

Notes: If you are using small sprouts, do not cut them into halves. The cooking time indicated for this recipe cooks the sprouts al dente. If you want then softer, cook them for 1-2 minutes more.

213. Beets and Greens with Horseradish Sauce

Prep: 5 minutes • pressure: 10 minutes • total: 15 minutes • pressure level: high • release: natural • Serves 4

Ingredients
2 large or 3 small beets with greens, scrubbed and root ends trimmed
1 cup water, for steaming
2 tablespoons sour cream
1 tablespoon whole milk
1 teaspoon prepared horseradish
¼ teaspoon lemon zest
⅛ teaspoon kosher salt, divided
2 teaspoons unsalted butter
1 tablespoon minced fresh chives

Directions
1. **Preparing the Ingredients.** Trim off the beet greens and set aside. If the beets are very large (3 inches or more in diameter), quarter them; otherwise, halve them. Add the water and insert the steamer basket or trivet. Place the beets on the steamer insert.
2. **High pressure for 10 minutes.** Lock the lid on the Crock-Pot Multi-Cooker® and then cook for 10 minutes. To get 10-minutes cook time, press "Soup" Button and use the TIME ADJUSTMENT button to adjust the cook time to 10 minutes

When the timer goes off, turn the cooker off. ("Keep Warm" setting, turn off).

3. **Pressure Release** Let the pressure to come down naturally .

   While the beets are cooking and the pressure is releasing, wash the greens and slice them into ½-inch-thick ribbons, removing any tough stems. In a small bowl, whisk together the sour cream, milk, horseradish, lemon zest, and $1/16$ teaspoon of kosher salt.

4. **Finish the dish.** When the pressure has released completely, unlock and remove the lid. Remove the beets and cool slightly; then use a paring knife or peeler to peel them. Slice them into large bite-size pieces and set aside.

   Remove the steamer from the Crock-Pot Multi-Cooker®, and pour out the water. Turn the Crock-Pot Multi-Cooker® to "brown." Add the butter to melt. When the butter stops foaming, add the beet greens and sprinkle with the remaining $1/16$ teaspoon of kosher salt. Cook for 3 to 4 minutes, stirring, until wilted. Return the beets to the Crock-Pot Multi-Cooker® and heat for 1 or 2 minutes, stirring. Transfer the beets and greens to a platter, and drizzle with the sour cream mixture. Sprinkle with the chives, and serve.

   It may be tempting to cool the beets completely before you peel them, but that would be a mistake. Beets are easiest to peel when they're just cool enough to handle; if they get too cool, the skins tend to stick.

   PER SERVING: CALORIES: 70; FAT: 4G; SODIUM: 162MG; CARBOHYDRATES: 9G; FIBER: 2G; PROTEIN: 2G

214. Steamed Artichokes

Preparation + Cook Time: 45 minutes | Servings: 4

Ingredients:
2 medium-sized whole artichokes (about 5 ½ oz each)
1 lemon wedge
1 cup water

Directions:
1. Rinse the artichokes clean and remove any damaged outer leaves.
2. With a sharp knife, trim off the stem and top third of each artichoke carefully. Rub the cut top with a lemon wedge to prevent browning.
3. Pour 1 cup of water into the Crock Pot Express™ and set the steamer basket or rack. Pout the artichokes on the steamer/rack.
4. Select "BEANS/CHILI" and cook at HIGH pressure for 20 minutes.
5. When the timer beeps, press CANCEL to turn off the warming function. Let the pressure release naturally for 10 minutes.
6. Open the lid and with tongs, remove the artichokes from the pot.

7. Serve warm with your dipping sauce of choice.

Notes: If cooking larger artichokes, set the timer to 25 minutes and if cooking smaller artichokes, set the timer to 15 minutes.

215. WARM QUINOA AND POTATO SALAD

Prep: 5 Minutes • Pressure: 10 Minutes • Total: 15 Minutes • Pressure Level: High • Release: Quick • Serves 6

Ingredients
¼ cup white balsamic vinegar
1 tablespoon Dijon mustard
1 teaspoon sweet paprika
½ teaspoon ground black pepper
¼ teaspoon celery seeds
¼ teaspoon salt
¼ cup olive oil
1½ pounds tiny white potatoes, halved
1 cup blond (white) quinoa
1 medium shallot, minced
2 medium celery stalks, thinly sliced
1 large dill pickle, diced

Directions
1. **Preparing the Ingredients.** Whisk the vinegar, mustard, paprika, pepper, celery seeds, and salt in a large serving bowl until smooth; whisk in the olive oil in a thin, steady stream until the dressing is fairly creamy.
    Place the potatoes and quinoa in the Crock-Pot Multi-Cooker®; add enough cool tap water so that the ingredients are submerged by 3 inches (some of the quinoa may float).
2. **High pressure for 10 minutes.** Lock the lid on the Crock-Pot Multi-Cooker® and then cook for 10 minutes. To get 10-minutes cook time, press "Soup" Button and use the TIME ADJUSTMENT button to adjust the cook time to 10 minutes.
3. **Pressure Release** Use the quick-release method to bring the pot's pressure back to normal.
4. **Finish the dish.** Unlock and open the pot. Drain the contents of the pot into a colander lined with paper towels or into a fine-mesh sieve in the sink. Do not rinse.
    Transfer the potatoes and quinoa to the large bowl with the dressing. Add the shallot, celery, and pickle; toss gently and set aside for a minute or two to warm up the vegetables.

216. Buttery Carrots With Pancetta

Prep: 5 minutes • pressure: 7 minutes • total: 12 minutes • pressure level: high • release: quick • Serves 4 - 6

Ingredients
4 ounces pancetta, diced
1 medium leek, white and pale green parts only, sliced lengthwise, washed, and thinly sliced
¼ cup moderately sweet white wine, such as a dry Riesling
1 pound baby carrots
½ teaspoon ground black pepper
2 tablespoons unsalted butter, cut into small bits

Directions
1. **Preparing the Ingredients.** Put the pancetta in the Crock-Pot Multi-Cooker® turned to the "browning" function. Fry until crisp and well browned, stirring occasionally, about 3 minutes.

   Add the leek; cook, stirring often, until softened, about 1 minute. Pour in the wine and scrape up any browned bits at the bottom of the pot as it comes to a simmer.

   Add the carrots and pepper; stir well. Scrape and pour the contents of the Crock-Pot Multi-Cooker® into a 1-quart, round, high-sided soufflé or baking dish. Dot with the bits of butter. Lay a piece of parchment paper on top of the dish, then a piece of aluminum foil. Seal the foil tightly over the baking dish.

   Set the Crock-Pot Multi-Cooker® rack inside, and pour in 2 cups water. Use aluminum foil to build a sling for the baking dish; lower the baking dish into the cooker.
2. **High pressure for 7 minutes.** Lock the lid on the Crock-Pot Multi-Cooker® and then cook for 7 minutes. To get 7-minutes cook time, press "Rice/Risotto" button and use the TIME ADJUSTMENT button to adjust the cook time to 7 minutes.
3. **Pressure Release.** Use the quick-release method to return the pot's pressure to normal.
4. **Finish the dish.** Unlock and open the pot. Use the foil sling to lift the baking dish out of the cooker. Uncover, stir well, and serve.

217. Breakfast Kale

Preparation + Cook Time: 10 minutes | Servings: 4

Ingredients:
10 oz kale
2 tsp vinegar, your favorite flavored
For the faux parmesan cheese:
1 cup raw cashews
½ cup nutritional yeast

1 tbsp salt-free seasoning (I used Benson's)
½ cup water

Directions:
1. Fill the Crock Pot Express™ container with washed and chopped kale.
2. Pour the water. Close and lock the lid. Select "BEANS/CHILI" and cook at HIGH pressure for 4 minutes.
3. Meanwhile, put all the faux Parmesan ingredients into a food processor. Process until the mixture is powdery. If you prefer it chunkier, process less.
4. When the timer beeps, use a quick release and carefully open the lid. Transfer the kale in a serving plate.
5. Pour about 2 teaspoons of your favorite flavored vinegar.
6. Top with the faux parmesan. Serve over cooked brown rice or with a small potato.

218. Braised Red Cabbage With Apples

Prep: 5 minutes • pressure: 13 minutes • total: 18 minutes • pressure level: high • release: quick • Serves 4

Ingredients
4 thin bacon slices, chopped
1 small red onion, chopped
1 medium tart green apple, such as Granny Smith, peeled, cored, and chopped
1 teaspoon dried thyme
¼ teaspoon ground allspice
¼ teaspoon ground mace
1 tablespoon packed dark brown sugar
1 tablespoon balsamic vinegar
1 medium red cabbage (about 2 pounds), cored and thinly sliced
½ cup chicken broth

Directions
1. **Preparing the Ingredients.** Fry the bacon in the Crock-Pot Multi-Cooker® turned to the "Browning" function, stirring often, until crisp, about 4 minutes.
   Add the onion to the pot; cook, stirring often, until soft, about 4 minutes. Add the apple, thyme, allspice, and mace. Cook about 1 minute, stirring all the while, until fragrant. Stir in the brown sugar and vinegar; keep stirring until bubbling, about 1 minute.
   Add the cabbage; toss well to mix evenly with the other ingredients. Drizzle the broth over the cabbage mixture.
2. **High pressure for 13 minutes.** Lock the lid on the Crock-Pot Multi-Cooker® and then cook for 13 minutes. To get 13-minutes cook time, press "Soup" Button, and use the TIME ADJUSTMENT button to adjust the cook time to 13 minutes.

3. **Pressure Release.** Use the quick-release method to return the pot to normal pressure. Unlock and open the pot. Stir well before serving.

219. Polenta with Honey and Pine Nuts

Preparation + Cook Time: 25 minutes | Servings: 6

Ingredients:
5 cups water
1 cup polenta
½ cup heavy cream
½ cup honey
¼ cup pine nuts
Salt to taste

Directions:
1. Mix pine nuts and honey with water in your Crock Pot Express™.
2. Turn on the "BROWN/SAUTÉ" function and bring to a boil while stirring.
3. Mix in polenta. Close and seal lid. Select "BEANS/CHILI" and adjust time to 12 minutes.
4. When time is up, press CANCEL and quick release the pressure.
5. Mix in cream and wait 1 minute before serving with a sprinkle of salt.

220. SAGE-BUTTER SPAGHETTI SQUASH

Prep: 5 minutes • pressure: 12 minutes • total: 17 minutes • pressure level: high • release: quick • Serves 6

Ingredients
One 3- to 3½-pound spaghetti squash, halved lengthwise and seeded
6 tablespoons unsalted butter
2 tablespoons packed fresh sage leaves, minced
½ teaspoon salt
½ teaspoon ground black pepper
½ cup finely grated Parmesan cheese (about 1 ounce)

Directions
1. **Preparing the Ingredients.** Put the squash cut side up in the cooker; add 1 cup water.
2. **High pressure for 12 minutes.** Lock the lid on the Crock-Pot Multi-Cooker® and then cook for 12 minutes. To get 12-minutes cook time, press "Soup" Button, and use the TIME ADJUSTMENT button to adjust the cook time to 12 minutes.

3. **Pressure Release** Use the quick-release method to bring the pot's pressure back to normal.
4. **Finish the dish.** Unlock and open the cooker. Transfer the squash halves to a cutting board; cool for 10 minutes. Discard the liquid in the cooker. Use a fork to scrape the spaghetti-like flesh off the skin and onto the cutting board; discard the skins.
   Melt the butter in the electric cooker turned to its browning function. Stir in the sage, salt, and pepper, then add all of the squash. Stir and toss over the heat until well combined and heated through, about 2 minutes. Add the cheese, toss well, and serve.

221. Polenta with Fresh Herbs
Preparation + Cook Time: 20 minutes | Servings: 6

Ingredients:
4 cups veggie broth
1 cup coarse-ground polenta
½ cup minced onion
1 bay leaf
3 tbsp fresh, chopped basil
2 tbsp fresh, chopped Italian parsley
2 tsp fresh, chopped oregano
2 tsp minced garlic
1 tsp fresh, chopped rosemary
1 tsp salt

Directions:
1. Select "BROWN/SAUTÉ" and preheat your Crock Pot Express™. Dry sauté the onion for about a minute.
2. Add the minced garlic and cook for one more minute.
3. Pour the broth, along with the oregano, rosemary, bay leaf, salt, half the basil, and half the parsley. Stir.
4. Sprinkle the polenta in the pot, but don't stir. Close and seal the lid.
5. Select "BEANS/CHILI" and cook at HIGH pressure for 5 minutes.
6. When the timer beeps, press CANCEL and wait 10 minutes.
7. Pick out the bay leaf. Using a whisk, stir the polenta to smooth it.
8. If it's thin, simmer on the "BROWN/SAUTÉ" setting until it reaches the consistency you like.
9. Season to taste with salt and pepper before serving.

221. BUTTERY RYE BERRY AND CELERY ROOT SALAD

Prep: 5 minutes • pressure: 40 minutes • total: 45 minutes • pressure level: high • release: quick • Serves 6

Ingredients
¾ cup rye berries
1 medium celeriac (celery root), peeled and shredded through the large holes of a box grater
2 tablespoons unsalted butter
2 tablespoons honey
2 tablespoons apple cider vinegar
½ teaspoon salt
½ teaspoon ground black pepper

Directions
1. **Preparing the Ingredients.** Place the rye berries in the Crock-Pot Multi-Cooker®; pour in enough cool tap water so the grains are submerged by 2 inches.
2. **High pressure for 40 minutes.** Lock the lid on the Crock-Pot Multi-Cooker® and then cook for 40 minutes. To get 40-minutes cook time, press "meat/stew" button and use the TIME ADJUSTMENT button to adjust the cook time to 40 minutes.
3. **Pressure Release** Use the quick-release method to bring the pot's pressure back to normal.
4. **Finish the dish.** Unlock and open the cooker. Stir in the shredded celeriac. Cover the pot without locking it and set aside for 1 minute. Drain the pot into a large colander set in the sink. Wipe out the cooker.
   Melt the butter in the Crock-Pot Multi-Cooker®; turned to its browning function. Add the honey and cook for 1 minute, stirring constantly. Add the drained rye berries and celeriac; cook, stirring constantly, for 1 minute. Stir in the vinegar, salt, and pepper to serve.

222. Pumpkin Puree

Preparation + Cook Time: 30 minutes | Servings: 6

Ingredients:
2 pounds small-sized sugar pumpkin or pie pumpkin, halved and seeds scooped out
½ cup water

Directions:
1. Pour the water into the Crock Pot Express™ and set the steamer rack.
2. Put the pumpkin halves on the rack. Select "BEANS/CHILI" and cook at HIGH pressure for 13 or 15 minutes.
3. When the timer beeps, turn the valve to quick release the pressure. Let the pumpkin cool.

4. When cool enough, scoop out the flesh into a bowl.
5. Puree using an immersion blender or puree in a blender.

Notes: You can stir pumpkin into your oatmeal, use it to make a dessert, stir some with an applesauce for instant pumpkin applesauce, mix with softened butter with some sugar and spices like cinnamon, nutmeg, or cloves to make a compound butter for biscuits, blend it to make a creamy soup, and much more.

223. Vegetable Stew with Barley

Prep: 10 minutes • pressure: 35 minutes • total: 55 minutes • pressure level: high • release: quick • Serves 6

Ingredients
6 tomatoes, diced
2 large carrots, cut into bite size pieces
3 potatoes cut into chunks
4 celery stalks cut into bite size pieces
2 cups of sliced white mushrooms
1 large onion, diced
6 cups vegetable stock (or beef/chicken stock)
½ cup red wine or rice wine (red wine is preferred)
1 cup pearl barley
3 gloves garlic, minced
1 tablespoon dried parsley flakes
1 tablespoon dried thyme
1 bay leaf

Directions
1. **Preparing the Ingredients.** In a nonstick pan add a drizzle of olive oil and quickly sauté the white mushrooms with the minced garlic and onions until golden brown (2-3 minutes on medium heat) then add in the red wine and cook for another minute. Set aside.
   In the Crock-Pot Multi-Cooker® add the rest of the ingredients not including the barley.
2. **High pressure for 20 minutes.** Lock the lid on the Crock-Pot Multi-Cooker® and then cook for 20 minutes. To get 20-minutes cook time, press "Beans/Chili" button.
3. **Pressure Release** Use the quick-release method to bring the pot's pressure back to normal.
   Add in the mushrooms and barley, give it a good stir and add 2 pinches of salt and pepper.

4. **High pressure for 10 minutes.** Lock the lid on the Crock-Pot Multi-Cooker® and then cook for 10 minutes. To get 10-minutes cook time, press "Soup" Button and use the TIME ADJUSTMENT button to adjust the cook time to10 minutes.
5. **Pressure Release** Use the quick-release method to bring the pot's pressure back to normal.
6. **Finish the dish** At this point the potatoes and carrots should have soften. Add salt and pepper to taste.
   Serve with your favorite pasta dish fresh baked biscuits.

224. Carrot Puree

Preparation + Cook Time: 25 minutes | Servings: 4

Ingredients:
1 ½ pounds carrots, peeled and roughly chopped
1 tbsp soy butter, softened
1 tbsp honey
½ tsp salt
1 cup water
Brown Sugar as needed for more sweetness

Directions:
1. Rinse peeled carrots, pat dry and then chop roughly into small pieces. Pour water and then insert a steamer basket in the Crock Pot Express™.
2. Place chopped carrots into the basket and secure pot with lid.
3. Select "BEANS/CHILI" and cook at HIGH pressure for 4 minutes.
4. When the timer beeps, switch off the Crock Pot Express™ and do a quick pressure release.
5. Then uncover the pot and transfer carrots to a food processor or blender.
6. Pulse until smooth and transfer puree to a bowl. Stir in honey, salt, and butter.
7. For more sweetness stir in brown sugar to taste and serve immediately.

225. Collard Greens In A Tomato Sauce

Prep: 5 minutes • pressure: 6 minutes • total: 11 minutes • pressure level: high • release: quick • Serves 6

Ingredients
2 tablespoons olive oil
1 tablespoon minced garlic

½ teaspoon red pepper flakes
1½ pounds collard greens, tough stems removed, the leaves chopped (about 8 packed cups)
½ cup canned tomato puree
½ cup vegetable or chicken broth
½ cup moderately sweet white wine, such as a dry Riesling
½ teaspoon salt

Directions

1. **Preparing the Ingredients.** Heat the oil in the Crock-Pot Multi-Cooker® turned to the "Browning" function. Add the garlic and red pepper flakes; cook, stirring all the while, until aromatic, less than 1 minute.

   Add the collards; toss over the heat for 2 minutes. Add the tomato puree, broth, wine, and salt, and stir well.

2. **High pressure for 6 minutes.** Lock the lid on the Crock-Pot Multi-Cooker® and then cook for 6 minutes. To get 6-minutes cook time, press "Rice/Risotto" button and use the TIME ADJUSTMENT button to adjust the cook time to 6 minutes.

3. **Pressure Release.** Use the quick-release method.

   Unlock and open the cooker. Stir well before serving.

226. Maple Glazed Carrots

Preparation + Cook Time: 40 minutes | Servings: 8

Ingredients:

2 pounds carrots, peeled and then diagonally sliced into thick pieces
¼ cup raisins
½ cup water
1 tbsp maple syrup
1 tbsp butter
Pepper to taste

Directions:

1. Wash the carrots. Peel them and then slice into thick diagonal pieces. Put the carrots into the Crock Pot Express™.
2. Add the raisins and the water. Close and lock the lid. Select the "Steam" setting, Set the PRESSURE to LOW and the timer to 3 or 4 minutes.
3. When the timer beeps, turn the valve to Venting to quick release the pressure.
4. Remove the carrots from the pot and strain. In the still warm Crock Pot Express™ bowl, melt the butter and the maple syrup.
5. Add the carrots and gently stir to coat. Sprinkle with pepper and serve.

227. with Lemon Sauce

Preparation time: **10 minutes** • Cooking time: **20 minutes** • Servings: **4**

Ingredients:
4 artichokes
1 tablespoon tarragon, chopped
2 cups chicken stock
2 lemons
1 celery stalk, chopped
½ cup extra virgin olive oil
Salt, to taste

Directions:
1. Discard the stems and petal tips from artichokes. Zest the lemons, cut into 4 slices and place them into the Crock pot Express™. Place an artichoke on each lemon slices, add the stock,
2. Cover the Crock pot Express™ and cook on the **"Steam" setting** for 20 minutes. Release the pressure, uncover the Crock pot Express™ and transfer artichokes to a platter. In a food processor, mix the tarragon with the lemon zest, the pulp from the second lemon, celery, salt, and olive oil and pulse well. Drizzle this over artichokes, and serve.

228. Carrots with Pancetta, Butter, and Leeks

Preparation + Cook Time: 20 minutes | Servings: 4

Ingredients:
1 pound baby carrots
4-ounces diced pancetta
1 sliced leek
2 cups water
¼ cup sweet white wine
2 tbsp chopped butter
Black pepper to taste

Directions:
1. Select "BROWN/SAUTÉ" and cook pancetta until crisp.
2. Add the white and green parts of the leek and wait for 1 minute. Pour the wine and deglaze the pot.
3. Add carrots and a dash of pepper before stirring.
4. Pour pot contents into a 1-quart baking dish. Add the butter.

5. Put a piece of parchment paper on top of the dish followed by foil, which you should seal over the dish.
6. Carefully wipe out the inner pot and add 2 cups of water. Lower in a trivet and then put the dish on top. Seal the lid.
7. Select "BEANS/CHILI" and cook at HIGH pressure for 7 minutes.
8. When time is up, quick-release the pressure.
9. Carefully take out the dish and stir before serving.

229. Artichokes and Spinach Dip

Preparation time: **10 minutes** • Cooking time: **5 minutes** • Servings: **6**

Ingredients:
14 ounces canned artichoke hearts
8 ounces cream cheese
16 ounces Parmesan cheese, grated
10 ounces spinach
½ cup chicken stock
8 ounces mozzarella cheese, shredded
½ cup sour cream
3 garlic cloves, peeled and minced
½ cup mayonnaise
1 teaspoon onion powder

Directions:
1. In the Crock pot Express™, mix the artichokes with the stock, garlic, spinach, cream cheese, sour cream, onion powder and mayonnaise, stir,
2. Cover and cook on the **"Steam" setting** for 5 minutes. Release the pressure, uncover the Crock pot Express™, add the cheeses, stir well, transfer to a bowl and serve with chips or crackers.

230. Steamed Carrot Flowers

Preparation + Cook Time: 15 minutes | Servings: 4

Ingredients:
1 pound thick carrots, peeled
1 cup water

Directions:

1. With a sharp knife, cut 4-5 long groves along the carrot body.
2. Cut the carrots into coins, which now makes them into flowers. Put the carrot flowers in the steaming basket.
3. Pour 1 cup of water into the Crock Pot Express™, then put the steamer basket in the pot.
4. Close and lock the lid. Select the "Steam" setting, set the pressure to LOW and the timer to 4 minutes. When the timer beeps, quick release the pressure.
5. Carefully remove the steamer basket from the pot to stop cooking.
6. Transfer the carrot flowers into a serving dish.
7. Serve naked or without seasoning or dressing or at least taste them before drizzling with a bit of olive oil and pinch of salt.

231. Artichoke Hearts

Preparation time: **10 minutes** • Cooking time: **40 minutes** • Servings: **4**

Ingredients:
4 artichokes, washed, stems and petal tips cut off
Salt and ground black pepper, to taste
2 tablespoons lemon juice
¼ cup extra virgin olive oil
2 teaspoons balsamic vinegar
1 teaspoon dried oregano
2 cups water
2 garlic cloves, peeled and minced

Directions:
1. Put the artichokes in the steamer basket of the Crock pot Express™. Add the water to the Crock pot Express™,
2. Cover and cook them on **"Steam" mode** for 8 minutes. In a bowl, mix lemon juice with vinegar, oil, salt, pepper, garlic, and oregano, and stir very well. Release the pressure from the Crock pot Express™, transfer artichokes to a plate, cut them into halves, take out the hearts and arrange them on a platter. Drizzle the vinaigrette over artichokes and let them marinate for 30 minutes. Heat up a grill over medium heat, add the artichokes, and cook for 3 minutes on each side. Serve them warm.

232. Wrapped Carrot with Bacon

Preparation + Cook Time: 25 minutes | Servings: 8

Ingredients:
1-pound carrot

9 oz bacon
1 tsp salt
½ tsp ground black pepper
1 tsp ground white pepper
1 tsp paprika
¼ cup chicken stock
1 tbsp olive oil
¼ tsp marjoram

Directions:
1. Wash the carrot carefully and peel it. Sprinkle the carrot with the ground black pepper.
2. Combine the salt, ground white pepper, paprika, and marjoram together. Stir the mixture.
3. Slice the bacon. Then combine the sliced bacon and spice mixture together. Stir it carefully.
4. Then wrap the carrot in the sliced bacon.
5. Pour the olive oil in the Crock Pot Express™ and add wrapped carrot. Close the lid and "BROWN/SAUTÉ" the carrot for 10 minutes.
6. Then add the chicken stock, close and lock the lid. Select "BEANS/CHILI" and cook at HIGH pressure for 8 minutes more.
7. When the time is over – quick release the remaining pressure and open the lid. Chill the carrot little.
8. Enjoy!

234. Savory Artichoke Dip

Preparation time: **10 minutes** • Cooking time: **22 minutes** • Servings: **2**

Ingredients:
2 artichokes, washed, stems and petal tips cut off
1 bay leaf
1 cup water
2 garlic cloves, chopped
1 lemon cut into halves
For the sauce:
¼ cup coconut oil
¼ cup extra virgin olive oil
3 anchovy fillets
3 garlic cloves

Directions:

1. Put the artichokes in the steamer basket of the Crock pot Express™, add the water to the Crock pot Express™, lemon halves, 2 garlic cloves, and bay leaf,
2. Cover, and cook on the "Steam" setting for 20 minutes. Release the pressure naturally for 10 minutes, uncover the Crock pot Express™ and divide the artichokes among plates. In a food processor, mix the coconut oil with the anchovies, garlic, and olive oil and blend well. Pour this into a bowl, and serve.

235. Zucchini and Mushrooms

Preparation + Cook Time: 20 minutes | Servings: 6

Ingredients:

8-12 oz mushrooms, sliced or separated depending on type of mushroom

4 medium zucchini, cut into ½-inch slices (about 8 cups)

1 can (15 ounce) crushed or diced tomatoes with juice

1 large sprig fresh basil, sliced

1 tbsp extra-virgin olive oil

½ tsp black pepper, or to taste

½ tsp salt, or to taste

2 cloves garlic, minced

1½ cups onions, diced

Directions:

1. Press the "BROWN/SAUTÉ" button of the Crock Pot Express™. Add the olive oil and heat.
2. Add the garlic, onions, and mushrooms; cook, frequently stirring, until the onions are soft and the mushrooms lose their moisture.
3. Add the basil and sprinkle with the salt and pepper. Sauté for 5 minutes until the mushrooms are soft.
4. Add the zucchini, stir. Add the tomatoes with the juices over the zucchini; do not stir.
5. Close and lock the lid. Press the "BEANS/CHILI" button. Set the pressure to LOW and the timer to 1 minute. (Allow cooking for 1 minute then Stop).
6. When the timer beeps, turn the steam valve to quick release the pressure. Carefully remove the cover.
7. If the zucchini are still a little undercooked, just cover the pot and let rest for 1 minutes to allow the zucchinis to soften.
8. Serve over pasta, rice, baked potatoes, or polenta. If desired, you can stir a can of white beans.

236. Mushroom Gravy

Preparation + Cook Time: 45 minutes | Servings: 4

Ingredients:
2 tbsp olive oil
8 oz sliced white mushrooms
4 tbsp all-purpose flour
4 tbsp vegan butter
2 fluid ounce vegetable broth
2 fluid ounce almond milk
22 fluid ounce water

Directions:
1. Select "BROWN/SAUTÉ" and preheat the Crock Pot Express™. Add olive oil.
2. Then add mushrooms and cook for 5-7 minutes or until nicely golden brown.
3. Pour in broth and continue cooking until mushrooms turn into dark color.
4. Press CANCEL, then pour the water and stir until just mixed. Close and lock the lid, select "BEANS/CHILI" and cook at HIGH pressure for 5 minutes.
5. Crock Pot Express™ will take 10 minutes to build pressure before cooking timer starts.
6. When the timer beeps, switch off the Crock Pot Express™ and let pressure release naturally for 10 minutes and then do quick pressure release.
7. Then uncover the pot, drain mushrooms and return to the pot, reserve broth.
8. Place a medium-sized saucepan over medium heat, add butter and let heat until melt completely.
9. Then gradually stir in flour and then slowly whisk in reserved broth until combined.
10. Pour in milk, stir in mushrooms and bring the mixture to simmer, whisk occasionally.
11. Simmer mixture for 8 minutes until gravy reaches desired thickness and then ladle into serving platters. Serve immediately.

237. Wrapped Asparagus Spears

Preparation time: **5 minutes** • Cooking time: **4 minutes** • Servings: **4**

Ingredients:
1 pound asparagus, trimmed
8 ounces prosciutto slices
2 cups water
Salt

Directions:

1. Wrap the asparagus spears in prosciutto slices and place them on the bottom of the steamer basket into the Crock pot Express™. Add the water to the Crock pot Express™, add a pinch of salt,
2. Cover and cook on the **"Steam" setting** for 4 minutes. Release the pressure naturally, uncover, transfer the asparagus spears on a platter, and serve at room temperature.

Main Dishes – Rice

238. Perfect Brown Rice

Prep: 5 minutes • pressure: 22 minutes • total: 27 minutes • pressure level: high • release: natural • Serves 4

Ingredients
1½ cups brown rice
2½ cups water
½ teaspoon salt
1 teaspoon olive oil

Directions
1. **Preparing the Ingredients** Place the rice, water, salt, and oil in the Crock-Pot Multi-Cooker® base.
2. **High pressure for 20 minutes.** Lock the lid on the Crock-Pot Multi-Cooker® and then cook for 20 minutes. To get 20-minutes cook time, press Meat/Chicken button and use the TIME ADJUSTMENT button to adjust the cook time to 20 minutes.
3. **Pressure Release.** When the time is up, open the Crock-Pot Multi-Cooker® with the 10-Minute Natural Release method.
4. Fluff the rice with a fork and serve.

239. Lentil and Wild Rice Pilaf

Preparation + Cook Time: 20 minutes + 30 min. soaking | Servings: 6

Ingredients:
For the lentils and rice (soak for 30 minutes before cooking):
¼ cup brown rice
¼ cup black/wild rice
½ cup black or green lentils
For the vegetables:
1 cup mushrooms, sliced
1 stalk celery, finely chopped
½ onion, medium-sized, finely chopped
3 cloves garlic, pressed/minced

For the spices:

1 bay leaf

1 tbsp Italian seasoning blend (no-salt added)

1 tsp dried coriander

1 tsp fennel seeds

½ tsp ground black pepper

¼ tsp red pepper flakes

2 cups vegetable broth

Directions:

1. Combine the rice and the lentils in a medium-sized bowl.
2. Let soak for 30 minutes. Drain and then rinse thoroughly.
3. Set the Crock Pot Express™ to "BROWN/SAUTÉ". Put the veggies in the inner pot and sauté for 3-5 minutes.
4. If needed, add a bit of water to prevent the veggies from burning.
5. Add the rice and lentils, vegetable broth, and spices into the pot. Close and lock the lid.
6. Press "BEANS/CHILI", set the pressure to HIGH, and set the timer to 9 minutes.
7. When the timer beeps, let the pressure release naturally. Open the lid. Stir the pilaf.
8. If liquid remains, let sit for 5 minutes uncovered to allow the pilaf to absorb more liquid.
9. Serve this dish with steamed or fresh veggies.

Notes: If you don't like fennel seeds, then use 1 tablespoon of your preferred dried herbs, such as thyme, rosemary, parsley, basil, or oregano. If you don't have black or wild rice on hand, you can use all brown rice.

240. Risotto with Peas and Shrimp

Prep: 5 minutes • pressure: 6 minutes • total: 11 minutes • pressure level: high • release: quick • Serves 4

Ingredients

1 tablespoon unsalted butter

½ cup chopped onion

1 cup Arborio rice

⅓ cup white wine

2¾ cups Chicken Stock or low-sodium broth, divided

½ pound raw medium shrimp, shelled and deveined

½ cup frozen peas, thawed

¼ cup grated Parmigiano-Reggiano or similar cheese

Directions

1. **Preparing the Ingredients.** Turn the Crock-Pot Multi-Cooker® to "brown," heat the butter until it stops foaming. Add the onion, and cook for about 2 minutes, stirring, until soft. Add the rice, and stir to coat with the butter. Cook for 1 minute, stirring. Stir in the white wine, and cook for 1 to 2 minutes, or until it's almost evaporated. Add 2½ cups of Chicken Stock, and stir to make sure no rice is sticking to the bottom of the cooker.

2. **High pressure for 6 minutes.** Lock the lid on the Crock-Pot Multi-Cooker® and then cook for 6 minutes. To get 6-minutes cook time, press "Rice/Risotto" button and use the TIME ADJUSTMENT button to adjust the cook time to 6 minutes.

3. **Pressure Release** Use the quick-release method.

4. **Finish the dish.** Unlock and remove the lid. Turn the Crock-Pot Multi-Cooker® to "brown," Continue to cook the rice, stirring, for 1 to 2 minutes more, or until the rice is firm just in the very center of the grain and the liquid has thickened slightly. Add the shrimp and peas, and continue to cook for about 4 minutes more, or until the shrimp are cooked. Stir in the Parmigiano-Reggiano. If the risotto is too thick, stir in a little of the remaining ¼ cup of Chicken Stock to loosen it up. Serve immediately. Risotto is one of those dishes that lend themselves to almost endless variation. Leftover ham is a great addition, as is smoked salmon or trout, or go vegetarian with "Sautéed" Mushrooms, roasted peppers, or even beets.

PER SERVING: CALORIES: 343; FAT: 6G; SODIUM: 292MG; CARBOHYDRATES: 45G; FIBER: 3G; PROTEIN: 21G

241. Rice-Stuffed Acorn Squash

Preparation + Cook Time: 20 minutes | Servings: 4

Ingredients:
3¾ cups veggie stock
2 medium-sized, halved acorn squash
1 cup white rice
1 cup diced onion
½ cup quinoa
½ cup vegan cheese
2 minced garlic cloves
1 tbsp Earth Balance spread (or any vegan butter)
1 tsp chopped rosemary
1 tsp chopped thyme
1 tsp chopped sage

Directions:

1. Turn your Crock Pot Express™ to "BROWN/SAUTÉ" and melt the Earth Balance. Add onion and salt, and cook for two minutes.
2. Toss in the garlic and cook for another minute or so. Add rice, quinoa, herbs, and pour in the broth. Stir.
3. Put your de-seeded squash halves with the cut-side up in a steamer basket.
4. Put the trivet in the cooker, and place the basket on top. Close and seal the lid.
5. Hit "BEANS/CHILI" and cook for 6 minutes on HIGH pressure.
6. When the timer beeps, carefully quick-release the pressure after hitting CANCEL.
7. Take out the steamer basket and drain any liquid that's hanging around in the squash.
8. Add vegan cheese to the pot and stir. Wait 5 minutes or so for the stuffing to thicken.
9. Fill the squash and sprinkle on some extra cheese. Serve!

242. Risotto With Butternut Squash And Porcini

Prep: 5 minutes • pressure: 10 minutes • total: 15 minutes • pressure level: high • release: quick • Serves 6

Ingredients
2 tablespoons unsalted butter
1 medium leek, white and pale green parts only, halved lengthwise, washed, and thinly sliced
1½ cups white Arborio rice
¼ cup dry vermouth
4 cups (1 quart) vegetable broth
2 cups seeded, peeled, and finely chopped butternut squash
½ ounce dried porcini mushrooms, crumbled
1 teaspoon dried thyme
¼ teaspoon saffron threads
½ cup finely grated Parmesan cheese (about 1 ounce)

Directions
1. **Preparing the Ingredients**. Melt the butter in the Crock-Pot Multi-Cooker® turned to the "browning" function. Add the leek and cook, stirring often, until softened, about 2 minutes.
   Add the rice; stir until coated in the butter. Pour in the vermouth; stir over the heat until fully absorbed into the grains, 1 to 2 minutes. Add the broth, squash, dried porcini, thyme, and saffron.
2. **High pressure for 10 minutes.** Lock the lid on the Crock-Pot Multi-Cooker® and then cook for 10 minutes. To get 10-minutes cook time, press "Rice/Risotto" button and use the TIME ADJUSTMENT button to adjust the cook time to 10 minutes.
3. **Pressure Release.** Use the quick-release method.
4. **Finish the dish.** Unlock and open the cooker. Turn the Crock-Pot Multi-Cooker® to its "browning" function. Bring to a simmer, stirring until thickened, about 2 minutes.

5. Stir in the cheese. Put the lid onto the cooker without locking it in place. Set aside for 5 minutes to melt the cheese and blend the flavors. Stir again before serving.
6. Serve and Enjoy!

243. Perfect Basmati Rice

Preparation + Cook Time: 15 minutes | Servings: 4

Ingredients:
1 cup white basmati rice
1¼ cups water
Salt to taste

Directions:
1. Put the rice in a colander.
2. Rinse until the water is clear.
3. Transfer into the Crock Pot Express™ and then add the water.
4. Set the pot to "BEANS/CHILI", set the pressure to LOW, and the timer to 8 minutes.
5. When the timer beeps, quick release the pressure.
6. Fluff the rice using a fork and serve.

244. Barley Risotto with Fresh Spinach

Prep: 6 minutes • pressure: 22 minutes • total: 26 minutes • pressure level: high • release: quick • Serves 6

Ingredients
1 tablespoon olive oil
1 tablespoon light margarine
1 yellow onion, diced
1 cup pearled barley
4 cups chicken stock or broth
Juice of 1 lemon
1 tablespoon minced garlic
4 cups baby spinach
1/4 cup grated Parmesan cheese
Salt and pepper

Directions

1. **Preparing the Ingredients.** With the cooker's lid off, heat oil and margarine on "brown," until oil is sizzling and margarine is melted.
   Place diced onion in the cooker, and sauté until translucent, 5 minutes.
   Stir in barley, and sauté 1 additional minute.
   Add the chicken broth, lemon juice, and minced garlic.
2. **High pressure for 25 minutes.** Lock the lid on the Crock-Pot Multi-Cooker® and then cook for 25 minutes. To get 25-minutes cook time, press "Beans/Chili" button and use the TIME ADJUSTMENT button to adjust the cook time to 25 minutes.
3. **Pressure Release.** Let the pressure release naturally 5 minutes before performing a quick release for any remaining pressure.
   With the cooker's lid off, set to "brown," to sauté, and stir in spinach and Parmesan cheese, simmering until spinach cooks down. Season with salt and pepper to taste before serving.

245. Crock Pot Express™ Brown Rice

Preparation + Cook Time: 30 minutes | Servings: 6

Ingredients:
2 cups brown rice
½ tsp of sea salt
2 ½ cups any kind vegetable broth or water

Directions:
1. Put the rice into the Crock Pot Express™.
2. Pour in the broth or water and salt. Close and lock the lid. Press the "BEANS/CHILI" and set the pressure to HIGH and the timer to 22 minutes.
3. When the timer beeps, naturally release the pressure for 10 minutes.
4. Carefully open the lid. Serve.

246. Quinoa Risotto With Bacon

Prep: 7 minutes • pressure: 9 minutes • total: 16 minutes • pressure level: high • release: quick • Serves 4

Ingredients
3 ounces slab bacon, diced
6 medium scallions, thinly sliced
12 cherry tomatoes, halved
¼ cup dry vermouth

3½ cups chicken broth
1½ cups white or red quinoa, rinsed if necessary
3 fresh thyme sprigs
¼ cup finely grated Parmesan cheese (about ½ ounce)
½ teaspoon ground black pepper

Directions

1. **Preparing the Ingredients.** Place the bacon in the Crock-Pot Multi-Cooker® turned to the "browning" function. Fry until crisp, stirring occasionally, about 4 minutes.
   Add the scallions; stir over the heat until softened, about 1 minute. Put in the tomatoes; cook just until they begin to break down, about 2 minutes, stirring occasionally. Pour in the vermouth; as it comes to a simmer, scrape up any browned bits in the bottom of the cooker.
   Stir in the broth, quinoa, and thyme sprigs.
2. **High pressure for 9 minutes.** Lock the lid on the Crock-Pot Multi-Cooker® and then cook for 9 minutes. To get 9-minutes cook time, press "Rice/Risotto" button and use the TIME ADJUSTMENT button to adjust the cook time to 9 minutes.
3. **Pressure Release.** Return the pot's pressure to normal with the quick-release method.
4. **Finish the dish.** Unlock and open the cooker. Turn the Crock-Pot Multi-Cooker® to its "browning" function. Discard the thyme sprigs. Bring the mixture in the pot to a simmer; cook, stirring often, until thickened, 2 to 3 minutes. Stir in the cheese and pepper to serve.

247. Brown Rice Medley

Preparation + Cook Time: 35 minutes | Servings: 4

Ingredients:
3-4 tbsp red, wild or black rice
¾ cup (or more) short grain brown rice
1½ cups water
3/8-1/2 tsp sea salt, optional

Directions:
1. Put as much as 3-4 tablespoons of red, wild, or black rice or use all three kinds in 1-cup measuring cup.
2. Add brown rice to make 1 cup total of rice. Put the rice in a strainer and wash. Put the rice in the Crock Pot Express™.
3. Add 1½ cups water in the pot. If desired, add salt.
4. Stir and then check the sides of the pot to make sure the rice is pushed down into the water. Close and lock the lid. Press "Beans/Chili" and set the time to 23 minutes.
5. When the timer beeps, let the pressure release naturally for 5 minutes, then turn the steam valve and release the pressure slowly.

6. If you have time, let the pressure release naturally for 15 minutes. Stir and serve.

248. Armenian Rice Pilaf

Prep: 7 minutes • pressure: 3 minutes • total: 10 minutes • pressure level: high • release: natural • Serves 4

Ingredients
2 tablespoons unsalted butter
1 tablespoon olive oil
½ cup vermicelli or angel hair pasta, broken into 1-inch pieces
2 cups long-grain white or basmati rice
4 cups salt-free Chicken Stock, preferably double-strength
2 teaspoons salt

Directions
1. **Preparing the Ingredients.** Heat the Crock-Pot Multi-Cooker® using the "Sauté" Function, add the butter and oil, and cook until the butter has melted. Add the vermicelli and stir well to coat. Sauté until the pieces just begin to turn golden. Add the rice; stir well to coat and toast for about 1 minute. Add the chicken stock and salt.
2. **High pressure for 3 minutes.** Lock the lid on the Crock-Pot Multi-Cooker® and then cook for 3 minutes. To get 3-minutes cook time, press "Steam" button and use the TIME ADJUSTMENT button to adjust the cook time to 3 minutes.
3. **Pressure Release.** When the time is up, open the Crock-Pot Multi-Cooker® with the 10-Minute Natural Release method.
4. Mix the pilaf well, pulling up the rice from the bottom of the Crock-Pot Multi-Cooker® to the top before serving.

249. Brown Rice-Stuffed Cabbage Rolls with Pine Nuts and Currants

Preparation + Cook Time: 35 minutes | Servings: 4

Ingredients:
1 large head green cabbage cored
1 tbsp olive oil
1½ cups onion finely chopped
3 cups brown rice cooked
3 ounces feta cheese crumbled, about 3/4 cup
½ cup currants dried
2 tbsp pine nuts toasted

2 tbsp parsley fresh chopped

¼ tsp salt

½ tsp black pepper freshly ground

½ cup apple juice

1 tbsp cider vinegar

1 can crushed tomatoes undrained, 14.5-ounce

Parsley additional, chopped and fresh, optional

Directions:

1. Steam cabbage head 8 minutes; cool slightly. Remove 16 leaves from cabbage head; discard remaining cabbage. Cut off raised portion of the center vein of each cabbage leaf (do not cut out vein); set trimmed cabbage leaves aside.
2. Heat oil in a large nonstick skillet over medium heat; swirl to coat. Add onion; cover and cook 6 minutes or until tender.
3. Remove from heat; stir in brown rice, add feta cheese, currants dried, pine nuts and parsley. Stir in 1/4 teaspoon of the salt and 1/8 teaspoon of the pepper.
4. Place cabbage leaves on a flat surface; place about 1/3 cup rice mixture into center of each cabbage leaf. Fold in edges of leaves over rice mixture; roll up. Arrange cabbage rolls in bottom of the inner pot of a 6-quart Crock Pot Express™.
5. Combine the remaining 1/4 teaspoon salt, remaining 1/8 teaspoon pepper, apple juice, vinegar, and tomatoes; pour evenly over cabbage rolls.
6. Close and lock the lid of the Crock Pot Express™. Turn the steam release handle to Venting position. Press SLOW COOK, and select 2 hours cook time.
7. Serve sprinkled with parsley, if desired. Enjoy!

250. Wild and Brown Rice Pilaf

Prep: 5 minutes • pressure: 27 minutes • total: 32 minutes • pressure level: high • release: combination •Serves 4

Ingredients
1 tablespoon olive oil

¾ cup diced onion

1 garlic clove, minced

⅓ cup wild rice

⅔ cup water

½ teaspoon kosher salt, divided, plus additional for seasoning

½ cup brown rice

¾ cup low-sodium vegetable broth

¼ cup dry white wine

1 bay leaf

1 fresh thyme sprig, or ¼ teaspoon dried thyme

2 tablespoons chopped fresh parsley

Directions

1. **Preparing the Ingredients.** Set the Crock-Pot Multi-Cooker® to "brown," heat the olive oil until it shimmers and flows like water. Add the onion and garlic, and cook for about 3 minutes, stirring, until the garlic is fragrant and the onions soften and separate. Add the wild rice, water, and ¼ teaspoon of kosher salt, and stir.
2. **High pressure for 15 minutes.** Lock the lid on the Crock-Pot Multi-Cooker® and then cook for 15 minutes. To get 15-minutes cook time, press "Poultry" button.
3. **Pressure Release.** Use the quick-release method.
   Unlock and remove the lid. Stir in the brown rice, vegetable broth, remaining ¼ teaspoon of kosher salt, white wine, bay leaf, and thyme.
4. **High pressure for 12 minutes.** Lock the lid on the Crock-Pot Multi-Cooker® and then cook for 12 minutes. To get 12-minutes cook time, press "Rice/Risotto" button. When the timer goes off, turn the cooker off. (""Keep Warm"" setting, turn off).
5. **Pressure Release.** After cooking, use the natural method to release pressure for 12 minutes, then the quick method to release the remaining pressure.
6. **Finish the dish.** Unlock and remove the lid. Remove the bay leaf and thyme sprig, and stir in the parsley. Taste and adjust the seasoning, as needed. Replace but do not lock the lid. Let the rice steam for about 4 minutes, fluff gently with a fork, and serve.

PER SERVING: CALORIES: 195; FAT: 4G; SODIUM: 309MG; CARBOHYDRATES: 32G; FIBER: 2G; PROTEIN: 5G

251. Beetroot Rice

Preparation + Cook Time: 35 minutes | Servings: 2-4

Ingredients:
1 cup Basmati rice
1¼ cup water
1 tbsp ghee or oil
½ tsp cumin seeds or Jeera
½ tbsp ginger paste
½ tbsp garlic paste
½ onion thinly sliced
1 beet cut into small pieces
½ cup green peas
1 tbsp lemon juice
Whole Spices (optional):
1 inch stick cinnamon or Dal chini
1 bay leaf or Tej Patta
1 star anise
6 black peppercorns
3 cloves or Laung
Spices:
2 tsp salt
½ tsp cayenne or red chili powder
½ tsp garam masala
1 tsp coriander or Dhania powder (optional)
¼ tsp turmeric or Haldi powder

Directions:
1. Start the Crock Pot Express™ In "Brown/Sauté" mode and heat it. Add ghee, cumin seeds and whole spices and sauté them for 30 seconds until the cumin seeds change color.
2. Add the sliced onions, ginger, garlic and sauté for 3 minutes.
3. Add the beets, green peas and spices. Mix well.
4. Add the rice and water to the pot. Stir the ingredients in the pot.
5. Change the Crock Pot Express™ setting to "BEANS/CHILI", close the lid and cook for 4 minutes at HIGH pressure.
6. When the Crock Pot Express™ beeps, do a 10 minute natural release, then release the remaining pressure "BEANS/CHILI"ly.
7. Add the lemon juice and fluff the rice. Beet Pulao is ready. Enjoy with homemade yogurt or raita.

Notes:
- Adding whole spices is optional. You can enjoy this beet pulao even if you don't have all the whole spices in your pantry.
- To reduce spice, skip the cayenne.
- I added green peas along with the beets, as that is what I had at hand. Other possible options to add are potatoes, bell peppers, carrots and edamame.

252. Wild Rice Salad with Apples

Prep: 5 minutes • pressure: 18 minutes • total: 23 minutes • pressure level: high • release: natural • Serves 4

Ingredients
4 cups water
1¼ teaspoons kosher salt, divided
1 cup wild rice
⅓ cup walnut or olive oil
3 tablespoons cider vinegar
¼ teaspoon celery seed
⅛ teaspoon freshly ground black pepper
Pinch granulated sugar
½ cup walnut pieces, toasted
2 or 3 celery stalks, thinly sliced (about 1 cup)
1 medium Gala, Fuji, or Braeburn apple, cored and cut into ½-inch pieces

Directions
1. **Preparing the Ingredients.** Add the water into the Crock-Pot Multi-Cooker®, and 1 teaspoon of kosher salt. Stir in the wild rice.
2. **High pressure for 18 minutes.** Lock the lid on the Crock-Pot Multi-Cooker® and then cook for 18 minutes. To get 18-minutes cook time, press Meat/Chicken button and use the TIME ADJUSTMENT button to adjust the cook time to 18 minutes.
3. **Pressure Release.** Use the natural-release method.
4. **Finish the dish.** Unlock and remove the lid. The rice grains should be mostly split open. If not, simmer the rice for several minutes more, in the Crock-Pot Multi-Cooker® set to "brown," until at least half the grains have split. Drain and cool slightly.

   To a small jar with a tight-fitting lid, add the walnut oil, cider vinegar, celery seed, the remaining ¼ teaspoon of kosher salt, the pepper, and the sugar, and shake until well combined.

   To a medium bowl, add the cooled rice, walnuts, celery, and apple. Pour half of the dressing over the salad, and toss gently to coat, adding more dressing as desired.
5. Serve.

253. Portuguese Tomato Rice with Shrimp

Preparation + Cook Time: 35 minutes | Servings: 4

Ingredients:
2 tbsp olive oil
1 large onion finely chopped
2 tbsp tomato paste
4 cloves garlic finely chopped
2 bay leaves
1½ cups Arborio rice
2 ¾ cups passata or thin tomato puree (if the passata is very thick use 2¼ cups passata and 1¼ cups of stock)
¾ cup chicken stock
2 tsp paprika
Kosher salt to taste
Black pepper to taste
1 cup tomato diced, heaping cup
3-4 tbsp butter
1 handful parsley freshly chopped
24 raw shrimp shelled and deveined, optional

Directions:
1. Hit the "Brown/Sauté" button on your Crock Pot Express™ and when says it's 'Hot', add in the oil and the onions and sauté for 3 or 4 minutes, until the onions are nice and soft.
2. Add in the tomato paste and cook for another couple of minutes, stirring constantly so the tomato paste doesn't burn.
3. Now add the garlic and bay leaves, stir another minute before adding in the rice.
4. Pour in the stock, the tomatoes, paprika and good pinch of kosher salt (start with 1 teaspoon and taste) and a few grinds of black pepper. Lastly, stir in the chopped tomatoes
5. Close up the lid, seal the vent and press the "Steam" button to program your Crock Pot Express™ to cook for 6 minutes at HIGH pressure.
6. When the time is up, quick release the pressure, open the lid and give the rice a good stir. It will be quite soupy.
7. If you are adding shrimp, add them now, stir them into the rice and add the lid back on and let the rice sit for 3 or 4 minutes to cook them. If you are NOT adding shrimp, you

can leave the lid off but continue to stir the rice occasionally for another minute or so to thicken the rice up a bit.

8. Just before serving, stir in the butter and parsley. Enjoy!

254. Seafood Risotto

Prep: 10 minutes • pressure: 6 minutes • total: 16 minutes • pressure level: high • release: natural • Serves 4

Ingredients
   3 cups mixed seafood (shrimp, calamari, clams, etc.)
   Water, as needed
   2 tablespoons olive oil, plus more to finish
   3 garlic cloves, chopped
   3 oil-packed anchovies
   2 cups Arborio or Carnaroli rice
   Freshly squeezed juice of 1 lemon
   2 teaspoons salt
   ¼ teaspoon ground white pepper
   1 bunch flat-leaf parsley, chopped
   Lemon wedges, for serving

Directions

1. **Preparing the Ingredients.** Separate the shellfish from the other seafood and set the shellfish aside. Add the remaining seafood to a 4-cup measuring cup and add water to just over the 4-cup mark.
   Heat the Crock-Pot Multi-Cooker® using the "Sauté" mode, add the oil, and heat briefly. Stir in the garlic and anchovies and sauté until the garlic is golden and the anchovies are broken up. Add the rice, stirring to coat well. While you continue to stir, look carefully at the rice, it will first become wet and look slightly transparent and pearly; then it will slowly begin to look dry and solid white again. At that point pour in the lemon juice. Scrape the bottom of the Crock-Pot Multi-Cooker® gently, and keep stirring until all of the juice has evaporated. Stir in the seafood and water and the salt and pepper. Place the shellfish on top without stirring any further.

2. **High pressure for 6 minutes**. Lock the lid on the Crock-Pot Multi-Cooker® and then cook for 6 minutes. To get 6-minutes cook time, press Rice / Risotto button and use the TIME ADJUSTMENT button to adjust the cook time to 6 minutes.

3. **Pressure Release** When the time is up, open the Crock-Pot Multi-Cooker® with the Natural Release method.
   Stir the risotto. Swirl some oil over the top and sprinkle with parsley. Serve with lemon wedges.

255. Rice and Lentils

Preparation + Cook Time: 55 minutes | Servings: 4

Ingredients:
For the sauté:
1 tbsp oil, OR dry sauté (or add a little water/vegetable broth)
½ cup onion, chopped
2 cloves garlic, minced
For the porridge:
1½ cups brown rice
1 cup rutabaga, peeled and diced, OR potato OR turnip
1 cup brown lentils
1 tbsp dried marjoram (or thyme)
2-inch sprig fresh rosemary
3½ cups water
Salt and pepper to taste

Directions:
1. Press the "Brown/Sauté" key of the Crock Pot Express™ and select the Normal option.
2. Put the oil/ broth in the pot and, if using oil, heat. When the oil is hot, add the onion and sauté for 5 minutes or until transparent.
3. Add the garlic and sauté for 1 minute.
4. Add the lentils, brown rice, rutabaga, marjoram, rosemary, and pour in the water into the pot and stir to combine. Press the CANCEL key to stop the "Brown/Sauté" function.
5. Press the "BEANS/CHILI" key, set the pressure to HIGH, and set the timer for 23 minutes.
6. When the Crock Pot Express™ timer beeps, press the CANCEL key. Let the pressure release naturally for 10-15 minutes or until the valve drops. Release remaining pressure. Unlock and carefully open the lid.
7. Taste and, if needed, season with pepper and salt to taste.
8. If needed, add more ground rosemary and more marjoram.

256. Brown Rice Pilaf With Cashews

Prep: 5 minutes • pressure: 33 minutes • total: 38 minutes • pressure level: high • release: quick • Serves 6

Ingredients
3 tablespoons unsalted butter
1 large leek, white and pale green parts only, halved lengthwise, washed, and thinly sliced

½ teaspoon dried thyme

½ teaspoon salt

⅛ teaspoon ground turmeric

1½ cups long-grain brown rice, such as brown basmati

3 cups vegetable or chicken broth

½ cup chopped roasted unsalted cashews

Directions

1. **Preparing the Ingredients.** Melt the butter in the Crock-Pot Multi-Cooker® turned to the "Browning" function. Add the leek and cook, stirring often, until softened, about 2 minutes. Stir in the thyme, salt, and turmeric until fragrant, less than half a minute. Add the rice and cook for 1 minute, stirring all the while. Pour in the broth and stir well to get any browned bits off the bottom of the cooker.
2. **High pressure for 33 minutes.** Lock the lid on the Crock-Pot Multi-Cooker® and then cook for 33 minutes. To get 33-minutes cook time, press "Soup" Button and use the TIME ADJUSTMENT button to adjust the cook time to 33 minutes.
3. **Pressure Release.** Use the quick-release method to return the pot's pressure to normal but do not open the cooker. Set aside for 10 minutes to steam the rice.
4. Unlock and open the pot. Stir in the chopped cashews before serving.

257. Rice &Chickpea Stew

Preparation + Cook Time: 35 minutes | Servings: 6

Ingredients:

3 medium-sized onions, peeled and sliced

1 pound sweet potato, peeled and diced

6 oz brown basmati rice, rinsed

30 oz cooked chickpeas

¼ tsp salt

¼ tsp ground black pepper

2 tsp ground cumin

2 tsp ground coriander

8 fluid oz orange juice

1 tbsp olive oil

4 cups vegetable broth

4 oz chopped cilantro

Directions:

1. Plug in and switch on a 6-quarts Crock Pot Express™, select "BROWN/SAUTÉ" option, add oil and onion and let cook for 8-10 minutes or until browned.
2. Stir in coriander and cumin and continue cooking for 15 seconds or until fragrant.

3. Add remaining ingredients into the pot except for black pepper and cilantro and stir until just mixed.
4. Press CANCEL and secure pot with lid. Then position pressure indicator, select "BEANS/CHILI" option and adjust cooking time on timer pad to 5 minutes and let cook on HIGH pressure.
5. Crock Pot Express™ will take 10 minutes to build pressure before cooking timer starts.
6. When the timer beeps, switch off the Crock Pot Express™ and let pressure release naturally for 10 minutes and then do quick pressure release.
7. Then uncover the pot and stir in pepper until mixed.
8. Garnish with cilantro and serve.

258. Wild Rice With Sweet Potatoes

Prep: 5 minutes • pressure: 45 minutes • total: 50 minutes • pressure level: high • release: quick • Serves 6

Ingredients
2 tablespoons olive oil
1 medium yellow onion, chopped
2 medium celery stalks, chopped
1 tablespoon packed fresh sage leaves, minced
2 teaspoons fresh thyme leaves
1½ cups black wild rice (about 8 ounces)
3 cups vegetable or chicken broth
1 large sweet potato (about 1 pound), peeled and diced
¼ cup dried cranberries
½ teaspoon salt
½ teaspoon ground black pepper

Directions
1. **Preparing the Ingredients.** Heat the olive oil in the Crock-Pot Multi-Cooker® turned to the "browning" function. Add the onion and celery; cook, stirring often, until the onion softens, about 4 minutes. Mix in the sage and thyme; cook until fragrant, about 30 seconds. Stir in the rice and toss well to coat. Pour in the broth; stir well to get up any browned bits in the bottom of pot.
2. **High pressure for 30 minutes.** Lock the lid on the Crock-Pot Multi-Cooker® and then cook for 30 minutes. To get 30-minutes cook time, press "Soup" Button.
3. **Pressure Release** Use the quick-release method to return the pot's pressure to normal. Unlock and open the cooker. Stir in the sweet potato, cranberries, salt, and pepper.
4. **High pressure for 15 minutes**. Lock the lid back on the Crock-Pot Multi-Cooker® and then cook for 15 minutes. To get 15-minutes cook time, press ""Poultry"" button.
5. **Pressure Release** Use the quick-release method to return the pot's pressure to normal.
6. **Unlock** and open the cooker. Stir well before serving.

259. Mexican Rice

Preparation + Cook Time: 25 minutes | Servings: 4

Ingredients:
1 tbsp olive oil
¼ cup onion, diced
2 cups long grain white rice
2⅓ cups chicken stock
1 cup salsa
1 tsp salt

Directions:
1. Set the Crock Pot Express™ to "Brown/Sauté" setting.
2. Sauté olive oil and onion until translucent about 1 to 2 minutes
3. Add in rice and sauté for 2 to 3 minutes.
4. Stir in chicken stock, salsa, and salt into the rice.
5. Close and lock the lid. Select "BEANS/CHILI" and cook at HIGH pressure for 10 minutes.
6. Once the time is up, let the pressure release naturally.
7. Fluff the rice with a fork and serve.

260. Brown Rice with Lentils

Prep: 5 minutes • pressure: 35 minutes • total: 40 minutes • pressure level: high • release: natural • Serves 8

Ingredients
5 tablespoons olive oil
3 large onions, halved through the root (flatter) end, then sliced into thin half-moons
1 teaspoon coriander seeds
1 teaspoon cumin seeds
½ teaspoon ground turmeric
½ teaspoon ground allspice
½ teaspoon ground cinnamon
2 cups long-grain brown rice, preferably basmati
1 teaspoon sugar
1 teaspoon ground black pepper

½ teaspoon salt

4½ cups vegetable or chicken broth

½ cup green lentils (French lentils or lentils de Puy)

Directions

1. **Preparing the Ingredients.** Heat 1½ tablespoons oil in the Crock-Pot Multi-Cooker® turned to the "Browning" function. Add half the onions and cook until well browned and crisp at the edges, at least 10 minutes, stirring occasionally. Transfer the cooked onions to a large bowl; repeat with 1½ tablespoons more oil and the rest of the onions. Add the remaining 2 tablespoons oil to the cooker; stir in the coriander, cumin, turmeric, allspice, and cinnamon until aromatic, about 1 minute. Add the rice, sugar, pepper, and salt; stir for 1 minute. Stir in the broth, scraping up any brown bits in the cooker. Stir in the lentils.

2. **High pressure for 35 minutes.** Lock the lid on the Crock-Pot Multi-Cooker® and then cook for 35 minutes. To get 35-minutes cook time, press "Soup" Button and use the TIME ADJUSTMENT button to adjust the cook time to 35 minutes.

3. **Pressure Release.** Turn off the Crock-Pot Multi-Cooker® or unplug it so it doesn't flip to the keep-warm setting. Let its pressure return normal naturally, 14 to 20 minutes.

4. **Finish the dish** Unlock and open the cooker. Spoon the caramelized onions on top of the rice; set the lid back on the cooker without locking it in place, and set aside for 10 minutes to warm the onions. Serve by scooping up big spoonfuls with onions and rice in each.

261. Spanish Rice

Preparation + Cook Time: 30 minutes | Servings: 4

Ingredients:

2 tbsp butter

2 cups long grain rice

1½ cups chicken stock or water

8 oz tomato sauce

1 tsp cumin

1 tsp chili powder

½ tsp garlic powder

½ tsp onion powder

½ tsp salt

Directions:

1. Set the Crock Pot Express™ to "Brown/Sauté" setting.

2. Sauté butter and dry rice together for 4 minutes.

3. Stir in chicken stock, tomato sauce, cumin, chili powder, garlic powder and onion powder into the rice.
4. Close and lock the lid. Select "BEANS/CHILI" and cook at HIGH pressure for 10 minutes.
5. Once the time is up, let the pressure release naturally.
6. Fluff the rice with a fork and serve.

262. Tiger Prawn Risotto

Prep: 10 minutes • pressure: 30 minutes • total: 40 minutes • pressure level: high • release: natural • Serves 2-4

Ingredients
½ pound frozen tiger prawns, thawed and peeled
1 teaspoon salt
1 teaspoon white pepper
3 tablespoons olive oil
4 tablespoons butter
1 shallot, minced
3 cloves garlic, minced
2 cups Arborio rice
¾ cup cooking sake
2 teaspoons soy sauce
4 cups fish stock or Japanese Dashi
20 grams Parmesan cheese, finely grated
2 stalk green onions, thinly sliced

Directions
1. **Preparing the Ingredients.** In mixing bowl season the prawns with salt and white pepper. Set the Crock-Pot Multi-Cooker® on brown and add the olive oil and butter and sauté prawns for 5-10 minutes with the shallot and garlic, the prawns should be about 80% cooked. Remove and set aside.

   Add the Arborio rice, cooking sake, soy sauce and fish stock into Crock-Pot Multi-Cooker® with a swirl of olive oil. Stir and combine, make sure the rice is coated with the liquids or Japanese Dashi

2. **High pressure for 25 minutes**. Lock the lid on the Crock-Pot Multi-Cooker® and then cook for 25 minutes. To get 25-minutes cook time, press "Rice/Risotto" button and use the TIME ADJUSTMENT button to adjust the cook time to 25 minutes.

3. **Pressure Release** Use the quick-release method to return the pot's pressure to normal. Place the prawns on top of the risotto and sprinkle the Parmesan cheese over the prawns and risotto.

4. **High pressure for 5 minutes.** Cover and lock the lid again and cook on High for another 5 minutes. To get 5-minutes cook time, press "Beans/Chili" button and use the TIME ADJUSTMENT button to adjust the cook time to 5 minutes.

5. **Pressure Release** Use the quick-release method to return the pot's pressure to normal.
    Garnish with the sliced green onions.

263. Delicious Rice and Artichokes

Preparation + Cook Time: 30 minutes | Servings: 4

Ingredients:
6 ounces graham crackers, crumbled
6 ounces arborico rice
16 ounces vegan cream cheese, soft
14 ounces artichoke hearts, chopped
1½ tbsp vegan cheese, grated
8 ounces veggie stock
8 ounces water
2 tbsp white wine
Salt and black pepper to taste
1 tbsp vegetable oil
2 garlic cloves, minced
1 ½ tbsp thyme, finely chopped

Directions:
1. Heat up a pan with the oil over medium high heat, add rice and garlic, stir and cook for 3 minutes.
2. Transfer everything to your Crock Pot Express™, add stock, wine, water, cover and Select "BEANS/CHILI" and cook at HIGH pressure for 10 minutes.
3. Release pressure naturally for 5 minutes.
4. Add crackers, add artichokes, vegan cheese, vegan cream cheese, salt, pepper and thyme, stir well, divide into bowls and serve right away.
5. Enjoy!

264. Pineapple Fried Rice

Preparation + Cook Time: 35 minutes | Servings: 2

Ingredients:
1½ cups jasmine rice

1½ cups water

2 tbsp sesame oil

3-4 garlic cloves, minced

½ tbsp grated ginger

1 small onion, chopped

3 stalks spring onion, chopped, white and green parts separated

½ red bell pepper

½ cup mix of carrots & peas (I used frozen carrot & peas and put them in warm water for 5 minutes before using in the recipe)

1¼ cups pineapple chunks, I used canned pineapple chunks

2½ tbsp soy sauce

¼ tsp white pepper powder, or to taste

Salt to taste

Directions:
1. Rinse rice with cold water till the water is no longer cloudy and turns clear. This might take 60-90 seconds and is an extremely important step in order to get the perfect texture of rice.
2. Drain the rice completely and then transfer it to the pot. Add water and stir.
3. Close the lid of the Crock Pot Express™, set valve to sealing.
4. Press "BEANS/CHILI" and cook at HIGH pressure for 3 minutes
5. Once the time is up, let the pressure release naturally for 10 minutes and then release the remaining pressure.
6. Open the lid and fluff the rice using a fork. Transfer rice to a bowl and set aside.
7. Now press the "BROWN/SAUTÉ" button.
8. Add oil to the pot (there's no need to clean it).
9. Once oil is hot, add garlic and ginger and sauté for few seconds.
10. Add in chopped onion and spring onion whites. Sauté for a minute.
11. Then add carrot, green peas and pepper. Sauté for another minute.
12. Stir in the pineapple chunks and cook for 1 more minute.
13. Push all the veggies to the side and add the soy sauce.
14. Put the cooked rice back in the pot again. You may press CANCEL button at this point.
15. Stir till everything is well combined and all the rice is coated with the sauce.
16. Add white pepper powder, salt and mix to combine.
17. Garnish with spring onion greens and enjoy the pineapple fried rice!

265. Long-Grain White Rice

Prep: 5 minutes • pressure: 22 minutes • total: 27 minutes • pressure level: high • release: natural • Serves 4

Ingredients

1½ cups long-grain white rice
3 cups water
½ teaspoon salt
1 teaspoon vegetable oil or unsalted butter

Directions

1. **Preparing the Ingredients.** Place the rice, water, salt, and oil in the Crock-Pot Multi-Cooker® base.
2. **High pressure for 4 minutes.** Lock the lid on the Crock-Pot Multi-Cooker® and then cook for 4 minutes. To get 4-minutes cook time, press "Steam" button and use the TIME ADJUSTMENT button to adjust the cook time to 4 minutes.
3. **Pressure Release.** When the time is up, open the Crock-Pot Multi-Cooker® with the 10-Minute Natural Release method.
4. Fluff the rice with a fork and serve.

266. Fried Rice

Preparation + Cook Time: 15 minutes | Servings: 4

Ingredients:

1 tbsp butter (or oil)
1 medium onion, diced
2 cloves garlic, minced
1 egg
1 cup basmati rice, uncooked
¼ cup soy sauce
1½ cups chicken stock
½ cups peas, frozen OR your preferred vegetable

Directions:

1. Select "BROWN/SAUTÉ" mode and preheat the Crock Pot Express™. Put the oil in the pot.
2. Add the garlic and the onion. Sauté for 1 minute.
3. Add the egg, scramble with the garlic mix for about 1-2 minutes.
4. Add the rice, stock, and soy sauce in the pot. Press CANCEL. Close and lock the lid. Press "RICE/RISOTTO" and set the time for 10 minutes.
5. When the timer beeps, quick release the pressure. Carefully open the lid. Stir in the frozen peas or veggies.
6. Let sit until the peas/ veggies are warmed through.

267. Multi-Grain Rice Millet Blend

Preparation + Cook Time: 15 minutes | Servings: 8

Ingredients:
2 cups jasmine rice OR long-grain white rice
½ cup millet
3¼ cups water
½ tsp sea salt (optional)

Directions:
1. Put all the ingredients in the Crock Pot Express™ and stir.
2. Cover and lock the lid.
3. Press the "RICE/RISOTTO" button and let the pot do all the cooking, about 10 minutes.
4. When the timer beeps, quick release the pressure. Carefully open the lid. Serve.

Main Dishes – Beans And Grains

268. Refried Beans

Prep: 5 minutes • pressure: 21 minutes • total: 26 minutes • pressure level: high • release: quick
Serves 8

Ingredients

1½ pounds (3 cups) dried pinto beans
One 3-ounce salt pork chunk
1 tablespoon minced garlic
¼ cup vegetable or canola oil
Up to 2 cups finely shredded smoked cheddar cheese (about 8 ounces)

Directions

1. **Preparing the ingredients.** Soak the beans in a big bowl of water on the counter overnight, for at least 12 hours or up to 16 hours.

   Drain the beans in a colander set in the sink; pour them into the Crock-Pot Multi-Cooker®. Add the salt pork and garlic; pour in enough cool tap water so that the ingredients are covered by 2 inches of water (the garlic will float).

2. **High pressure for 21 minutes.** Lock the lid on the Crock-Pot Multi-Cooker® and then cook for 21 minutes. To get 21-minutes cook time, press "Multigrain" button and use the TIME ADJUSTMENT button to adjust the cook time to 21 minutes.

3. **Pressure Release** Use the quick-release method to drop the pot's pressure back to normal.

4. **Finish the dish.** Unlock and open the cooker. Discard the salt pork. Scoop out 1 cup of the soaking water and set aside. Drain the remaining contents of the cooker into a colander set in the sink.

   Transfer the beans and garlic to a large bowl. Use a potato masher to create a thick paste, adding the soaking water in small bits until you've added just enough to get a smooth but not wet paste.

   Heat the oil in a large pot over medium heat. Add the bean paste and cook, stirring often, until hot and bubbling, about 5 minutes. Spread the mixture on a large serving platter or individual plates and top with the shredded cheese.

269. Spice Black Bean and Brown Rice Salad

Preparation + Cook Time: 35 minutes | Servings: 8

Ingredients:
1 can (14 oz) black beans, drained and rinsed
1 cup brown rice
1 avocado, diced
1½ cups water
¼ cup cilantro, minced
¼ tsp salt
12 grape tomatoes, quartered
For the spicy dressing:
3 tbsp lime juice, fresh squeezed
3 tbsp extra-virgin olive oil
2 tsp Tabasco or Cholula
2 garlic cloves, pressed or minced
1/8 tsp salt
1 tsp agave nectar

Directions:
1. Combine the rice with the water and salt in the Crock Pot Express™. Close and lock the lid. Select "BEANS/CHILI" and cook at HIGH pressure for 24 minutes.
2. When the timer beeps, release the pressure naturally for 10 minutes. Turn the steam valve to release any remaining pressure. Carefully open the lid.
3. Using a fork, fluff the rice and let cool to room temperature.
4. When cool, refrigerate until ready to use. In a large-sized bowl, stir the brown rice with the black beans, avocado, tomato, and cilantro.
5. In a small-sized bowl, except for the olive oil, whisk the dressing ingredients together. While continuously whisking, slowly pour in the olive oil.
6. Pour the dressing over the brown rice mix and stir to combine.

270. Rich and creamy lentils

Prep: 5 minutes • pressure: 15 minutes • total: 20 minutes • pressure level: high • release: quick • Serves 6

Ingredients
2 tablespoons olive oil
1 large yellow onion, chopped
1 tablespoon minced garlic

1 tablespoon minced fresh ginger
1 tablespoon garam masala
2 cups brown lentils
1½ cups chicken broth
¾ cup canned crushed tomatoes
2 bay leaves
1 cup plain whole-milk yogurt

Directions

1. **Preparing the ingredients.** Heat the oil in the crock-pot multi-cooker® turned to the browning function. Add the onion and cook, stirring often, until softened, about 4 minutes. Add the garlic and ginger; cook, stirring constantly, until aromatic, about 1 minute.
   Stir in the garam masala until aromatic, less than a minute; then add the lentils, broth, tomatoes, and bay leaves. Stir well.
2. **High pressure for 15 minutes.** Lock the lid on the crock-pot multi-cooker® and then cook for 15 minutes. To get 15-minutes cook time, press "Poultry" button.
3. **Pressure release** use the quick-release method to bring the pot's pressure back to normal.
4. **Finish the dish.** Unlock and open the cooker. Turn the electric cooker to its browning function. Bring to a simmer, stirring often. Cook, stirring almost constantly, until the liquid has evaporated, 5 to 10 minutes. Discard the bay leaves. Stir in the yogurt before serving.

271. Refried Beans

Preparation + Cook Time: 55 minutes | Servings: 8

Ingredients:

2 tsp dried oregano
2 pounds pinto beans, dried, sorted
1-2 tsp sea salt
3 tbsp vegetable OR shortening lard
½ tsp ground black pepper
4 cups vegetable broth
1 jalapeno, seeds removed and chopped
4 cups water
1½ tsp ground cumin
4-5 garlic cloves, roughly chopped
1 ½ cups onion, chopped

Directions:

1. Put the sorted pinto beans into a large-sized mixing bowl.

2. Fill the bowl with just enough water to cover the beans by several inches. Set aside to soak for 15 minutes.
3. Meanwhile, put the garlic cloves, onion, dried oregano, jalapeno, cumin, lard, vegetable broth, black pepper, and water in the Crock Pot Express™. Stir to mix.
4. Put the soaked beans in a colander to strain. Discard the soaking liquid. Rinse the beans with fresh water.
5. Add the beans into the pot. Stir to mix. It's ok if the lard is still a lump. It will melt as the pot heats up. Cover and lock the lid.
6. Press the "BEANS/CHILI" button and adjust the time to 45 minutes.
7. When the timer beeps, let the pressure down naturally, about 40 minutes.
8. When the pressure is released, carefully open the lid and season the beans with sea salt to taste.
9. With an immersion blender, blend the beans to desired consistency. It will appear soupy, but as the beans cool, it will thicken.

272. White Bean, Sausage, And Escarole Stew

Prep: 5 Minutes • Pressure: 15 Minutes • Total: 20 Minutes • Pressure Level: High • release: quick • Serves 6

Ingredients
2 cups dried great northern beans
2 tablespoons olive oil
1 pound mild italian sausage, cut into 1-inch pieces
4 cups (1 quart) chicken broth
2 small escarole heads, cored and chopped
2 tablespoons white wine vinegar
½ cup finely grated parmesan cheese (about 1 ounce)

Directions
1. **Preparing the ingredients.** Soak the beans in a big bowl of water on the counter overnight, for at least 12 hours or up to 16 hours. Drain them in a colander set in the sink.
   Heat the oil in the crock-pot multi-cooker® turned to the browning function. Add the sausage and brown on all sides, turning occasionally with kitchen tongs, about 6 minutes. Pour in the broth and the drained beans.
2. **High pressure for 15 minutes.** Lock the lid on the crock-pot multi-cooker® and then cook for 15 minutes. To get 15-minutes cook time, press "Poultry" button.
3. **Pressure release.** Use the quick-release function to bring the pot's pressure back to normal.
   Unlock and open the pot. Stir in the escarole and vinegar.

4. **High pressure for 3 minutes.** Lock the lid on the crock-pot multi-cooker® and then cook for 3 minutes. To get 3-minutes cook time, press "Steam" button and use the time adjustment button to adjust the cook time to 3 minutes.
5. **Pressure release.** Use the quick-release method to bring the pressure back to normal.
6. **Finish the dish** then open the pot. Stir well and serve with the cheese sprinkled over each bowlful.

273. Italian Cannellini Beans and Mint Salad

Preparation + Cook Time: 15 minutes | Servings: 4

Ingredients:
1 cup cannellini beans, soaked overnight
4 cups water
1 clove garlic smashed
1 bay leaf
1 sprig mint fresh
1 dash vinegar
Olive oil
Salt to taste
Pepper to taste

Directions:
1. Add soaked beans, water, garlic clove and bay leaf to the Crock Pot Express™.
2. Close and lock the lid. Press "BEANS/CHILI" and cook at HIGH pressure for 8 minutes.
3. When time is up, open the Crock Pot Express™ using natural release.
4. Strain the beans and mix with mint, vinegar, olive oil, salt and pepper. Enjoy!

274. Hummus

Prep: 5 minutes • pressure: 12 minutes • total: 17 minutes • pressure level: high • release: quick • Serves 8

Ingredients
2 cups dried chickpeas
1 teaspoon baking soda
¼ cup olive oil
¼ cup tahini
6 tablespoons fresh lemon juice
2 or 3 medium garlic cloves
½ teaspoon ground cumin

½ teaspoon dried oregano
½ teaspoon dried sage
½ teaspoon salt
½ teaspoon ground black pepper

Directions

1. **Preparing the ingredients.** Soak the chickpeas in a big bowl of water on the counter for at least 12 hours or up to 16 hours.

   Drain the chickpeas in a colander set in the sink, then pour them into the crock-pot multi-cooker®. Add enough cool tap water so they're submerged by 2 inches. Stir in the baking soda.

2. **High pressure for 12 minutes.** Lock the lid on the crock-pot multi-cooker® and then cook for 12 minutes. To get 12-minutes cook time, press soup button and use the time adjustment button to adjust the cook time to 12 minutes.

3. **Pressure release** use the quick-release method to bring the pot's pressure back to normal.

4. **Finish the dish.** Unlock and open the cooker. Drain the chickpeas into a colander set in the sink; rinse with cool water to bring them back to room temperature. Pour the chickpeas into a large bowl and cover with cool tap water; agitate the water to loosen their skins. Rub off and discard the skins. (you should have about 4 cups of peeled chickpeas.)

   Pour the peeled chickpeas into a food processor fitted with the chopping blade. Add the olive oil, tahini, lemon juice, garlic, cumin, oregano, sage, salt, and pepper. Cover and process until a thick, velvety spread, scraping down the inside of the canister at least once and adding a tablespoon or more of water if the paste is too thick. Scrape into a serving bowl, cover, and refrigerate for at least 2 hours or up to 3 days.

275. Easy Aloo Beans

Preparation + Cook Time: 25 minutes | Servings: 3

Ingredients:
1 tbsp oil
½ tsp cumin seeds or Jeera
4 cloves garlic chopped
1 green chili chopped (optional)
2 cup green beans chopped in ½ inch pieces
1 potato cubed into small pieces
Spices:
2 tsp coriander or Dhania powder
¼ tsp turmeric or Haldi powder
¼ tsp red chili or Mirchi powder

1½ tsp salt

1 tsp dry mango or Amchur powder, can also be replaced with lemon juice

Directions:
1. Start the Crock Pot Express™ In "Brown/Sauté" mode, heat it and then add oil. Heating the pot first helps later, so the veggies don't stick to the bottom. Then add cumin seeds, garlic and green chili.
2. When the cumin seeds start to splutter, add chopped green beans and potatoes. Add spices except dry mango powder and mix properly. Sprinkle water with your hand.
3. Close the Crock Pot Express™ lid, and change setting to "BEANS/CHILI" mode and cook at HIGH pressure for 2 minutes. When the Crock Pot Express™ beeps, let the pressure release naturally.
4. Mix in the dry mango powder or lemon juice. If there is any water, change the setting to "Brown/Sauté" mode and get it to your desired consistency. Aloo Beans are ready to be served with roti or naan.

Notes:

If you like firm beans do a 5 minute NPR, which means release the pressure "BEANS/CHILI"ly 5 minutes after the Crock Pot Express™ beeps.

276. Cuban-style black beans with ham

Prep: 5 minutes • pressure: 18 minutes • total: 17 minutes • pressure level: high • release: quick • Serves 8

Ingredients
2 cups dried black beans

2 tablespoons olive oil

½ pound smoked ham, any rind removed, the meat chopped

2 medium yellow onions, chopped

1 large green bell pepper, stemmed, cored, and chopped

1 tablespoon finely grated orange zest

2 teaspoons minced garlic

½ tablespoon dried oregano

½ teaspoon red pepper flakes

2 bay leaves

One 4-inch cinnamon stick

3 tablespoons sherry vinegar

1 tablespoon packed dark brown sugar

4 cups (1 quart) chicken broth

¼ cup packed fresh cilantro leaves, chopped

Directions

1. **Preparing the ingredients** soak the beans in a big bowl of water on the counter overnight, for at least 12 hours or up to 16 hours. Drain in a colander set in the sink. Heat the oil in the crock-pot multi-cooker® turned to the browning function. Add the ham and fry until well browned, about 5 minutes, stirring occasionally. Add the onions and pepper; cook, stirring often, until the onion turns translucent, about 4 minutes. Stir in the orange zest, garlic, oregano, red pepper flakes, bay leaves, and cinnamon stick until aromatic, less than 1 minute. Add the vinegar and brown sugar; stir until the brown sugar melts. Pour in the broth and scrape up any browned bits in the bottom of the cooker. Stir in the beans and cilantro.

2. **High pressure for 18 minutes.** Lock the lid on the crock-pot multi-cooker® and then cook for 18 minutes. To get 18-minutes cook time, press rice / risotto button and use the time adjustment button to adjust the cook time to 18 minutes.

3. **Pressure release** use the quick-release method to return the pot's pressure to normal.

4. **Finish the dish** unlock and open the cooker. Discard the bay leaves and cinnamon stick. Turn the electric cooker to its browning function. Bring to a simmer; cook, uncovered and stirring often, until the remaining liquid in the pot is reduced by half, between 5 and 10 minutes.

277. Steamed Green Beans

Preparation + Cook Time: 20 minutes | Servings: 4

Ingredients:
1 pound green beans, washed
1 cup water
2 tbsp fresh parsley, chopped, for garnish
For the dressing:
1 pinch ground black pepper
1 pinch salt
2 tbsp white wine vinegar
3 tbsp
3 tbsp olive oil
3 cloves garlic, sliced

Directions:
1. Pour the water into the Crock Pot Express™ and set the steamer basket. Put the green beans in the basket.
2. Press "STEAM", set the pressure to HIGH and the timer to 4 minute.

3. When the timer beeps, turn the valve to Venting to quick release the pressure.
4. Transfer the beans into a serving bowl.
5. Toss with the dressing Ingredients and let stand for 10 minutes.
6. Remove the slices of garlic and then garnish with the parsley. Serve.

278. One minute quinoa

Prep: 5 minutes • pressure: 1 minutes • total: 6 minutes • pressure level: high • release: natural • Serves 6-8

Ingredients

2 cups whole-grain quinoa, rinsed and drained
3 cups water
2 teaspoons salt

Directions
1. **Preparing the ingredients.** Place the quinoa, water, and salt in the crock-pot multi-cooker® base.
2. **High pressure for 1minute.** Bring the cooker to high pressure by pressing the "Steam" button. Allow to cook for 1 minute and press start/stop
3. **Pressure release.** When the time is up, open the crock-pot multi-cooker® with the 10-minute natural release method.
4. Fluff the quinoa with a fork and serve.

279. Green Bean Sweet Potato & Spinach Risotto

Preparation + Cook Time: 45 minutes | Servings: 4

Ingredients:
1 ½ cups carnaroli (or other risotto) rice
1 ½ cups green beans, cut into 1/3-inch pieces, or 1 ½ cups peas (thawed, if frozen)
1 cup spinach, chopped (or 1 cup kale, torn)
1 pinch saffron (or ¼ tsp turmeric)
1 sweet potato, medium-sized, peeled and diced into 1/3-inch cubes
1 tbsp sage, finely minced
2 cloves garlic, minced
3 ½ cups vegetable broth
4 shallots, finely diced
Sea salt and freshly ground black pepper

Directions:

1. Preheat the oven to 410F. Line a shallow baking tray with silicone mat or parchment paper.
2. In a large-sized bowl, toss the sweet potatoes with 2 tablespoons veggie broth. Using your fingers, remove from the bowl, letting the excess broth run off the potatoes. Spread them in the prepared baking tray, put in the oven, and roast in the center of the oven for about 10-15 minutes or until beginning to brown.
3. Remove the tray from the oven, flip the sweet potatoes, return the tray in the oven, and roast for 5 minutes.
4. When the sweet potatoes are baked, let them rest in the baking tray.
5. While the sweet potatoes are cooking, press the "BROWN/SAUTÉ" key of the Crock Pot Express™ and wait until the display shows 'Hot'.
6. When hot. Add the onion and sauté for about 2-3 minutes, frequently stirring, until slightly caramelized. Add the garlic and sauté for 30 seconds.
7. Pour in 1/4 cup of the stock to deglaze the pot. Add the rice, the remaining broth, saffron, and sage. Press the CANCEL key to stop the "Brown/Sauté" function.
8. Cover and lock the lid. Turn the steam valve to Sealing. Press the "BEANS/CHILI" key, set the pressure to HIGH, and set the timer for 5 minutes. When the Crock Pot Express™ timer beeps, press the CANCEL key.
9. Using an oven mitt or a long handled spoon, turn the steam valve to quick release the pressure. Unlock and carefully open the lid.
10. Stir in the spinach and the beans in the rice mixture in the pot.
11. Cover the lid and let steam with the rice for 3 minutes to cook.
12. Add the roasted sweet potatoes and then season with pepper and salt. Serve!

280. Pinto beans with bacon

Prep: 5 minutes • pressure: 18 minutes • total: 23 minutes • pressure level: high • release: quick • Serves 4

Ingredients
1 cup dried pinto beans
1 tablespoon unsalted butter
3 thin bacon slices, chopped
½ cup chopped pecans
1 medium yellow or white onion, chopped
½ teaspoon dried oregano
½ teaspoon ground cumin
¼ teaspoon ground coriander
One 4½-ounce can chopped mild green chiles (about ½ cup)

Directions

1. **Preparing the ingredients.** Soak the beans in a large bowl of water on the counter overnight, for at least 12 hours or up to 16 hours.
   Drain the beans in a colander set in the sink; pour them into the crock-pot multi-cooker®. Add enough cool tap water that they're submerged by 2 inches.
2. **High pressure for 18 minutes.** Lock the lid on the crock-pot multi-cooker® and then cook for 18 minutes. To get 18-minutes cook time, press rice / risotto button and use the time adjustment button to adjust the cook time to18 minutes.
3. **Pressure release** use the quick-release method.
4. **Finish the dish.** Unlock and open the cooker. Scoop out 1 cup of the cooking liquid and reserve it. Drain the beans in a colander set in the sink. Wipe out the cooker.
   Melt the butter in the crock-pot multi-cooker® turned to its "browning" function. Add the bacon and pecans; fry until both are lightly browned, stirring occasionally, about 3 minutes. Add the onion and cook, stirring often, until softened, about 3 minutes.
   Stir in the oregano, cumin, and coriander until aromatic, about 20 seconds. Then pour in the drained beans, green chiles, and ¼ cup of the reserved cooking liquid. Cook, stirring often, until the beans are just heated through, adding more of the reserved cooking liquid in ¼-cup increments when the mixture gets too dry.

281. Green Bean Casserole

Preparation + Cook Time: 30 minutes | Servings: 4

Ingredients:
16 ounces green beans (I used Frozen)
12 ounces mushroom, sliced
½ cup French's onions, for garnishing
1 onion, small-sized
1 cup heavy cream
1 cup chicken broth
2 tbsp butter

Directions:
1. Press "BROWN/SAUTÉ" key of the Crock Pot Express™.
2. Put the butter in the pot and melt. Add the onion and mushrooms; sauté for about 2-3 minutes or until the onions are soft.
3. Add the green beans, heavy cream, and chicken broth. Press the CANCEL key to stop the "Brown/Sauté" function. Cover and lock the lid.
4. Press the "BEANS/CHILI" key, set the pressure to HIGH, and set the timer for 15 minutes.

5. When the Crock Pot Express™ timer beeps, press the CANCEL key and unplug the Crock Pot Express™. Turn the steam valve to quick release the pressure. Unlock and carefully open the lid.
6. While the dish is still hot, add 2 tablespoons cornstarch to thicken.
7. Serve topped with French's onions.

282. Spicy black-eyed peas

Prep: 5 minutes • pressure: 22 minutes • total: 27 minutes • pressure level: high • release: quick • Serves 6

Ingredients
4 ounces slab bacon, chopped
1 medium yellow onion, chopped
2 cups dried black-eyed peas
One 14-ounce can diced tomatoes (about 1¾ cups)
One 4½-ounce can chopped hot green chiles (about ½ cup)
1 tablespoon dried oregano

Directions
1. **Preparing the ingredients.** Fry the bacon in the crock-pot multi-cooker® turned to its "browning"function until it begins to brown and give off its fat, about 2 minutes. Add the onion and cook, stirring often, until it turns translucent, about 4 minutes. Pour in 3 cups water; add the black-eyed peas, tomatoes, chiles, and oregano, and stir well.
2. **High pressure for 22 minutes.** Lock the lid on the crock-pot multi-cooker® and then cook for 22 minutes. To get 22-minutes cook time, press rice / risotto button and use the time adjustment button to adjust the cook time to 22 minutes.
3. **Pressure release.** Use the quick-release method.
4. **Finish the dish** unlock and open the cooker. Stir well before serving.
5. Serve and enjoy!

283. Refried Bean Nachos

Preparation + Cook Time: 35 minutes | Servings: 6

Ingredients:
2 cups pinto beans dried, (rinsed well, but not soaked)
1 onion, large-sized, cut into fourths (or diced if you like to leave your beans chunky)
4 cloves garlic, peeled and roughly chopped
1 jalapeno pepper, seeded (more or less to taste, optional)
1 tsp salt
1 tsp paprika
1 tsp chili powder

1 tsp cumin
½ tsp black pepper
½ cup salsa Cilantro, to taste (optional)
3 cups vegetable broth OR water OR combination of the two

Directions:
1. Put all of the ingredients in the Crock Pot Express™ and stir well to incorporate. Close and lock the lid. Press "BEANS/CHILI" and cook at HIGH pressure for 28 minutes.
2. When the timer beeps, let the pressure release naturally for 10 minutes. Turn the valve to release any remaining pressure. Carefully open the lid and stir the dish.
3. With a potato masher or in a blender, mash or blend the beans to desired consistency – be careful because the beans are hot.
4. If you prefer your beans thick, drain some of the water before mashing or blending.
5. Serve warm.

Notes: This dish is freezer-friendly. Store in portion-sized containers and freeze.

284. White beans with prosciutto

Prep: 5 minutes • pressure: 12 minutes • total: 17 minutes • pressure level: high • release: quick • Serves 4

Ingredients
1 tablespoon kosher salt
1 quart water
½ pound dried navy beans
1 tablespoon olive oil
3 ounces prosciutto or ham, diced
2 medium garlic cloves, minced
1¾ cups chicken stock or low-sodium broth
1 or 2 fresh rosemary sprigs
2 tablespoons dry white wine

Directions
1. **Preparing the ingredients.** In a large bowl, dissolve the kosher salt in the water. Add the beans, and soak at room temperature for 8 to 24 hours. Drain and rinse. Set the crock-pot multi-cooker® to its "brown" function, heat the olive oil until it shimmers and flows like water. Add the prosciutto, and cook for about 3 minutes, stirring, until the prosciutto starts to crisp. Add the garlic, and cook for 1 more minute, or until fragrant. Add the chicken stock and rosemary to the crock-pot multi-cooker®, then pour in the beans.

2. **High pressure for 12 minutes.** Lock the lid on the crock-pot multi-cooker® and then cook for 12 minutes. To get 12-minutes cook time, press "Soup" Button and use the time adjustment button to adjust the cook time to12 minutes.
3. **Pressure release** use the quick-release method.
4. **Finish the dish.** Unlock and remove the lid. Remove the rosemary sprig, but don't worry if some of the needles have fallen off; they'll be tender enough to eat. If the beans are too soupy, turn the crock-pot multi-cooker® to "simmer," and simmer until some of the liquid has evaporated. Stir in the white wine, and serve.

Per serving: calories: 271; fat: 6g; sodium: 602mg; carbohydrates: 36g; fiber: 14g; protein: 17g

285. Black Bean + Sweet Potato Hash

Preparation + Cook Time: 15 minutes | Servings: 4

Ingredients:
1 cup chopped onion
2 cups peeled, chopped sweet potatoes
2 tsp hot chili powder
1 minced garlic clove
⅓ cup veggie broth
1 cup cooked and drained black beans
¼ cup chopped scallions

Directions:
1. Prep your veggies.
2. Turn your Crock Pot Express™ to "BROWN/SAUTÉ" and cook the chopped onion for 2-3 minutes, stirring so it doesn't burn.
3. Add the garlic and stir until fragrant. Add the sweet potatoes and chili powder, and stir.
4. Pour in the broth and give one last stir before locking the lid. Select "BEANS/CHILI" and cook at HIGH pressure for 3 minutes.
5. When time is up, quick-release the pressure carefully.
6. Add the black beans and scallions, and stir to heat everything up.
7. Season with salt and more chili powder if desired.

286. Black bean and corn salad

Prep: 5 minutes • pressure: 18 minutes • total: 23 minutes • pressure level: high • release: quick

Serves 8

Ingredients
2 cups dried black beans
2 tablespoons olive oil
2 teaspoons cumin seeds
2 teaspoons minced garlic
1 medium fresh jalapeño chili, stemmed and split lengthwise
2 cups fresh corn kernels (about 2 large ears), or frozen kernels, thawed
1 large globe or beefsteak tomato, chopped
Up to 6 medium scallions, thinly sliced
1 medium yellow bell pepper, stemmed, cored, and diced
¼ cup fresh lime juice
3 tablespoons olive oil
1 tablespoon sherry vinegar
1 tablespoon honey
1 teaspoon salt

Directions
1. **Preparing the ingredients.** Soak the beans in a large bowl of water on the counter overnight, for at least 12 hours or up to 16 hours. Drain them in a colander set in the sink.
   Heat the oil in the crock-pot multi-cooker® turned to the "browning" function. Add the cumin seeds and garlic; cook for 1 minute, stirring constantly, just until the garlic begins to brown. Pour in the drained beans; add the jalapeño. Add enough cool tap water so that the ingredients are submerged by 2 inches (the seeds will float).
2. **High pressure for 18 minutes.** Lock the lid on the crock-pot multi-cooker® and then cook for 18 minutes. To get 18-minutes cook time, press rice / risotto button and use the time adjustment button to adjust the cook time to18 minutes.
3. **Pressure release** use the quick-release method.
   Unlock and open the cooker. Drain the contents of the cooker into a colander set in the sink. Discard the jalapeño.
4. **Finish the dish** transfer the bean mixture to a large bowl; stir in the corn, tomato, scallions, and bell pepper. Whisk the lime juice, olive oil, vinegar, honey, and salt in a small bowl until smooth; pour over the salad and toss well.

287. Barley and Mushroom Risotto

Preparation time: **10 minutes** • Cooking time: **30 minutes** • Servings: **4**

Ingredients:
2 cups yellow onions, peeled and chopped
1 tablespoon olive oil
1 cup pearl barley

1 teaspoon fennel seeds
2 tablespoons black barley
3 cups chicken stock
⅓ cup dry sherry
1½ cups water
1.5 ounce dried mushrooms
Salt and ground black pepper, to taste
¼ cup Parmesan cheese, grated

Directions:
1. Set the Crock pot Express™ on "Brown/Sauté" mode, add the oil, and heat it up. Add the fennel and onions, stir, and cook for 4 minutes. Add the barley, sherry, mushrooms, stock, water, salt, and pepper and stir well.
2. Cover the Crock pot Express™, cook on the "Rice/Ristto" setting for 18 minutes, release the pressure, uncover the Crock pot Express™, and set it on "Brown/Sauté" mode. Add more salt and pepper, if needed, stir and cook for 5 minutes. Divide into bowls, add the cheese on top, and serve.

288. White Bean Dip with Tomatoes

Preparation + Cook Time: 15 minutes | Servings: 8

Ingredients:
1 can cannellini beans, soaked overnight
1 small white onion, peeled and diced
1½ tsp minced garlic, divided
6 sun-dried tomatoes
3 tbsp chopped parsley
1¼ cups water
1 tsp salt
1/8 tsp ground black pepper
1 tsp paprika
3 tbsp olive oil
2 tbsp lemon juice
1 tbsp capers

Directions:
1. Drain beans and place in the Crock Pot Express™. Pour in water and add 1 teaspoon garlic, salt, and black pepper.

2. Plug in and switch on the Crock Pot Express™ and secure with lid. Then position pressure indicator, select "BEANS/CHILI" and cook at HIGH pressure for 14 minutes.
3. When the timer beeps, switch off the Crock Pot Express™ and let pressure release naturally for 10 minutes and then do quick pressure release.
4. In the meantime, place a small non-stick frying pan over medium heat, add oil and let heat.
5. Then add onion and remaining garlic and cook for 3-5 minutes or until onions are nicely golden brown.
6. When the onions are done, set pan aside until required. Then uncover the pot and drain beans, reserve ½ cup of cooking liquid.
7. Let beans cool slightly and then transfer to a food processor and add onion-garlic mixture, paprika, and lemon juice.
8. Pulse until smooth; slowly blend in reserved cooking liquid until dip reaches to desired thickness. Tip mixture into a serving bowl.
9. Dice tomatoes and stir together with capers and parsley.
10. Add this mixture into bean dip and stir until mixed well.
11. Adjust the seasoning and serve immediately.

289. Barley with Vegetables

Preparation time: **10 minutes** • Cooking time: **25 minutes** • Servings: **4**

Ingredients:
1 tablespoon extra virgin olive oil
1 tablespoon butter
1 white onion, peeled and chopped
1 garlic clove, peeled and minced
1½ cups pearl barley, rinsed
1 celery stalk, chopped
⅓ cup mushrooms, chopped
4 cups vegetable stock
2¼ cups water
Salt and ground black pepper, to taste
3 tablespoons fresh parsley, chopped
1 cup Parmesan cheese, grated

Directions:
1. Set the Crock pot Express™ on "Brown/Sauté" mode, add the oil and butter and heat them up. Add the onion and garlic, stir, and cook for 4 minutes. Add the celery and barley and toss to coat. Add the mushrooms, water, stock, salt, and pepper, stir,

2. Cover the Crock pot Express™ and cook on the "Multigrain" setting for 18 minutes. Release the pressure, uncover the Crock pot Express™, add the cheese and parsley and more salt and pepper, if needed, stir for 2 minutes, divide into bowls, and serve.

290. White Bean with Greens and Lemon

Preparation + Cook Time: 20 minutes | Servings: 4-6

Ingredients:
1 onion, chopped
2 tsp olive oil
1 cup white beans, soaked overnight
2 bay leaves
½ - ¾ cup vegetable stock or water
3 cloves garlic minced
3-4 cups greens kale, chard or spinach (stems removed), chopped
1 tsp lemon zested,
1-2 tbsp lemon juice
Salt to taste
Pepper to taste

Directions:
1. Press "Brown/Sauté" to pre-heat the Crock Pot Express™. When the display says "Hot", add the olive oil and sauté the onion.
2. Turn off "Brown/Sauté" function. Add beans, vegetable stock and bay leaves to the Crock Pot Express™. Select "BEANS/CHILI" and cook at HIGH pressure for 7 minutes.
3. Begin preparing greens while contents of Crock Pot Express™ continue to cook (If using kale, remove stems and finely chop).
4. Zest and juice lemon. Peel and mince the garlic.
5. When pressure cooking is complete, allow for natural pressure release. Open up the Crock Pot Express™ and add greens, lemon zest, and garlic.
6. Close up the Crock Pot Express™, press "BEANS/CHILI" and cook at HIGH pressure for 1 minute. Allow to cook 1 Minute then press Stop.
7. Quick release pressure, open the lid add lemon juice, and remove bay leaves
8. Serve alone or with your favorite noodles or grain. Enjoy!

291. Barley Salad

Preparation time: **10 minutes** • Cooking time: **20 minutes** • Servings: **4**

Ingredients:
1 cup hulled barley, rinsed
2½ cups water
¾ cup jarred spinach pesto

1 green apple, chopped
¼ cup celery, chopped
Salt and ground white pepper, to taste

Directions:
1. Put the barley, water, salt, and pepper into the Crock pot Express™, stir, cover and cook on the "Multigrain" setting for 20 minutes. Release the pressure, uncover the Crock pot Express™,
2. Strain the barley, and put in a bowl. Add the celery, apple, spinach pesto, and more salt and pepper, toss to coat, and serve.

292. Stewed Tomatoes and Green Beans

Preparation + Cook Time: 15 minutes | Servings: 10)

Ingredients:
1 pound trimmed green beans
2 cups fresh, chopped tomatoes
1 crushed garlic clove
1 tsp olive oil
½ cup water
Salt to taste

Directions:
1. Set "BROWN/SAUTÉ" setting and preheat your Crock Pot Express™.
2. When warm, add 1 teaspoon of olive oil and garlic.
3. When the garlic has become fragrant and golden, add tomatoes and stir. If the tomatoes are dry, add ½ cup water.
4. Fill the steamer basket with the green beans and sprinkle on salt. Lower into cooker.
5. Close and seal the lid. Select "BEANS/CHILI" and cook at HIGH pressure for 5 minutes.
6. When the timer beeps, turn off cooker and quick-release the pressure.
7. Carefully remove the steamer basket and pour beans into the tomato sauce.
8. If the beans aren't quite tender enough, simmer in sauce for a few minutes.
9. Serve.

293. Wheat Berry Salad

Preparation time: **10 minutes** • Cooking time: **35 minutes** • Servings: **6**

Ingredients:
1½ cups wheat berries
1 tablespoon extra virgin olive oil
Salt and ground black pepper, to taste
4 cups water
For the salad:
1 tablespoon balsamic vinegar
1 tablespoon extra virgin olive oil
1 cup cherry tomatoes, cut into halves
2 green onions, chopped
2 ounces feta cheese, crumbled
½ cup Kalamata olives, pitted and chopped
½ cup fresh basil leaves, chopped
½ cup fresh parsley, chopped

Directions:
1. Set the Crock pot Express™ on "Brown/Sauté", add the tablespoon oil and heat it up. Add the wheat berries, stir, and cook for 5 minutes. Add the water, salt, and pepper,
2. Cover the Crock pot Express™, and cook on "Multigrain" mode for 30 minutes. Release the pressure for 10 minutes, uncover the Crock pot Express™, drain the wheat berries, and put them in a salad bowl. Add the salt and pepper, 1 tablespoon oil, balsamic vinegar, tomatoes, green onions, olives, cheese, basil, and parsley, toss to coat, and serve.

294. Baked Beans

Preparation + Cook Time: 1 hour 20 minutes | Servings: 8

Ingredients:
1 pound dried navy beans, soaked overnight for at least 8 - 16 hours
1½ tbsp fine table salt
6 cups cold water
Baked Beans Sauce and Aromatics:
6 strips thick-cut bacon, roughly diced
1 small onion, roughly diced
2 cloves garlic, roughly chopped
1¾ cup cold water
¼ cup blackstrap molasses
¼ cup maple syrup
1 tbsp light soy sauce, not low sodium soy sauce
¼ tsp fine table salt

2 bay leaves
Ground black pepper to taste
2 tsp Dijon mustard
1 tsp apple cider vinegar

Directions:

Overnight Soaking Method: Place 1 pound dried navy beans and 1 1/2 tbsp fine table salt in a large container. Pour 6 cups cold water in the large container and give it a few stir. Allow beans to soak overnight for at least 8 - 16 hours. If your house is very warm, place the large container in the fridge to avoid fermentation.

Quick Soaking Method: If you're short on time or forgot to soak the beans overnight, you can use this quick soaking method instead. The result will not be as good as the overnight soaking method. Place 1 pound dried navy beans, 1.5 tablespoons fine table salt, and 6 cups cold water in the pressure cooker. Close lid and pressure cook at HIGH pressure for 0 minute + 30 minutes natural release.

1. Pour out the soaked water and drain the navy beans through a mesh strainer. Rinse the beans with cold tap water. Drain well. The soaked beans should almost double in weight.
2. Place chopped bacon in the Crock Pot Express™ and Press "Brown/Sauté" button to heat the pot to Medium. Stir occasionally and allow the bacon bits to crisp (~3 minutes). Add in diced onion, freshly ground black pepper and sauté for a minute. Add in chopped garlic cloves and sauté until fragrant (~30 seconds).
3. While the bacon is rendering in pressure cooker, combine 1/4 cup blackstrap molasses, 1/4 cup maple syrup, 1 tablespoon light soy sauce, and 1 3/4 cup cold water in a 1 liter glass measuring cup. Mix well.
4. Pour 1/2 cup of the molasses mixture in the Crock Pot Express™. Deglaze by scrubbing all the flavorful brown bits off the bottom of the pan and mix them into the mixture.
5. Add 1/4 teaspoon fine table salt, 2 bay leaves, soaked navy beans and the remaining molasses mixture in the Crock Pot Express™. Mix well and make sure all the beans are submerged in the molasses mixture. Close lid, Select "BEANS/CHILI" and cook at HIGH pressure for 20 minutes + 20 minutes natural release. After 20 minutes, turn the venting knob to Venting position to release the remaining pressure. Open the lid carefully.
6. Add 2 teaspoons Dijon mustard, and 1 teaspoon apple cider vinegar into the cooked baked beans. Mix well. Press "Brown/Sauté" button to heat the pot and stir to thicken the baked beans to desired consistency. Taste and adjust the seasoning by adding more blackstrap molasses, salt, or vinegar if necessary. For reference, we added in another tablespoon of blackstrap molasses.
7. Serve this delicious sweet 'n smokey baked beans as a side dish at your BBQ, picnics, potlucks, or dinner.

295. Cracked Wheat and Vegetables

Preparation time: **10 minutes** • Cooking time: **15 minutes** • Servings: **4**

Ingredients:
½ cup cracked whole wheat
1½ cups water
2 tomatoes, cored and chopped
2 small potatoes, cubed
5 cauliflower florets, chopped
Salt and ground black pepper, to taste
¼ teaspoon mustard seeds
¼ teaspoon cumin seeds
1 teaspoon ginger, grated
1 tablespoon yellow split peas, rinsed
2 garlic cloves, peeled and minced
1 yellow onion, peeled and chopped
2 curry leaves
3 teaspoons vegetable oil
¼ teaspoon garam masala
Cilantro leaves, chopped, for serving

Directions:
1. Set the Crock pot Express™ on "Brown/Sauté" mode, add the oil and heat it up. Add the cumin and mustard seeds, stir, and cook for 1 minute. Add the onion, garlic, split peas, garam masala, ginger, and curry leaves, stir, and cook for 2 minutes. Add the cauliflower, potatoes, and tomatoes, stir, and cook for 4 minutes. Add the wheat, salt, pepper, and water, stir,
2. Cover, and cook on "Multigrain" mode for 5 minutes. Release the pressure, uncover the Crock pot Express™, transfer the wheat and vegetables to plates, sprinkle cilantro on top, and serve.

296. Quick Soaking Dry Beans

Preparation + Cook Time: 15 minutes | Servings: 3

Ingredients:
4 cups water
1 cup beans
1 tsp salt, optional

Directions:

1. Place water, beans and salt into the Crock Pot Express™
2. Set Crock Pot Express™ to "BEANS/CHILI" and cook for 2-8 minutes at HIGH pressure.
3. Once time is up, slow release the pressure from the Crock Pot Express™.
4. Strain, rinse and drain the beans.
5. You are now able to use these beans in any recipe at normal cooking time!

Notes: You can double, triple, or half this recipe as long as you keep the ratio of beans to water at 1:4.

297. Cracked Wheat Surprise

Preparation time: **5 minutes** • Cooking time: **17 minutes** • Servings: **2**

Ingredients:
2 cups cracked wheat
1 teaspoon fennel seeds
2½ cups butter
2 cups light brown sugar
3 cloves
1 cup milk
Salt
3 cups water
Almonds, chopped

Directions:
1. Set the Crock pot Express™ on "Brown/Sauté" mode, add the butter and heat it up. Add the cracked wheat, stir, and cook for 5 minutes. Add the cloves and fennel seeds, stir, and cook for 2 minutes. Add the sugar, a pinch of salt, milk, and water, stir,
2. Cover, and cook on the "Multigrain" setting for 10 minutes. Release the pressure, uncover the Crock pot Express™, divide into bowls, and serve with chopped almonds on top.

Snacks, Appetizers and Side Dishes

298. Wild Rice and Farro Pilaf

Preparation time: **10 minutes** • Cooking time: **35 minutes** • Servings: **12**

Ingredients:
1 shallot, peeled and diced
1 teaspoon garlic, minced
Extra virgin olive oil
1½ cups whole grain faro
¾ cup wild rice
6 cups chicken stock
Salt and ground black pepper, to taste
½ tablespoons dried parsley, minced
½ tablespoons dried sage, minced
½ cup hazelnuts, toasted and chopped
¾ cup cherries, dried
Minced chives, for serving

Directions:
1. Set the Crock pot Express™ on "Brown/Sauté" mode, add a drizzle of olive oil and heat it up. Add the onion and garlic, stir, and cook for 2-3 minutes. Add the farro, rice, salt, pepper, stock, sage, and parsley, stir,
2. Cover the Crock pot Express™ and cook on "Multigrain" mode for 25 minutes. Put the cherries in a pot, add enough hot water to cover, set aside for 10 minutes, and drain. Release the pressure from the Crock pot Express™ for 5 minutes, drain the excess liquid, add the hazelnuts and cherries, stir gently, divide among plates, and garnish with chopped chives.

299. Red White and Green Brussels Sprouts

Preparation + Cook Time: 20 minutes | Servings: 4

Ingredients:
1 pound Brussels Sprouts
¼ cup pine nuts toasted
1 Pomegranate
1 tbsp extra-virgin olive oil

½ tsp salt
1 grate pepper

Directions:
1. Remove the outer leaves and trim the stems of the washed Brussels Sprouts. Cut the largest ones in half to get them to a uniform size for even cooking.
2. Prepare the Crock Pot Express™ by pouring in one cup of water, and adding the steamer basket. Put the sprouts in the basket.
5. Close the lid and set the valve to pressure cooking position. Cook for 3 minutes on at HIGH pressure. To get 3-minutes cook time, press "Steam" button and use the TIME ADJUSTMENT button to adjust the cook time to 3 minutes.
3. When time is up, quick release the pressure.
4. Move the sprouts to a serving dish and dress in olive oil, salt and pepper prior to sprinkling with toasted pine nuts and pomegranate seeds.
5. Serve warm or room temperature. Enjoy!

300. Rigatoni with Meat Sauce

Preparation + Cook Time: 45 minutes | Servings: 4-6

Ingredients:
2 tbsp olive oil
2-3 cloves garlic
3.5 oz white mushrooms, finely chopped (pulse in food processor or chop by hand)
1 onion finely chopped
1 tbsp tomato paste
2 tsp basil dried
2 tsp oregano dried
Kosher salt to taste
Black pepper to taste
1 lb italian sausage a combo of sweet and hot tastes delicious
1 can tomatoes 28-ounce can
1 can tomato puree 14.5-ounce can
3½ cups water
1 pound rigatoni dried

Directions:
1. Heat the oil in your Crock Pot Express™ on "Brown/Sauté" mode. When display reads "Hot" add in and sauté the onions, mushrooms, garlic and a pinch of kosher salt and a few grinds of black pepper until softened, at least five minutes.
2. Stir in the oregano, basil and tomato paste and cook another minute, stirring constantly with a wooden spoon.

3. Add in the sausage meat that you have removed from the casings and brown, breaking it up with your spoon, until no pink remains.
4. Pour in the water, the tomato puree and, using your hand, squish the tomatoes in to break them up and then pour in all of the liquid from the can.
5. Give the pot a good stir to make sure you get up all of the fond on the bottom of the pot and then add in the dry rigatoni.
6. Give it one more good stir, close and lock the lid. Select "BEANS/CHILI" and cook at HIGH pressure for 6 minutes.
7. When the time is up, quick release the pressure and open the lid.
8. Let it sit for another minute or two, giving it a couple of stirs, to thicken up a bit. If the sauce seems too thin, you can turn the "BROWN/SAUTÉ" feature back on and simmer it for a couple of minutes as well.
9. Serve in big bowls with freshly grated parmesan. Enjoy!

Variation: When you have the extra time, you can make the sauce right up to the point where you would add in the dry pasta. Instead, close up the Crock Pot Express™ and seal the vent, hit "BEANS/CHILI" and cook the sauce for 15 minutes on HIGH pressure. Release the steam, add in the dry rigatoni at this point, close it back up and then program it for 6 more minutes at HIGH pressure and proceed as instructed. The extra 15 minutes of cook time give even deeper depth of flavor to the sauce.

301. Couscous and Vegetable Medley

Preparation + Cook Time: 30 minutes | Servings: 3

Ingredients:
1 tbsp olive oil
2 bay leaves or Tej Patta
½ large onion chopped
1 large red bell pepper chopped
1 cup carrot grated
1¾ cup couscous Isreali
1¾ cup water
2 tsp salt or to taste
½ tsp garam masala
1 tbsp lemon juice
Cilantro to garnish

Directions:
1. Heat the Crock Pot Express™ In "Brown/Sauté" mode and add olive oil to it. Add the bay leaves and onions. Sauté for 2 minutes.
2. Add the bell peppers and carrots. Sauté for one more minute.

3. Add the couscous, water, garam masala and salt. Stir well.
4. Change the Crock Pot Express™ setting to "BEANS/CHILI" and cook at HIGH pressure for 2 minutes. When the Crock Pot Express™ beeps, do 10 minutes natural pressure release.
5. Fluff the couscous, it is fully cooked. Mix in the lemon juice. Garnish with cilantro and serve hot.

Notes: Prepare with vegetables of your choice. I used bell peppers, carrots and onions, which I had at home. Other options are cauliflower, broccoli, edamame and green peas. If you like, you can add more spices.

302. Quinoa Pilaf

Preparation time: **10 minutes** • Cooking time: **2 minutes** • Servings: **4**

Ingredients:
2 cups quinoa
2 garlic cloves, peeled and minced
2 tablespoons extra virgin olive oil
Salt, to taste
2 teaspoons turmeric
3 cups water
½ cup fresh parsley, chopped
2 teaspoons cumin

Directions:
1. Set the Crock pot Express™ on "Brown/Sauté" mode, add the oil and heat it up. Add the garlic, stir, and cook for 30 seconds. Add the water, quinoa, cumin, turmeric, and salt, stir,
2. Cover and cook on the Steam setting for 1 minute, (press Stop when complete 1 minute). Release the pressure naturally for 10 minutes, fluff the quinoa with a fork, transfer to plates, season with more salt, if needed, sprinkle the parsley on top, and serve.

303. Slow Cook Spinach and Goat Cheese Lasagna

Preparation + Cook Time: 2 hours 20 minutes | Servings: 8

Ingredients:
1 tsp extra-virgin olive oil
1¾ cups onion, chopped

1 cup zucchini, diced
½ cup carrot, shredded
2 cloves garlic, chopped
½ tsp salt
½ tsp black pepper freshly ground
1 can tomatoes crushed, undrained, 28-ounce can
Cooking Spray
1 cup basil fresh, chopped
¾ cup part-skim ricotta cheese
20 ounces spinach frozen and chopped, thawed, drained, and squeezed dry
2 ounces goats cheese roughly 1/4-cup
8 gluten free lasagna noodles
1 ounce Parmesan cheese, shredded fresh, about 1/4-cup
Basil leaves, optional

Directions:
1. Heat a 4-quart saucepan over medium heat. Add oil to the pan; swirl to coat.
2. Add onion, zucchini, and carrot; cook, stirring constantly for 5 minutes.
3. Add garlic; cook, stirring constantly for 1 minute. Stir in the salt, pepper and tomatoes; bring to a simmer, and cook for 5 minutes, stirring occasionally.
4. Coat the inner pot of a 6 quart Crock Pot Express™ with cooking spray.
5. Combine basil, ricotta, spinach and goat cheese in a medium bowl.
6. Spread 1/2 cup spinach mixture in the cooker, Arrange 1/3 of the lasagna noodles over spinach mixture in the pot, breaking noodles as necessary to fit in the pot; top with half of the remaining spinach mixture and 1 cup tomato mixture. Repeat procedure once, ending with noodles.
7. Pour the remaining tomato mixture over noodles, being careful to cover noodles completely.
8. Close and lock the lid of the Crock Pot Express™. Turn the steam release handle to Venting position. Press SLOW COOK function and adjust to select Less mode. Adjust time to 2 hours cooking.
9. When time is up, uncover and sprinkle with Parmesan cheese; cover and let stand 15 minutes before serving. Garnish with basil leaves, if desired.

304. Quinoa with Almonds

Preparation time: **10 minutes** • Cooking time: **11 minutes** • Servings: **4**

Ingredients:
½ cup yellow onion, peeled and diced
1 tablespoon butter

1 celery stalk, chopped
1½ cups quinoa, rinsed
14 ounces chicken stock
Salt and ground black pepper, to taste
¼ cup water
½ cup almonds, toasted and sliced
2 tablespoons parsley, chopped

Directions:
1. Set the Crock pot Express™ on "Brown/Sauté" mode, add the butter and melt it. Add the onion and celery, stir, and cook for 5 minutes. Add the quinoa, water, stock, salt, and pepper, stir,
2. Cover and cook on the "Steam" setting for 3 minutes. Release the pressure for 5 minutes, uncover, fluff with a fork, add the almonds and parsley, stir, divide among plates, and serve.

305. Pink Rice

Preparation time: **10 minutes** • Cooking time: **5 minutes** • Servings: **8**

Ingredients:
1 teaspoon salt
2½ cups water
2 cups pink rice

Directions:
1. Put the rice into the Crock pot Express™. Add the water and salt, stir,
2. Cover and cook on the "Steam" setting for 5 minutes. Release the pressure naturally for 10 minutes, uncover the Crock pot Express™, fluff rice with a fork, divide among plates, and serve.

306. Crock Pot Express™ Carbonara

Preparation + Cook Time: 25 minutes | Servings: 4

Ingredients:
1 pound pasta dry, rigatoni, penne or cavatappi are great
4 cups water
Pinch kosher salt
4 large eggs
8 ounces bacon pancetta or guanciale

1 cup Pecorino Romano finely grated, can also use parmesan
Black pepper as much as you like

Directions:
1. Put the pasta and the water, with a pinch of kosher salt, in the Crock Pot Express™ and program it to cook on "BEANS/CHILI" for 5 minutes at HIGH pressure.
2. While the cooker heats up, crack the eggs in a bowl, add in the cheese and the black pepper, whisk it until it's all mixed together and put aside until you need it.
3. Cook the bacon (pancetta or, if you can find it, the guanciale), in a frying pan over medium heat for a few minutes until it's crispy and has rendered lots of fat and then remove the pan from the heat.
4. When the cooking time on the Crock Pot Express™ is up, do a controlled quick release. Pasta can foam up so release with small spurts until you are sure it's not going to spew all over the place and then release it all at once.
5. Put the pan with the bacon/pancetta back on the heat and dump in the pasta and any liquid left in the pot, wait for the water to come to a fierce bubbling up and cook for about 30 seconds until there is just a bit of water left. You want to see some liquid but you don't it to be all soupy.
6. Now, remove the pan from the heat again so that you can add in the eggs/cheese and quickly stir it all together until the eggs thicken into a sauce.
7. If you like it super peppery, season with a bit more, more grated cheese if you like and serve right away. Enjoy!

307. Mushroom Risotto

Preparation time: **10 minutes** • Cooking time: **15 minutes** • Servings: 4

Ingredients:
2 cups risotto rice
4 cups chicken stock
2 garlic cloves, peeled and crushed
2 ounces extra virgin olive oil
1 yellow onion, peeled and chopped
8 ounces mushrooms, sliced
4 ounces heavy cream
4 ounces sherry vinegar
2 tablespoons Parmesan cheese, grated
1 ounce fresh basil, minced

Directions:

1. Set the Crock pot Express™ on "Brown/Sauté" mode, add the oil and heat it up. Add the onions, garlic, and mushrooms, stir and cook for 3 minutes. Add the rice, stock and vinegar, stir,
2. Cover the Crock pot Express™ and cook on the "STEAM" setting for 10 minutes. Release the pressure, uncover the Crock pot Express™, add the cream and Parmesan and stir. Divide among plates, sprinkle with the basil, and serve.

308. Vegetarian Rigatoni Bolognese
Preparation + Cook Time: 30 minutes | Servings: 6

Ingredients:
3 tbsp olive oil
½ cup onion, chopped fine
½ cup celery, chopped fine
½ cup carrots, chopped fine
½ cup bell peppers, chopped fine
1 tbsp garlic, minced
2 cups mushrooms, chopped
1 cup water
1 ounce dried porcini mushrooms, chopped
1 can crushed tomatoes 28-ounce can
½ tsp black pepper
1 tsp salt or to taste
¼ tsp dried thyme
1 tsp dried oregano
1 tsp dried basil
1 tsp sugar
1 tbsp balsamic vinegar
1 tbsp tomato paste
½ tsp crushed red pepper flakes or to taste
12 ounces rigatoni pasta
1 cup whole milk
1 cup red wine
4 ounces Mascarpone cheese
¼ cup Parmesan cheese finely grated
3 tbsp parsley fresh, chopped

Directions:
1. Press "Brown/Sauté" and add olive oil to inner pot of Crock Pot Express™. Add onions, celery, carrots, bell peppers and garlic and sauté for 3 minutes, stirring frequently.

2. Add fresh mushrooms and sauté for 2 minutes. Turn off Crock Pot Express™ by pressing CANCEL.
3. If there's food stuck to the bottom, deglaze pot with 2 tablespoons of water.
4. Add in dried porcini mushrooms, crushed tomatoes, black pepper, salt, thyme, oregano, basil, sugar, balsamic vinegar, tomato paste, crushed red pepper, pasta, milk, wine and water. Stir to combine.
5. Close Crock Pot Express™ lid, and make sure steam release handle is in the Sealing position. Select "BEANS/CHILI" and cook at HIGH pressure for 7 minutes. Use a quick release.
6. There might seem to be more liquid than you'd like, but don't worry, the liquid will get absorbed by the pasta.
7. Stir in mascarpone cheese. Let the pasta rest for a few minutes and it will thicken up.
8. Sprinkle each serving with Parmesan and fresh parsley.

309. Pumpkin Risotto

Preparation time: **5 minutes** • Cooking time: **10 minutes** • Servings: 4

Ingredients:
2 ounces extra virgin olive oil
1 small yellow onion, peeled and chopped
2 garlic cloves, peeled and minced
12 ounces Arborio rice
4 cups chicken stock
6 ounces pumpkin puree
½ teaspoon nutmeg
1 teaspoon fresh thyme, chopped
½ teaspoon ginger, grated
½ teaspoon ground cinnamon
½ teaspoon allspice
4 ounces heavy cream

Directions:
1. Set the Crock pot Express™ on "Brown/Sauté" mode, add the oil and heat it up. Add the onion and garlic, stir and cook for 1-2 minutes. Add the rice, chicken stock, pumpkin puree, thyme, nutmeg, cinnamon, ginger and allspice, and stir.
2. Cover the Crock pot Express™ and cook on the "Steam" setting for 10 minutes. Release the pressure, add the cream, stir well, and serve.

310. Vegetables and Rice

Preparation time: **6 minutes** • Cooking time: **15 minutes** • Servings: 4

Ingredients:
2 cups basmati rice
1 cup frozen mixed vegetables
2 cups water
½ teaspoon canned green chilies, minced
½ teaspoon ginger, grated
3 garlic cloves, peeled and minced
2 tablespoons butter
1 cinnamon stick
1 tablespoon cumin seeds
2 bay leaves
3 whole cloves
5 black peppercorns
2 whole cardamoms
1 tablespoon sugar
Salt, to taste

Directions:
1. Put the water into the Crock pot Express™. Add the rice, vegetables, chilies, grated ginger, garlic, cinnamon, cloves, butter, cumin seeds, bay leaves, cardamoms, peppercorns, salt, and sugar.
2. Stir, cover, and cook on the ""Rice/Risotto"" setting for 15 minutes. Release the pressure, remove the cinnamon stick, bay leaves, peppercorns, cloves, and cardamoms, divide among plates, and serve.

311. Sushi Rice

Preparation + Cook Time: 15 minutes | Servings: 18 sushi pieces)

Ingredients:
1 cup sushi rice
1½ cups water
3 tbsp rice wine vinegar or 1 tbsp apple cider vinegar and a pinch of sugar

Directions:

1. Rinse the sushi rice well, rubbing it around in the strainer as the water passes through. Rinse until the water runs clear (about 3 minutes). Measure the rice and cooking water carefully
2. To the inner pot, add the rinsed rice and water and mix to evenly distribute the rice. Close and lock the lid. Press "Beans/Chili" button and Cook for 7 minutes at HIGH pressure.
3. When cooking time is up, count 5 minutes of natural pressure release. Then, quick release the rest of the pressure slowly using the valve. Even if all of the pressure is naturally released before the 5 minutes are up keep the lid closed the entire time. Otherwise, release any remaining pressure slowly using the valve.
4. Stir the rice-wine vinegar into the rice handling it delicately without over-working it.
5. Tumble the rice into a large wooden bowl or wooden cutting board and smooth-out into an even layer.
6. Let cool for about 10 minutes, and it's ready to be used to make sushi! Cool the cooked sushi rice by spreading in an even layer in a wooden bowl or cutting-board.
7. For making sushi: Slice fresh vegetables for filling into long thin, even strips – use avocado, fresh tomatoes, even peppers Layout nonlinear ingredients in a rectangular shape. Use cooked, smoked or pickled fish for filling – only experts should be purchasing and handling raw fish.

312. Flavored Mashed Sweet Potatoes

Preparation time: **10 minutes** • Cooking time: **9 minutes** • Servings: **8**

Ingredients:
2 garlic cloves
3 pounds sweet potatoes, peeled and chopped
Salt and ground black pepper, to taste
½ teaspoon dried parsley
¼ teaspoon dried sage
½ teaspoon dried rosemary
½ teaspoon dried thyme
1½ cups water
¼ cup milk
½ cup Parmesan cheese, grated
2 tablespoon butter

Directions:
1. Put the potatoes and garlic in the steamer basket of the Crock pot Express™, add 1½ cups water to the Crock pot Express™,
2. Cover, and cook on the "Steam" setting for 10 minutes. Release the pressure, drain water, transfer the potatoes and garlic to a bowl and mix them using kitchen hand

mixer. Add the butter, cheese, milk, salt, pepper, parsley, sage, rosemary, and thyme and blend everything well. Divide among plates, and serve.

313. Honey Garlic Chicken Lettuce Wraps

Preparation + Cook Time: 70 minutes | Servings: 4

Ingredients:
1/8 cup honey garlic sauce store bought or recipe below
2 tbsp coconut aminos (or soy sauce)
¼ tsp chilies
1 tbsp onion minced
½ tsp salt
1 tsp black pepper
8-10 chicken thighs boneless, skinless
1 jalapeno thinly sliced (optional)
1 head lettuce
1 medium carrot grated
½ bell pepper, thinly sliced
1 green onion diced
1 avocado thinly sliced
1/8 cup cashews crushed or chopped
Fermented Honey Garlic Sauce (Optional):
1 Fido Jar or a jar with cover
Cloves garlic peeled
Raw honey enough to cover the amount of garlic cloves being used

Instructions:
1. Combine coconut aminos (soy sauce), onions, chilies, salt, pepper and honey garlic sauce (if using the recipe below, crush the garlic cloves and include some of the honey) in a bowl.
2. Put boneless skinless chicken thighs into the mixture and let marinate for 20 to 40 minutes.
3. Put chicken and sauce into the Crock Pot Express™. Close and lock the lid. Select "BEANS/CHILI" and cook at HIGH pressure for 6 minutes.
4. While you are waiting for the chicken to cook (likely 10 minutes to reach pressure, 6 minutes cooking time and a 6-8 minute natural pressure release). Prepare the remaining vegetables, chopping and dicing as needed.
5. Prepare the washed lettuce into full leaves. You can use whatever type of lettuce you prefer.

6. Once the natural pressure release time readout reaches 6 minutes open up the valve and release any remaining pressure. The chicken should shred easily with a fork. Leave the shredded chicken marinating in the sauce until you are ready to assemble wraps.
7. Lay chicken, grated carrot, pepper slices, chopped cashews, green onion, and avocado, in slices inside the lettuce, drizzling sauce over top of the chicken and veggies before rolling the lettuce around ingredients.
8. Serve and Enjoy!

Making the Honey Garlic Sauce
1. In a clean dry jar, place the garlic cloves, you want to leave a little room at the top.
2. Pour the honey into the jar coving the cloves but again making sure there is some space at the top. As the garlic ferments in the honey, it can bubble up.
3. _Make sure the garlic cloves stay covered with honey, and that you regularly "burp" the lid of the fido jar or covering.
4. Let sit for 4 weeks, or 28 days. The garlic will darken, and the honey slightly more liquid, and then you know it is ready!

314. Tasty Saffron Risotto

Preparation time: **10 minutes** • Cooking time: **10 minutes** • Servings: **10**

Ingredients:
2 tablespoons extra virgin olive oil
½ teaspoon saffron threads, crushed
½ cup onion, peeled and chopped
2 tablespoons hot milk
1½ cups Arborio rice
3½ cups vegetable stock
Salt, to taste
1 tablespoon honey
1 cinnamon stick
⅓ cup almonds, chopped
⅓ cup dried currants

Directions:
1. In a bowl, mix the milk with the saffron, stir and set aside. Set the Crock pot Express™ on "Brown/Sauté" mode, add the oil and heat it up. Add the onions, stir and cook for 5 minutes. Add the rice, stock, saffron and milk, honey, salt, almonds, cinnamon stick, and currants. Stir,
2. Cover the Crock pot Express™ and cook on the "Rice/Risotto" setting for 5 minutes. Release the pressure, fluff the rice a bit, discard the cinnamon stick, divide it among plates, and serve.

315. Candied Cajun Trail Mix

Preparation + Cook Time: 25 minutes | Servings: 5)

Ingredients:
1 ½ cups raw pecan halves
1 cup raw almonds
1 cup chickpeas drained, or more if preferred, omit for paleo friendly
1/3 - ½ cup cashews
¼ cup raw sunflower seeds
2-3 tbsp vegan butter or regular butter
1 tbsp water optional
½ cup pure maple syrup
½ -1 tbsp spicy cajun seasoning or mix, you can also use use 1/4 to ½ tsp each of cayenne, garlic, onion powder, paprika, and pepper
1 pinch ground ginger
1 pinch sea salt
6 ounces dried mango or spicy chili dried mango to add after (if desired)

Directions:
1. Heat the Crock Pot Express™ In "Brown/Sauté" mode.
2. Place all ingredients into the Crock Pot Express™. Mix thoroughly.
3. Sauté with plastic spatula until butter is melted and nuts/ chickpeas are coated with the seasoning and maple syrup. If batter seems too sticky/thick once sautéing, add the 1 tablespoon of water.
4. Close and lock the lid. Select "BEANS/CHILI" and cook at HIGH pressure for 10 minutes. Use a quick release one timer is done.
5. Remove from pot and spread the nut mix onto a lined cooking sheet.
6. Bake on 375F for 7-10 minutes in the oven; turning nuts/seeds half way. Any longer might burn the nuts. The chickpeas will be a little less cooked but still tasty! See notes for other options.
7. Remove from oven and Let Cajun trail mix completely cool.
8. Lastly, dice you mango into small pieces. Then add to your candied Cajun trail mix and stir all together. It's easiest to this in large zip lock or air tight container. If you are using plain dried mango, feel free to add more spices to the mix to coat.
9. Store in air tight container. Makes 5 cups or so.

Notes: If want crispier chickpeas, try adding in roasted chickpeas snacks after cooking, instead of cooking the canned.

316. Cherry Farro

Preparation time: **10 minutes** • Cooking time: **40 minutes** • Servings: **6**

Ingredients:
1 tablespoon apple cider vinegar
1 cup whole grain farro
1 teaspoon lemon juice
Salt, to taste
3 cups water
1 tablespoon extra virgin olive oil
½ cup cherries, dried and chopped
¼ cup green onions, chopped
10 mint leaves, chopped
2 cups cherries, pitted and cut into halves

Directions:
1. Put the water into the Crock pot Express™, add the rinsed farro, stir,
2. Cover and cook on the "Multigrain" setting for 40 minutes. Release the pressure, drain the farro, transfer to a bowl and mix with the salt, oil, lemon juice, vinegar, dried cherries, fresh cherries, green onions, and mint. Stir well, divide among plates, and serve.

317. Pepper Jack Mac'n Cheese

Preparation + Cook Time: 10 minutes | Servings: 4

Ingredients:
2 ½ cups elbow macaroni
2 cups chicken stock
1 ½ cups shredded pepper jack cheese
1 ½ cups mozzarella cheese
1 cup heavy cream
½ cup whole milk
1 tbsp butter
1 tsp salt
1 tsp black pepper

Directions:

1. Pour chicken stock and cream into the Crock Pot Express™. Add macaroni, salt, and pepper. Seal and close the lid.
2. Select "BEANS/CHILI" and cook at HIGH pressure for 7 minutes.
3. When time is up, press CANCEL and use a quick release.
4. Mix in butter, milk, and cheese.
5. Stir well and serve!

Stocks and Sauces

318. Simple Spaghetti Sauce

Preparation time: **10 minutes** • Cooking time: **40 minutes** • Servings: **6**

Ingredients:
1 and ⅔ pounds beef, ground
2 carrots, peeled and chopped
4 garlic cloves, peeled and minced
2 celery ribs, chopped
28 ounces canned crushed tomatoes
1 yellow onion, peeled and chopped
2 bay leaves
1 tablespoon olive oil
Dried basil
Dried oregano
Red wine
Salt and ground black pepper, to taste
For the chicken stock mix:
1 cup chicken stock
2 tablespoons soy sauce
3 tablespoons tomato paste
2 tablespoons fish sauce
1 tablespoon Worcestershire sauce

Directions:
1. Set the Crock pot Express™ on "Brown/Sauté" mode, add the beef, salt, pepper, and oil, stir and brown for 7 minutes. Transfer the beef to a bowl when it's brown and set it aside for now. In a bowl, mix the stock with the fish sauce, soy sauce, tomato paste, and Worcestershire sauce and stir well. Heat up you Crock pot Express™ again, add the onions, garlic, bay leaves, basil, and oregano, stir and cook for 5 minutes. Add the celery, carrots, salt, and pepper, stir and cook for 3 minutes. Add the wine, chicken stock, beef, and crushed tomatoes on top.
2. Cover the Crock pot Express™ and cook on the "Steam"setting for 10 minutes. Release the pressure, uncover the Crock pot Express™, add more salt and pepper, if needed, set the Crock pot Express™ on "Brown/Sauté" mode and cook the sauce for 4 minutes. Serve with your favorite pasta.

319. Tabasco Sauce

Preparation + Cook Time: 25 minutes | Cups: 2

Ingredients:
12 oz fresh hot peppers OR any kind, stems removed
2 tsp smoked or plain salt
1¼ cups apple cider

Directions:
1. Press the "BROWN/SAUTÉ" key of the Crock Pot Express™.
2. Roughly chop the hot peppers and put into the Crock Pot Express™. Pour in just enough apple cider to cover the peppers. Add the salt.
3. Press the CANCEL key to stop the "Brown/Sauté" function. Cover and lock the lid.
4. Press the "BEANS/CHILI" key, set the pressure to HIGH, and set the timer for 1 minute. (Press Stop when completes 1 Minute).
5. When the Crock Pot Express™ timer beeps, press the CANCEL key and unplug the Crock Pot Express™. Let the pressure release naturally for 10-15 minutes or until the valve drops. Turn the steam valve to release remaining pressure. Unlock and carefully open the lid.
6. Using an immersion blender, puree the contents and strain into a fresh dished-washed or sterilized bottle.
7. Refrigerate for up to 3 months or transfer into a suitable container and freeze for up to 1 year.

320. Marinara Sauce

Preparation time: **10 minutes** • Cooking time: **20 minutes** • Servings: **8**

Ingredients:
56 ounces canned crushed tomatoes
3 garlic cloves, peeled and minced
½ cup red lentils
1 cup sweet potato, diced
Salt and ground black pepper, to taste
1½ cups water

Directions:
1. Set the Crock pot Express™ on "Brown/Sauté" mode, add the lentils, sweet potatoes, salt, pepper, and garlic, stir and cook them for 2 minutes. Add the water and tomatoes, stir,

2. Cover the Crock pot Express™ and cook on the "Beans/Chili" setting for 13 minutes. Release the pressure, uncover the Crock pot Express™, puree everything using an immersion blender, add more salt and pepper, if needed, set the Crock pot Express™ on "Brown/Sauté" mode, and cook the sauce for 4 minutes.

321. Salted Caramel Sauce

Preparation + Cook Time: 20 minutes | Cups: 1)

Ingredients:
½ tsp sea salt
1/3 cup heavy cream
3 tbsp butter, cut into ½-inch pieces
1 cup sugar
½ tsp vanilla
1/3 cup water

Directions:
1. Press the "BROWN/SAUTÉ" key of the Crock Pot Express™.
2. Add the water and the sugar. Stir to combine and let cook for 13 minutes without touching the pot.
3. When 13 minutes are up, immediately whisk the butter in the pot, followed by the cream. Whisk until smooth.
4. Add the vanilla and the salt.
5. Press the CANCEL key and with an oven mitt gloved hand, remove the inner pot from the housing to remove from heat.
6. Pour the salted caramel into a heat-safe glass and let cool. Store in the fridge for up to 5 days.

322. Applesauce

Preparation time: **10 minutes** • Cooking time: **8 minutes** • Servings: **4**

Ingredients:
8 apples, cored and chopped
2 drops cinnamon oil
1 cup water
1 teaspoon ground cinnamon

Directions:

1. Put apples into the Crock pot Express™, add the water, cover the Crock pot Express™ and cook on the "Beans/Chili" setting for 8 minutes. Release the pressure, uncover the Crock pot Express™, add the oil and cinnamon and puree using an immersion blender. Serve chilled.

323. Cranberry Sauce

Preparation time: **10 minutes** • Cooking time: **15 minutes** • Servings: **4**

Ingredients:
2½ teaspoons orange zest
12 ounces cranberries
¼ cup orange juice
2 tablespoons maple syrup
Salt
1 cup sugar

Directions:
1. In the Crock pot Express™, mix the orange juice with maple syrup and stir well. Add the orange zest and almost all of the cranberries, stir,
2. Cover and cook on the "Steam" setting for 3 minutes. Release the pressure, uncover the Crock pot Express™, and set it on "Brown/Sauté" mode. Add the rest of the cranberries, a pinch of salt, and the sugar, stir and cook until sugar dissolves. Serve chilled.

324. Vegan Alfredo Sauce

Preparation + Cook Time: 20 minutes | Servings: 4

Ingredients:
12-ounces cauliflower florets
½ cup water
Almond milk if needed
Garlic salt to taste
Black pepper to taste

Directions:
1. Pour water into your Crock Pot Express™.
2. Put cauliflower florets into your steamer basket and lower into cooker. Seal the lid.
3. Select "BEANS/CHILI" and cook at HIGH pressure for 3 minutes.
4. When the timer beeps, press CANCEL and wait for a natural pressure release.

5. Remove steamer basket and cool cauliflower for a few minutes.
6. Pulse cauliflower with pot liquid in a blender until very smooth. If it isn't quite creamy enough, add a splash of almond milk.
7. Season with garlic salt and black pepper.

325. Ancho Chili Sauce

Preparation time: **10 minutes** • Cooking time: **10 minutes** • Servings: **8**

Ingredients:
5 ancho chilies, dried, seedless and chopped
2 garlic cloves, peeled and crushed
Salt and ground black pepper, to taste
1½ cups water
1½ teaspoons sugar
½ teaspoon dried oregano
½ teaspoon cumin
2 tablespoons apple cider vinegar

Directions:
1. In the Crock pot Express™ mix the water chilies, garlic, salt, pepper, sugar, cumin, and oregano, stir, cover and cook on the "Beans/Chili" setting for 8 minutes. Release the pressure for 5 minutes, uncover the Crock pot Express™, and pour sauce into a blender. Add the vinegar, blend well and transfer everything to a bowl.

326. Bolognese Eggplant Sauce

Preparation + Cook Time: 45 minutes | Servings: 8

Ingredients:
1 pound ground meat, your choice (I used ground pork)
1 can (28 ounces) tomatoes, drained, and then gently pureed
1 can (5.5 ounces) tomato paste
5 cloves garlic, smashed
½ sweet onion, large-sized, chopped
1 eggplant, sliced into halves and then diced
½ cup olive oil
1 cup bone broth OR filtered water
½ tsp turmeric
½ tsp dried dill
1 tbsp apple cider vinegar

¼ cup fresh parsley, chopped
1 tsp sea salt
Pepper to taste
Fresh lemon to serve

Directions:
1. Plug the Crock Pot Express™ and press the "BROWN/SAUTÉ" key.
2. Add the ground meat of your choice in the pot and cook until no longer pink.
3. Remove the meat and cooking liquid and transfer into a plate. Set aside. Add the olive oil into the pot.
4. Add the onion and sauté until starting to turn translucent and soft. Sprinkle with a pinch of salt to release the juices and bring out the flavors.
5. Add the garlic and cook for 1 minute or until the garlic is fragrant.
6. Add the apple cider vinegar and stir well to combine. Continuously stirring the mix, cook for about 1-2 minutes.
7. Scrape up any browned bits off from the bottom of the pot. If it starts to brown quickly, add a little more olive oil or water to prevent from burning.
8. Add the can of tomato paste into the pot. Stir well and cook for about 1-2 minutes to soften the flavor of the tomato paste.
9. Add the can of pureed tomatoes, 1 teaspoon salt, spices, ground meat with any juices accumulated on the plate, and fresh parsley.
10. Stir to combine and pour in 1 cup of water or bone broth. Stir to mix. Press the CANCEL key to stop the "Brown/Sauté" function. Cover and lock the lid.
11. Press the "BEANS/CHILI" key, set the pressure to HIGH, and set the timer for 15 minutes. When the Crock Pot Express™ timer beeps, keep the pot in "KEEP WARM" mode for 10 minutes. Press CANCEL and turn the steam valve to quick release the pressure. Unlock and carefully open the lid.
12. Taste for seasoning. Add more fresh cracked pepper, salt, and freshly squeezed lemon to taste.
13. Enjoy with fresh cracked pepper, avocado chunks, and lemon wedges.
14. You can also serve over spiralized veggies, rice, or pasta.

327. Orange and Ginger Sauce

Preparation time: **5 minutes** • Cooking time: **7 minutes.** • Servings: **4**

Ingredients:
1 cup fish stock
Salt and ground black pepper, to taste
1 tablespoon olive oil
4 green onions, chopped
1-inch ginger piece, chopped
Zest and juice from 1 orange

Directions:

1. In the Crock pot Express™, mix the fish stock with the salt, pepper, olive oil, onions, ginger, orange juice, and zest and stir well.
2. Cover the Crock pot Express™ and cook on the "Beans/Chili" setting for 7 minutes. Release the pressure, uncover the Crock pot Express™, and serve your sauce.

328. Bone Broth

Preparation + Cook Time: 1 hour 40 minutes | Servings: 8

Ingredients:

1 tsp unrefined sea salt

1-2 tbsp apple cider vinegar

2-3 pounds bones (2-3 pounds lamb, beef, pork, or non-oily fish, or 1 carcass of whole chicken)

Assorted veggies (1/2 onion, a couple carrots, a couple stalks celery, and fresh herbs, if you have them on hand)

Filtered water

Directions:

1. Put the bones in the Crock Pot Express™. Top with the veggies. Add the salt and apple cider vinegar.
2. Pour in enough water to fill the pot 2/3 full.
3. If you have enough time, let the pot sit for 30 minutes to allow the vinegar to start pulling the minerals out of the bones.
4. Cover and lock the lid. Press the "Soup" Button, set the pressure to LOW, and set the timer for 120 minutes.
5. When the Crock Pot Express™ timer beeps, press the CANCEL key and unplug the Crock Pot Express™. Let the pressure release naturally for 10-15 minutes or until the valve drops.
6. Unlock and carefully open the lid. Strain the broth.
7. Discard the veggies and bones. Pour the broth into jars. Store in the refrigerator or freeze.

Notes: If you are using pork, lamb, or beef bones, roast them in a preheated 350F oven for 30 minutes. This step is optional, but it does wonders to the flavors of the broth.

329. Barbecue Sauce

Preparation time: **10 minutes** • Cooking time: **10 minutes** • Servings: **8**

Ingredients:
1 tablespoon sesame seed oil
½ cup tomato puree
1 yellow onion, peeled and chopped
½ cup water
4 tablespoons white wine vinegar
4 tablespoons honey
1 teaspoon salt
½ teaspoon garlic powder
1 teaspoon liquid smoke
1 teaspoon Tabasco sauce
1/8 teaspoon cumin
1/8 teaspoon ground cloves
5 ounces dried seedless plums

Directions:
1. Set the Crock pot Express™ on "Brown/Sauté" mode, add the oil and heat it up. Add the onion, stir and cook for 5 minutes. Add the tomato puree, honey, water, vinegar, salt, garlic, Tabasco sauce, liquid smoke, cumin, and cloves and stir everything very well. Add the plums and stir well.
2. Cover the Crock pot Express™ and cook on the "Beans/Chili" setting for 10 minutes. Release the pressure, uncover the Crock pot Express™, blend everything with an immersion blender, transfer sauce to a bowl, and serve.

330. Beef Bone Broth

Preparation + Cook Time: 90 minutes | Servings: 8

Ingredients:
5 ounces carrots
4-5 sprigs thyme
4 cloves garlic
3 pounds beef bones (oxtail or neck bones preferred)
3 bay leaves
1 onion, roughly chopped
Half head celery, chopped
Filtered water
Pepper to taste
Salt to taste

Directions:
1. Cut the celery and onion. Add into the Crock Pot Express™.
2. Add the rest of the ingredients into the pot.
3. Fill the pot with water up to the line before the max line of the Crock Pot Express™.
4. Cover and lock the lid. Turn the steam valve to Sealing. Press the "BEANS/CHILI" key, set the pressure to HIGH, and set the timer for 90 minutes.
5. When the Crock Pot Express™ timer beeps, press the CANCEL key and unplug the Crock Pot Express™. Turn the steam valve to quick release the pressure.
6. Unlock and carefully open the lid. Strain the broth and store in freezer.

331. Gravy

Preparation time: **10 minutes** • **Cooking time:** 1 hour and 30 minutes • Servings: **2**

Ingredients:
Turkey neck, gizzard, livers, and heart
1 tablespoon vegetable oil
½ cup dry vermouth
1 yellow onion, peeled and chopped
1 quart turkey stock
1 bay leaf
4 tablespoons butter
2 thyme sprigs
4 tablespoons white flour
Salt and ground black pepper, to taste

Directions:
1. Set the Crock pot Express™ on "Brown/Sauté" mode, add the oil and heat it up. Add the turkey pieces and onion, stir and cook for 3 minutes. Stir again and cook for 3 minutes. Add the vermouth, stock, bay leaf, and thyme and stir.
2. Cover the Crock pot Express™ and cook on the "Beans/Chili" setting for 36 minutes. Release the pressure for 20 minutes, strain the stock, reserve the turkey giblets and let them cool down, remove gristle and dice them into small pieces. Heat up a pan with the butter over medium heat, add the flour, stir, and cook for 3 minutes. Add the strained stock, stir well, increase heat to medium high and simmer for 20 minutes, stirring frequently. Add salt, pepper, and the giblets, stir well, and serve.

332. Chicken Stock

Preparation + Cook Time: 120 minutes | Liters: 4

Ingredients:
1 chicken carcass
1 onion, cut into quarters
10-15 whole pieces peppercorns
2 bay leaves
2 tbsp apple cider vinegar
Veggie scraps, optional
Water Equipment: 4-5 mason jars

Directions:
1. Put the chicken carcass in the Crock Pot Express™. If desired, feel free to add the skin.
2. Add the vegetable scraps, onion, apple cider vinegar, peppercorns, and bay leaves.
3. Fill the pot with water to 1/2-inch below the max line. Cover and lock the lid. Press the "Soup" Button and set the timer for 120 minutes.
4. When the Crock Pot Express™ timer beeps, press the CANCEL key and unplug the Crock Pot Express™. Let the pressure release naturally for 10-15 minutes or until the valve drops – do not turn the steam valve for at least 30 minutes. Turn the steam to release remaining pressure.
5. Unlock and carefully open the lid. Strain out everything else from the stock and discard.
6. Pour the stock into the mason jar – do not overfill. If you are planning to freeze your stock, use 5 mason jars.
7. Let the stock cool and then store in the fridge or freeze within 3 days.

Notes: Let the jars cool completely before putting them in the fridge or freezing them. If not freezing, be sure to use in 3 days. If not using within 3 days, then freeze.

333. Zucchini Pesto

Preparation time: **10 minutes** • Cooking time: **10 minutes** • Servings: **4**

Ingredients:
1 yellow onion, peeled and chopped
1 tablespoon extra virgin olive oil
1½ pounds zucchini, chopped
Salt, to taste
½ cup water
1 bunch fresh basil, chopped
2 garlic cloves, peeled and minced

Directions:

1. Set the Crock pot Express™ on "Brown/Sauté" mode, add the oil and heat it up. Add the onion, stir and cook 4 minutes.
2. Add the zucchini, salt and water, stir, cover, and cook on the "Steam" setting for 3 minutes. Release the pressure, uncover the Crock pot Express™, add the garlic and basil and blend everything using an immersion blender. Transfer to a bowl, and serve.

334. Fish Stock

Preparation + Cook Time: 65 minutes | Quarts: 3

Ingredients:
2 salmon heads, large-sized, cut into quarters
2 lemongrass stalks, roughly chopped
1 cup carrots, roughly chopped
1 cup celery, roughly chopped
2 cloves garlic
Filtered water
Handful fresh thyme, including stems
Oil, for frying the fish heads

Directions:
1. Wash the fish heads with cold water – make sure there is no blood – and then pat them dry.
2. Put the oil in a pan and lightly sear the fish heads – this will minimize the fish meat from falling apart.
3. Slice the vegetables and put them in the Crock Pot Express™.
4. Add the fish and thyme. Pour water in the pot until the level reaches 3 quarts or just cover the fish. Cover and lock the lid.
5. Press the "Soup" Button, set the pressure to HIGH, and set the timer for 45 minutes.
6. When the Crock Pot Express™ timer beeps, press the CANCEL key and unplug the Crock Pot Express™. Let the pressure release naturally for 10-15 minutes or until the valve drops. Unlock and carefully open the lid.
7. Strain the fish and vegetable and store the stock.

335. Vegetarian Sauce

Preparation time: **10 minutes** • Cooking time: **20 minutes** • Servings: **8**

Ingredients:
1 yellow onion, peeled and chopped

2 tablespoons olive oil
5 celery ribs
8 carrots, peeled and chopped
4 beets, peeled and chopped
1 butternut squash, peeled and chopped
8 garlic cloves, peeled and minced
1 cup vegetable stock
¼ cup lemon juice
1 bunch fresh basil, chopped
2 bay leaves
Salt and ground black pepper, to taste

Directions:

1. Set the Crock pot Express™ on "Brown/Sauté" mode, add the oil and heat it up. Add the celery, onion, and carrots, stir and cook for 4 minutes. Add the beets, squash, garlic, stock, lemon juice, basil, bay leaves, salt, and pepper, stir,
2. Cover and cook for 12 minutes at "Beans/Chili". Release the pressure, uncover the Crock pot Express™, discard the bay leaves, puree sauce using an immersion blender, transfer to a bowl, and serve.

336. Vegetable Stock

Preparation + Cook Time: 30 minutes | Cups: 8

Ingredients:
2 green onions, sliced
2 tsp minced garlic
4 medium-sized carrots, peeled and chopped
4 celery stalks, chopped
6 parsley sprigs
4 thyme sprigs
8 cups water
2 bay leaves
8 black peppercorns
1½ tsp salt

Directions:
1. Prepare vegetables. In a 6-quarts Crock Pot Express™, pour the water and add all the ingredients except salt.
2. Plug in and switch on the Crock Pot Express™, and secure pot with lid.
3. Select SOUP option, and adjust cooking time to 30 minutes and let cook. Crock Pot Express™ will take 10 minutes to build pressure before cooking timer starts.

4. When the timer beeps, switch off the Crock Pot Express™ and let pressure release naturally for 10 minutes and then do quick pressure release.
5. Then uncover the pot and pass the mixture through a strainer placed over a large bowl to collect stock and vegetables on the strainer.
6. Stir salt into the stock and let cool completely before storing or use it later for cooking.

337. Cheese Sauce

Preparation time: **10 minutes** • Cooking time: **5 minutes** • Servings: **4**

Ingredients:
2 cups processed cheese, cut into chunks
1 cup Italian sausage, cooked and chopped
5 ounces canned tomatoes and green chilies, diced
4 tablespoons water

Directions:
1. In the Crock pot Express™, mix sausage with cheese, tomatoes, and chilies and water.
2. Stir, Cover and cook on the "Beans/Chili" setting for 5 minutes. Release the pressure, uncover the Crock pot Express™, transfer sauce to a bowl, and serve with your favorite pasta or vegetables.

338. Cranberry Apple Sauce

Preparation + Cook Time: 20 minutes | Cups: 2

Ingredients:
1-2 apples, medium-sized, peeled, cored, and then cut into chunks
10 oz cranberries, frozen or fresh, preferably organic
¼ tsp sea salt
¼ cup lemon juice
½ cup maple syrup OR honey OR omit
1 tsp cinnamon

Directions:
1. Put all of the ingredients in the Crock Pot Express™ and combine.
2. Cover and lock the lid. Press the "BEANS/CHILI" key, set the pressure to HIGH, and set the timer for 1 minute.

3. When the Crock Pot Express™ timer beeps, let the pressure release naturally for 10-15 minutes or until the valve drops. Press the CANCEL key and unplug the Crock Pot Express™.
4. Unlock and carefully open the lid. Using a wooden spoon, mash the fruit a bit.
5. Select the "BROWN/SAUTÉ" key and simmer for 1-2 minutes to allow some of the water to evaporate and the mix to thicken.
6. Press the CANCEL key. If you omitted the maple syrup/ honey and want to sweeten with stevia, then add to taste.
7. Stir to combine. Transfer into a pint jar and refrigerate.

339. Mushroom Sauce

Preparation time: **10 minutes** • Cooking time: **35 minutes** • Servings: **6**

Ingredients:
1 yellow onion, peeled and chopped
¼ cup olive oil
1 tablespoon flour
Salt and ground black pepper, to taste
1 tablespoon thyme, chopped
3 garlic cloves, peeled and minced
1¼ cup chicken stock
¼ cup dry sherry
10 ounces shiitake mushrooms, chopped
10 ounces cremini mushrooms, chopped
10 ounces button mushrooms, chopped
1-ounce Parmesan cheese, grated
½ cup heavy cream
1 tablespoons parsley, diced

Directions:
1. Set the Crock pot Express™ on "Brown/Sauté" mode, add the oil and heat it up. Add the onion, salt, and pepper, stir and cook for 5 minutes. Add the garlic, flour, and thyme, stir and cook for 1 minute. Add sherry, stock, and the mushrooms, stir,
2. Cover, and cook on the "Beans/Chili" setting for 25 minutes. Release pressure, uncover the Crock pot Express™, add the cream, cheese, and parsley, stir, and set the Crock pot Express™ on "Beans/Chili" mode. Cook for 5 minutes, transfer to a bowl, and serve.

Dessert Recipes

340. Chocolate pudding

Prep: 5 minutes • pressure: 15 minutes • total: 20 minutes • pressure level: high • release: natural • Serves 6

Ingredients
6 ounces semisweet or bittersweet chocolate, chopped
½ ounce unsweetened chocolate, chopped
6 tablespoons sugar
1½ cups light cream
4 large egg yolks, at room temperature and whisked in a small bowl
1 tablespoon vanilla extract
¼ teaspoon salt

Directions
1. **Preparing the ingredients.** Place all the chopped chocolate and the sugar in a large bowl. Heat the cream in a saucepan over low heat until small bubbles fizz around the inside edge of the pan.

   Pour the warmed cream over the chocolate; whisk until the chocolate has completely melted. Cool a minute or two, then whisk in the yolks, vanilla, and salt. Pour the mixture into six ½-cup heat-safe ramekins, filling each about three-quarters full. Cover each with foil.

   Set the rack in the crock-pot multi-cooker®; pour in 2 cups water. Set the ramekins on the rack, stacking them as necessary without any one ramekin sitting directly on top of another.
2. **High pressure for 15 minutes.** Lock the lid on the crock-pot multi-cooker® and then cook for 15 minutes. To get 15-minutes cook time, press "Poultry" button.
3. **Pressure release** turn off the crock-pot multi-cooker® or unplug it so it doesn't flip to its keep-warm setting. Let its pressure return to normal naturally, 10 to 14 minutes.
4. **Finish the dish.** Unlock and open the cooker. Transfer the hot ramekins to a cooling rack, uncover, and cool for 10 minutes before serving—or chill in the refrigerator for up to 3 days, covering again once the puddings have chilled.

341. Chocolate Cheesecake

Preparation + Cook Time: 2 hours 10 minutes | Servings: 6

Ingredients:
12 cups cashews, soaked
5 oz almond flour
2 tbsp coconut flour
2 oz melted coconut oil
½ tsp salt
2/3 cup brown sugar
1 tbsp cocoa powder
3 tsp vanilla extract, divided
2 tbsp honey
4 oz maple syrup
8 fluid ounce almond milk
16 fluid ounce water
2 oz vegan chocolate chips

Directions:
1. Add almond flour, maple syrup and coconut oil in a food processor and blend until mixture comes together. Add 1-2 tablespoons of water if the mixture is too dry.
2. Take a 7-inch spring form pan, then spoon oats mixture into it and press into the bottom and a little on the sides.
3. Place pan in a refrigerator until filling is prepared.
4. Drain cashews and reserve their soaking liquid.
5. In a food processor add cashew and half of the soaking liquid and blend until smooth.
6. Then add salt, sugar, vanilla and milk and blend until combined well and pour this mixture into a bowl and then add coconut flour and chocolate chip, stir thoroughly.
7. Pour out into prepared spring form pan and smooth the top. Pour water in the Crock Pot Express™ and insert a trivet.
8. Place prepared spring form pan on the trivet and secure pot with lid.
9. Select "BEANS/CHILI" and cook at HIGH pressure for 55 minutes.
10. When the timer beeps, switch off the Crock Pot Express™ and let pressure release naturally for 10 minutes and then use a quick release.
11. Then uncover the pot, carefully remove pan and let the pan cool completely.
12. Chill cake in the refrigerator for 2 hours. Serve and enjoy.

342. White chocolate lemon pudding

Prep: 5 Minutes • Pressure: 15 Minutes • Total: 20 Minutes • Pressure Level: High • Release: Natural • Serves 6

Ingredients
6 ounces white chocolate, chopped
1 cup heavy cream
1 cup half-and-half
4 large egg yolks, at room temperature and whisked in a small bowl
1 tablespoon sugar
1 tablespoon finely grated lemon zest (about 1 medium lemon)
¼ teaspoon lemon extract

Directions
1. **Preparing the ingredients.** Put the chopped white chocolate in a large bowl. Mix the cream and half-and-half in a small saucepan and warm over low heat until bubbles fizz around the edges of the pan.

   Pour the warm mixture over the white chocolate and whisk until melted. Whisk in the egg yolks, sugar, zest, and extract. Pour the mixture into six ½-cup heat-safe ramekins; cover each tightly with aluminum foil.

   Set the crock-pot multi-cooker® rack in the crock-pot multi-cooker®; pour in 2 cups water. Set the ramekins on the rack, stacking them as necessary without any one ramekin sitting directly on top of another.
5. **High pressure for 15 minutes.** Lock the lid on the crock-pot multi-cooker® and then cook for 15 minutes. To get 15-minutes cook time, press "Poultry" button.
2. **Pressure release.** Turn off the crock-pot multi-cooker® or unplug it so it doesn't jump to its "Keep Warm" setting. Let its pressure return to normal naturally, 10 to 14 minutes.
3. **Finish the dish.** Unlock and open the cooker. Transfer the (hot!) Ramekins to a cooling rack; uncover each and cool for a few minutes before serving—or store in the refrigerator for up to 3 days, covering the ramekins again after they have chilled.

343. Chocolate Zucchini Muffins

Preparation + Cook Time: 35 minutes | Servings: 24

Ingredients:
1 cup water
1 cup flour
1 cup grated zucchini
2 eggs
¾-1 cup cane juice
½ cup coconut oil

⅓ cup chocolate chips

3 tbsp cocoa powder

1 tbsp melted butter

2 tsp pure vanilla extract

¾ tsp cinnamon

½ tsp baking soda

¼ tsp salt

Directions:
1. Mix cane juice, eggs, coconut oil, and vanilla.
2. In a separate bowl, mix melted butter with cocoa powder.
3. Add to the egg mixture and mix. Add dry ingredients (flour, baking soda, cinnamon, and salt). Add the chocolate chips and zucchini.
4. Pour 1 cup of water into your Crock Pot Express™ and lower the trivet.
5. Select "BROWN/SAUTÉ" to preheat the pressure cooker.
6. Fill silicone muffin cups ⅔ of the way full with muffin batter. Put cups in the pressure cooker.
7. For the second layer, separate with a piece of parchment paper, foil, and another trivet.
8. Finish layering muffins, and cover again with parchment paper, foil, and then a plate. Close and seal the lid.
9. Select "Beans/Chili" and cook at HIGH pressure for 8 minutes.
10. Once cooking is complete, press CANCEL and wait 15 minutes. Then quick release any leftover pressure.
11. If a toothpick comes out clean from the muffins, they're ready!

344. Blackberry swirl cheesecake

Prep: 10 minutes • pressure: 20 minutes • total: 30 minutes • pressure level: high • release: natural • Serves 4-6

Ingredients
1 cup fresh blackberries

½ cup powdered sugar

4 tablespoons unsalted butter

1 cup crushed graham crackers

14 ounces cream cheese (one 8-ounce and two 3-ounce packages)

½ cup granulated sugar

Freshly grated zest from 1 lemon

Freshly grated zest from half an orange

2 large eggs

Directions

1. **Preparing the ingredients.** Add 2 cups of water to the crock-pot multi-cooker® base; insert the steamer basket and set aside. Cut a piece of wax paper to fit the bottom of a wide, flat-bottomed 4-cup baking dish; also cut a strip sized to fit the sides of the dish. Line the dish with the paper.

   Puree the blackberries and powdered sugar in a blender and set aside.

   Melt the butter in a medium saucepan on medium heat. Remove the pan from the heat and mix in the crushed crackers. Scoop the mixture into the prepared baking dish and, using the back of your hand, push it into a flat, thin, even layer that covers the bottom of the dish, and, if there is enough, partway up the sides. Put the dish in the refrigerator to chill, uncovered, while you prepare the filling.

   In a medium bowl, using an electric mixer on medium speed, mix together the cream cheese, granulated sugar, and lemon and orange zests. Add the eggs and mix into a smooth batter, about 5 minutes.

   Remove the dish with the crust from the refrigerator. Slowly pour the batter over the crust, spreading level. To add the blackberry swirl, pour the puree into a squirt bottle (or food storage bag with one corner clipped off) and with it draw a spiral from the center out on top of the batter. Then use a toothpick or skewer to drag radiating lines from the center to the edge of the dish. Using a foil sling, lower the dish into the crock-pot multi-cooker®; do not cover the dish.

2. **High pressure for 20 minutes.** Lock the lid on the crock-pot multi-cooker® and then cook for 20 minutes. To get 20-minutes cook time, press "meat/stew" button and use the time adjustment button to adjust the cook time to 20 minutes.

3. **Pressure release.** When the time is up, open the crock-pot multi-cooker® using the 10-minute natural release method.

4. **Finish the dish.** Lift the dish out of the crock-pot multi-cooker® and check the cake for doneness, transfer the dish to a wire rack.

   Let the cake cool, uncovered, for about 30 minutes. Then cover the dish with plastic wrap and refrigerate until ready to serve, for at least 4 hours.

   Work quickly and delicately to unmold the chilled cake: invert a plate over the dish and flip the dish and plate over together. Lift the dish off the cake and then peel off the wax paper circle on the base and the strip on the sides. Then invert a serving plate on the cake and gently flip all three components over together; lift off the top plate. Serve the cake cold, cut into wedges.

345. Chocolate Fondue with Coconut Cream

Preparation + Cook Time: 5 minutes | Servings: 4

Ingredients:
2 cups water
3.5 oz 70% dark bittersweet chocolate
3.5 oz coconut cream
1 tsp sugar

Directions:
1. Pour 2 cups of water into your Crock Pot Express™ and insert trivet.
2. In a heatproof bowl, add chocolate chunks.
3. Add coconut cream and sugar.
4. Put the bowl on top of the trivet. Close and seal the lid.
5. Select "BEANS/CHILI" and cook at HIGH pressure for 2 minutes. (Press Stop when complete 2 Minute).
6. When time is up, press CANCEL and use a quick release.
7. Carefully remove bowl and whisk with a fork until it becomes smooth. Serve!

346. Poached peach cups with ricotta and honey

Prep: 5 minutes • pressure: 4 minutes • total: 9 minutes • pressure level: low • release: quick • Serves 4

Ingredients
4 peaches, cut in half and pitted
1/4 cup apple juice
1/4 cup water
3 tablespoons light brown sugar
1/8 teaspoon ground cinnamon
1 cup part-skim ricotta cheese
2 tablespoons honey
1/4 teaspoon vanilla extract

Directions
1. **Preparing the ingredients.** Add peaches, apple juice, water, brown sugar, and cinnamon to the cooker.
2. **High pressure for 5 minutes.** Lock the lid on the crock-pot multi-cooker® and then cook for 5 minutes. To get 5-minutes cook time, press "Dessert" button, and use the time adjustment button to adjust the cook time to 5 minutes.

3. **Pressure release.** Perform a quick release to release the cooker's pressure. Remove peaches from cooking liquid, and set aside.
4. **Finish the dish.** Combine ricotta cheese, honey, and vanilla extract, and serve spooned into the center of each peach half.

347. Chocolate Custard

Preparation + Cook Time: 55 minutes | Servings: 6

Ingredients:
13-ounces chopped dark chocolate
6 whisked egg yolks Just over
1 cup cream (1.2 cups)
1 cup whole milk
½ cup sugar
1 tsp vanilla extract

Directions:
1. In a saucepan, simmer milk, cream, vanilla, and sugar until sugar has dissolved.
2. Take the pan off the heat and add chocolate.
3. When melted, slowly add whisked egg yolks, being careful that they don't cook.
4. Pour into an 7.2-8 -inch baking dish.
5. Pour 4 cups of water into your Crock Pot Express™ and insert trivet. Put the custard pan on the trivet and seal the lid.
6. Select "BEANS/CHILI" and cook at HIGH pressure for 30 minutes.
7. When time is up, press CANCEL and let the pressure release naturally for 10 minutes before quick-releasing.
8. The custard will have a wobbly center, like a jelly. Serve hot or cold.

348. Molten gingerbread cake

Prep: 5 minutes • pressure: 15 minutes • total: 20 minutes • pressure level: high • release: combination • Serves 2

Ingredients
3 tablespoons very hot water
¼ cup vegetable oil
¼ cup packed brown sugar
¼ cup molasses
1 large egg

⅔ cup all-purpose flour
¾ teaspoon ground ginger
½ teaspoon ground cinnamon
¼ teaspoon kosher salt
¼ teaspoon baking powder
¼ teaspoon baking soda
1 cup water, for steaming (double-check the crock-pot multi-cooker® manual to confirm amount, and follow the manual if there is a discrepancy)

Directions

1. **Preparing the ingredients.** In a small bowl, using a hand mixer, mix together the hot water, vegetable oil, brown sugar, molasses, and egg. In another small bowl, sift together the flour, ground ginger, cinnamon, kosher salt, baking powder, and baking soda. Add the dry ingredients to the liquid mixture. Mix on medium speed until the ingredients are thoroughly combined, with no lumps. Pour the batter into a nonstick mini (3-by-5-inch) loaf pan. Cover the pan with aluminum foil, making a dome over the pan.
   Add the water and insert the steamer basket or trivet. Carefully place the loaf pan on the steamer insert.
2. **High pressure for 15 minutes**. Lock the lid on the crock-pot multi-cooker® and then cook for 15 minutes. To get 15-minutes cook time, press "Dessert" button and use the time adjustment button to adjust the cook time to15 minutes.
   When the timer goes off, turn the cooker off. ("""Keep Warm"" setting, turn off).
3. **Pressure release.** After cooking, use the natural method to release pressure for 5 minutes, then the quick method to release the remaining pressure.
4. **Finish the dish.** Unlock and remove the lid. Using tongs, carefully remove the pan from the crock-pot multi-cooker®. Let the cake rest for 2 to 3 minutes; remove the foil, slice, and serve.
    to sift the dry ingredients, place a medium-coarse sieve over a small bowl or on a sheet of wax paper or parchment paper. Measure the dry ingredients into the sieve. Tap the side of the sieve to move the contents through the sieve to the bowl or parchment paper; then transfer the sifted ingredients to the wet ingredients.

Per serving: calories: 639; fat: 30g; sodium: 506mg; carbohydrates: 87g; fiber: 2g; protein: 8g

349. Two-Ingredient Chocolate Fondue

Preparation + Cook Time: 5 minutes | Servings: 4

Ingredients:
3.5-ounces of dark chocolate (minimum 70% cocoa)
3.5-ounces of cream

Directions:

1. Pour two cups of water into the Crock Pot Express™ and lower the trivet.
2. Put chocolate chunks in a ceramic, heat-proof container that fits into the pressure cooker, and pour over the cream.
3. Put into the Crock Pot Express™. Close and lock the lid. Select "BEANS/CHILI" and cook at HIGH pressure for 2 minutes.
4. When time is up, press CANCEL and carefully quick release the pressure.
5. Open the lid and remove the container.
6. Whisk quickly until the chocolate becomes smooth.
7. Serve right away!

Notes: If you want to make your fondue unique, add 1 teaspoon of Amaretto liquor before closing up the pressure. Other flavor options include chili powder, peppermint extract, orange extract, or Bailey's.

350. Pineapple upside-down cake

Prep: 5 minutes • pressure: 25 minutes • total: 30 minutes • pressure level: high • release: natural • Serves 6

Ingredients

1 cup all-purpose flour
¾ teaspoon baking powder
¼ teaspoon salt
¼ teaspoon ground cinnamon
¼ cup packed dark brown sugar
4 canned pineapple rings packed in syrup
2 large eggs, at room temperature
½ cup regular or low-fat sour cream
½ cup granulated sugar
3 tablespoons unsalted butter, melted and cooled
2 teaspoons vanilla extract

Directions

1. **Preparing the ingredients.** Generously butter the inside of a 2-quart round, high-sided soufflé or baking dish. Place a rack inside the crock-pot multi-cooker®; pour in 2 cups water. Whisk the flour, baking powder, salt, and cinnamon in a small bowl; set aside. Sprinkle the brown sugar evenly over the bottom of the prepared dish. Lay the pineapple rings in the baking dish. Whisk the eggs, sour cream, sugar, butter, and vanilla in a large bowl until smooth. Whisk in the flour mixture until moistened and uniform; pour into the baking dish. Do not cover.

Make an aluminum foil sling, set the baking dish on it, and lower it onto the rack in the cooker. Crimp the ends of the sling to fit into the pot.

2. **High pressure for 25 minutes.** Lock the lid on the crock-pot multi-cooker® and then cook for 25 minutes. To get 25-minutes cook time, press "Dessert" button and use the time adjustment button to adjust the cook time to25 minutes.
3. **Pressure release.** Turn off the crock-pot multi-cooker® or unplug it so it doesn't flip to its "Keep Warm" setting. Let its pressure return to normal naturally, 8 to 12 minutes.
4. **Finish the dish.** Unlock and open the cooker. Use the foil sling to transfer the hot baking dish to a wire rack. Cool for 10 minutes, then set a serving platter over the baking dish, invert it all, and remove the baking dish, thereby unmolding the cake. Serve warm or at room temperature.

351. Chocolate-Chip Banana Cake

Preparation + Cook Time: 75 minutes | Servings: 6

Ingredients:
1½ cups flour
2 eggs
2 ripe bananas
½ cup milk + 1 tbsp
⅔ cup water
⅓ cup dark chocolate chips
¼ cup honey
3 tbsp coconut oil
1 tbsp vinegar
1 tsp baking soda
½ tsp cinnamon
⅛ tsp ground nutmeg

Directions:
1. Grease the 3-cup Bundt Pan.
2. Pour vinegar into milk and let the bowl sit until the milk curdles and turns to buttermilk.
3. In a separate bowl, mix bananas, honey, vanilla, eggs, coconut oil, and nutmeg.
4. Add buttermilk. When combined, add the cinnamon, baking soda, and flour.
5. With a spatula, fold the chocolate chips into your batter.
6. Pour batter into your Bundt Pan.
7. Pour ⅔ cup of water into the Crock Pot Express™ and place the trivet. Put the Bundt Pan on top of the trivet. Close and seal the lid.
8. Select "BEANS/CHILI" and cook at HIGH pressure for 25 minutes.

9. Once cooking is complete, use a quick release. Take out the Bundt Pan and cool for 10 minutes.
10. Invert the cake and wait until fully cooled before serving.

352. Chocolate–peanut butter brownies

Prep: 10 minutes • pressure: 45 minutes • total: 55 minutes • pressure level: high • release: natural • Serves 8

Ingredients
Nonstick vegetable oil cooking spray
4 ounces (115 g) bittersweet chocolate, chopped
3/4 cup (1 1/2 sticks, or 180 g) unsalted butter
2 teaspoons instant espresso powder
1 teaspoon pure vanilla extract
3 large eggs
1 cup (200 g) sugar
1 cup (120 g) all-purpose flour
1/2 teaspoon kosher salt
1/4 teaspoon baking powder
1 cup (175 g) peanut butter chips
1/2 cup (88 g) bittersweet chocolate chips

Directions
1. **Preparing the ingredients.** Insert the steam rack into the crock-pot multi-cooker®. Add 1 1/2 cups (350 ml) water. Coat a deep 8-inch (20 cm) round soufflé or casserole dish with cooking spray.
   In a medium microwave-safe bowl, melt the chocolate and butter on high, stirring every 30 seconds, until melted and smooth, about 60 seconds total. Stir in the espresso powder and vanilla.
   In a large bowl, beat the eggs and sugar until combined. Add the chocolate mixture and mix to combine. Add the flour, salt, and baking powder, and mix until fully incorporated. Fold in the peanut butter chips and chocolate chips, then scrape the batter into the prepared dish.
   Cover the dish with aluminum foil. Using another piece of foil, make a "sling" measuring about 3 × 20 inches (7.5 × 51 cm). Use it to lower the dish into the pot.
2. **High pressure for 45 minutes.** Lock the lid on the crock-pot multi-cooker® and then cook for 45 minutes. To get 45-minutes cook time, press "Dessert" button and use the time adjustment button to adjust the cook time to 45 minutes
3. **Pressure release.** Use the "natural release" method for 10 minutes, then vent any remaining steam and open the lid.
4. **Finish the dish.** Transfer the dish to a wire cooling rack, uncover, and let cool for at least 20 minutes before serving.

353. Rich Chocolate Pudding

Preparation + Cook Time: 35 minutes | Servings: 6

Ingredients:
1½ cups whipping cream
4 ounces bittersweet chocolate chopped
4 egg yolks
1/3 cup brown sugar packed
1 tbsp unsweetened cocoa powder
1 tsp Vanilla
¼ tsp salt
1½ cups water

Directions:
1. Heat cream to a simmer in medium saucepan over medium heat. Remove from heat. Add chocolate; stir until chocolate is melted and mixture is smooth.
2. Whisk egg yolks, brown sugar, cocoa, vanilla and salt in large bowl until well blended. Gradually add hot chocolate mixture, whisking constantly until blended.
3. Strain into 6- to 7-inch (1½ -quart) soufflé dish or round baking dish that fits inside Crock Pot Express™. Cover dish tightly with foil.
4. Pour water into Crock Pot Express™. Place soufflé dish on rack; lower into pot using handles of rack.
5. Close and lock the lid. Select "BEANS/CHILI" and cook at LOW pressure for 22 minutes.
6. When cooking is complete, use natural release for 5 minutes, then release remaining pressure.
7. Use handles of rack to remove dish from pot. Remove foil; cool to room temperature. Cover and refrigerate at least 3 hours or up to 2 days.

354. Blueberry clafouti

Prep: 5 minutes • pressure: 11 minutes • total: 16 minutes • pressure level: high • release: quick • Serves 2

Ingredients
1 teaspoon unsalted butter, at room temperature, divided
½ cup fresh blueberries, divided
⅓ cup whole milk
3 tablespoons heavy (whipping) cream
3 tablespoons sugar
¼ cup all-purpose flour

1 large egg
¼ teaspoon vanilla extract
¼ teaspoon lemon zest
⅛ teaspoon ground cinnamon
Pinch fine salt
1 cup water, for steaming (double-check the crock-pot multi-cooker® manual to confirm amount, and follow the manual if there is a discrepancy)
2 teaspoons confectioners' sugar or powdered sugar

Directions

1. **Preparing the ingredients.** Using ½ teaspoon of butter each, coat the insides of each of 2 custard cups or small ramekins. Put ¼ cup of blueberries in each cup.

   In a medium bowl, combine the milk, heavy cream, sugar, flour, egg, vanilla, lemon zest, cinnamon, and fine salt. Using a hand mixer, beat the ingredients for about 2 minutes on medium speed, or until the batter is smooth. Evenly divide the batter between the 2 cups, filling them about three-fourths full with batter.

   Add the water and insert the steamer basket or trivet. Place the custard cups on the steamer insert. Place a square of aluminum foil over the pan, but don't crimp it down; it's just to keep steam from condensing on the surface of the clafouti.
2. **High pressure for 11 minutes.** Lock the lid on the crock-pot multi-cooker® and then cook for 11 minutes. To get 11-minutes cook time, press "Dessert" button, and use the time adjustment button to adjust the cook time to 11 minutes.
3. **Pressure release** use the quick-release method.
4. **Finish the dish.** Unlock and remove the lid. Using tongs, remove the foil. Transfer the cups to a small baking sheet. Preheat the broiler, and position a rack close to the broiler element. Place the baking sheet under the broiler for 3 to 4 minutes, or until the tops brown slightly. Cool for at least 10 minutes. Sift the confectioners' sugar over the clafouti, and serve warm.

Per serving: calories: 314; fat: 15g; sodium: 153mg; carbohydrates: 41g; fiber: 1g; protein: 7g

355. Apple Crumb Cake

Preparation + Cook Time: 55 minutes | Servings: 6

Ingredients:
6 small red apples
¾ cup melted butter
½ cup sugar
1½ cups water
⅔ cup dry bread crumbs

Juice and zest from ½ lemon
2 tbsp flour
1 tsp cinnamon
1 tsp ginger

Directions:
1. To make the filling, mix bread crumbs, sugar, cinnamon, melted butter, ginger, lemon juice, and lemon zest.
2. Core the apples, leaving the peels on, and slice very thin.
3. Grease your baking dish with butter and coat with a dusting flour. Lay down the apple slices in fan shapes.
4. Add a layer of the crumb filling, followed by apples, and keep going until everything is used up.
5. Wrap the dish tightly in foil. Pour 1½ cups of water into your Crock Pot Express™ and lower in the trivet.
6. Put the wrapped dish on top and seal the lid.
7. Select "BEANS/CHILI" and cook at HIGH pressure for 23 minutes.
8. Once cooking is complete, press CANCEL and wait 10 minutes before quick-releasing.
9. Take out the cake and remove the foil.
10. Flip the cake on a dish. To finish, sprinkle raw sugar on top and broil for just 3 minutes, or until the sugar caramelizes. Serve!

356. Strawberry freezer jam recipe

Prep: 10 minutes • pressure: 8 minutes • total: 18 minutes • pressure level: high • release: natural • Serves 4 cups

Ingredients
1 lb. (450 grams) strawberries (fresh or frozen)
1 /2 to 1 lb. (225 to 450 grams) granulated sugar
1 navel orange
1 tbs. Butter (optional, vegans can omit)

Directions
1. **Preparing the ingredients.** If you are using fresh berries, remove the stems, leaves and any bruised spots from the strawberries, lightly wash them, and cut into halves or quarters, depending on size. For frozen berries, defrost before use, cut them up if necessary.
   Peel the navel orange, removing the bitter white pith and any white connective tissues. I do this by slicing a bit off the top, so i can see how thick the peel is. I then take the knife and cut slices of peel down the sides of the orange. (it is better to remove a little of the orange than to leave the bitter pith on the orange.) Once you have removed all the peel

and any pith attached to the outside of the orange, break it apart into segments, remove any white pithy connective tissues inside, and roughly chop the segments. Reserve the chopped segments and any juice.

For a very smooth jam, place the sliced strawberries and chopped orange segments and juice into a food processor or blender and puree until smooth, then add to the sugar. If you would like your jam more like preserves (with small pieces of fruit mixed in), combine the sliced strawberries, orange pieces, and orange juice into the sugar.

Once mixed, use a potato masher to roughly mash the strawberries. The mixture should macerate in the refrigerator for at least an hour, but if you can let it set for 8 – 24 hours, that's even better.

Once the mixture has macerated, add to the crock-pot multi-cooker®. Using the "browning" setting, bring the jam up to a hard boil for 3 minutes to dissolve the sugar and reduce the excess water content. Stir frequently with the longest handled spatula you own.

Stir in 1 tablespoon of butter

2. **High pressure for 8 minutes.** Lock the lid on the crock-pot multi-cooker® and then cook for 8 minutes. To get 8-minutes cook time, press "Rice/Risotto" button, and use the time adjustment button to adjust the cook time to 8 minutes.

3. **Pressure release.** Let its pressure return to normal naturally, 8 to 12 minutes.

4. **Finish the dish.** After pressure has released, unlock and remove the lid, tilting the front side down and the back side up to direct any residual heat and steam away from you. With the lid off and the "browning" setting, bring the mixture back to the boil for 3 minutes, stirring frequently. Turn the unit off after the 3 minutes are up. Allow mixture to cool to room temperature, stirring periodically. Once cooled, put the jam in a container in the refrigerator to finish setting.

357. Mango Cake

Preparation + Cook Time: 50 minutes | Servings: 8

Ingredients:
1¼ cups flour
¾ cup milk
1 cup water
½ cup sugar
¼ cup coconut oil
1 tbsp lemon juice
1 tsp mango syrup
1 tsp baking powder
¼ tsp baking soda
⅛ tsp salt

Directions:
1. Grease a baking pan that will fit in your Crock Pot Express™.
2. Mix the sugar, oil, and milk in a bowl until the sugar has melted.
3. Pour in mango syrup and mix again.
4. Pour all the dry ingredients through a sieve into the wet.
5. Add lemon juice and mix well.
6. Pour into the baking pan.
7. Pour 1 cup of water into the Crock Pot Express™ and place a trivet in the pot.
8. Lower the baking pan into the cooker and close the lid.
9. Select "BEANS/CHILI", and cook at HIGH pressure for 35 minutes.
10. When time is up, press CANCEL and let the pressure release naturally.
11. Check the cake for doneness before cooling for 10 minutes.
12. Serve!

358. Apricot jam

Prep: 10 minutes • pressure: 8 minutes • total: 18 minutes • pressure level: high • release: natural • Serves 4 cups

Ingredients
2 pounds (907 grams) apricots
1 – 1 ½ pounds (450 – 680 grams) white sugar
2 large navel oranges
1 tablespoon butter or margarine (optional)
1 – 2 teaspoons fresh orange zest
¼ - ½ teaspoon almond extract

Directions

1. **Preparing the Ingredients.** Clean the fruit, removing stems, leaves and any bad spots. Cut each apricot in half, discard the pit, and add the fruit halves to the bowl of a blender or food processor. If you want pieces of fruit in your jam to make it more like preserves, peel some of the fruit and add it back in after the rest has been pureed. Remove the colorful surface layer of zest from the orange. You want only the thin outer layer, the white part underneath is bitter. Place the zest in a bag or container and refrigerate. Cut a thin slice off the top of the zested oranges. Cut an additional slice if needed to see how thick the orange peel is. Using your knife, cut down the sides of the oranges, in curves along the lines of the oranges, to remove the peel. Cut any remaining pith away from the outside of the orange segments. Separate the segments and remove the connective tissue inside. If any orange remains on the peel, hold it over the jam mixture and use your finger to press the juice out. Discard the peel. Either chop the orange segments up very finely with your

knife or your food processor. Add the sugar and the finely chopped orange segments to the jam mixture.

2. Let the jam macerate at least an hour, but preferably overnight or 24 hours. If you only have an hour, let it sit on the counter, for longer than that, it should be refrigerated. After maceration, place the apricot jam in the Crock-Pot Multi-Cooker® bowl. With the lid off and set on "Browning", bring the jam mixture to a hard rolling boil, and cook for 6 minutes. Ignore any foaming at the surface, this will disappear after pressure cooking. As soon as the 6 minutes are up, turn the machine off.
3. **High pressure for 8 minutes.** Lock the lid on the Crock-Pot Multi-Cooker® and then cook for 8 minutes. To get 8-minutes cook time, press "Rice/Risotto" button, and use the TIME ADJUSTMENT button to adjust the cook time to 8 minutes.
4. **Pressure Release.** Let its pressure return to normal naturally, 8 to 12 minutes.
5. **Finish the dish**. After your pressure cooker has released pressure, carefully remove the lid, and allow any hot liquid to fall back into the pot. Stir in the orange zest and almond extract to taste. Once the jam has cooled, refrigerate.

359. Apple-Ricotta Cake

Preparation + Cook Time: 45 minutes | Servings: 6

Ingredients:
2 cups water
1 cup ricotta cheese
1 cup flour
1 egg
¼ cup raw sugar
⅓ cup sugar
1 sliced apple
1 diced apple
3 tbsp olive oil
1 tbsp lemon juice
2 tsp baking powder
1 tsp baking soda
1 tsp vanilla extract
⅛ tsp cinnamon

Directions:
1. Pour water into your Crock Pot Express™ and lower in steamer basket or trivet.
2. Mix your diced and sliced apple in lemon juice.
3. Put a piece of wax paper on the bottom of a 4-cup baking dish (shallow and wide), and oil it, and then dust it with flour.
4. Sprinkle in raw sugar before laying down the apple slices. In a bowl, whisk ricotta, sugar, olive oil, vanilla, and egg.

5. Sift in the cinnamon, flour, baking soda, and baking powder. Stir in the diced apples and then pour into your baking dish. Seal the lid.
6. Select "BEANS/CHILI" and cook for 20 minutes at HIGH pressure.
7. When time is up, press CANCEL and wait 10 minutes before quick-releasing any leftover pressure.
8. To test for doneness, poke a toothpick in the middle.
9. If batter sticks to it, put back in the cooker and bake another 2 minutes under pressure.
10. To serve, chill or eat warm.

360. Pumpkin Chocolate Cake

Preparation time: **10 minutes** • Cooking time: **45 minutes** • Servings: **12**

Ingredients:
¾ cup white flour
¾ cup whole wheat flour
Salt
1 teaspoon baking soda
¾ teaspoon pumpkin pie spice
¾ cup sugar
1 banana, mashed
½ teaspoon baking powder
2 tablespoons canola oil
½ cup Greek yogurt
8 ounces canned pumpkin puree
Vegetable oil cooking spray
1 quart water
1 egg
½ teaspoon vanilla extract
⅔ cup chocolate chips

Directions:
1. In a bowl, mix the flours, salt, baking soda, baking powder, and pumpkin spice, and stir. In another bowl, mix the sugar with the oil, banana, yogurt, pumpkin puree, vanilla, and egg, and stir using a mixer. Combine the 2 mixtures, add the chocolate chips and mix well. Pour into a greased Bundt pan, cover the pan with paper towels and aluminum foil, and place in the steamer basket of the Crock pot Express™.
2. Add the quart water to the Crock pot Express™, cover, and cook on the "Beans/Risotto" setting for 35 minutes. Release the pressure for 10 minutes, uncover the Crock pot Express™, leave the cake to cool down before cutting and serving it.

361. Cookies and Cream Cheesecake

Preparation + Cook Time: 70 minutes | Servings: 8

Ingredients:
16 ounces cream cheese
¼ cup sour cream
½ cup sugar
1 tsp vanilla
1 bag of bite-sized Caco Chocolate sandwich cookies
2 eggs
2 tbsp butter, melted
1 cup water
Equipment: 7-inch springform pan

Directions:
1. Use a rolling pin or any other heavy tool to convert ½ your cookies into sweet crumbs.
2. Mix crumbled cookies with the melted butter and press the mixture into the springform pan.
3. Put the eggs, cream cheese, sugar, and sour cream into a mixer. Mix until well combined.
4. Crumble the remaining cookies and then add into the mixture.
5. Transfer the batter into the pan and spread into an even layer.
6. Cover the spring-form pan with unbleached parchment paper, top it with foil, and secure around the edges.
7. Put a trivet in the Crock Pot Express™ and pour 1 cup of water. Take a long piece of foil and fold it lengthwise to create a strip long enough to allow you to place the cheesecake onto the trivet and retrieve it later when the cooking time is done.
8. Using the foil sling, place the pan onto the trivet. Cover and lock the lid.
9. Press the "BEANS/CHILI" key, set the pressure to HIGH, and set the timer for 40 minutes.
10. When the Crock Pot Express™ timer beeps, press the CANCEL key and unplug the Crock Pot Express™. Let the pressure release naturally for 10-15 minutes or until the valve drops. Unlock and carefully open the lid.
11. Using the foil sling, carefully remove the cheesecake from the pot.
12. Put on the counter and let cool completely. Slice and serve.

362. Chocolate Cheesecake

Preparation time: **60 minutes** • Cooking time: **50 minutes** • Servings: **12**

Ingredients:
For the crust:
4 tablespoons melted butter
1½ cups chocolate cookie crumbs
For the filling:
24 ounces cream cheese, softened
2 tablespoons cornstarch
1 cup sugar
3 eggs
1 tablespoon vanilla extract
Vegetable oil cooking spray
1 cup water
½ cup Greek yogurt
4 ounces white chocolate
4 ounces milk chocolate
4 ounces bittersweet chocolate

Directions:
1. In a bowl, mix the cookie crumbs with the butter and stir well. Spray a springform pan with some cooking oil, line with parchment paper, press the crumbs and butter mixture on the bottom and keep in the freezer. In a bowl, mix the cream cheese with cornstarch and sugar and stir using a mixer. Add the eggs, yogurt, and vanilla, stir to combine everything and divide into 3 bowls. Put the milk chocolate in a heatproof bowl and heat up in the microwave for 30 seconds. Add this to one of the bowls with the batter you made earlier and stir well. Put dark and white chocolate in separate heatproof bowls and heat them up in the microwave for 30 seconds each. Add these to the other 2 bowls with cheesecake batter, stir, and place them all in the refrigerator for 30 minutes. Take the bowls out of the refrigerator and layer your cheesecake. Pour the dark chocolate batter in the center of the crust. Add white chocolate batter on top and spread evenly and end with milk chocolate batter. Put the pan in the steamer basket of the Crock pot Express™, add 1 cup water to the Crock pot Express™,
2. Cover, and cook on the "Beans/Risotto" setting for 45 minutes. Release the pressure for 10 minutes, take the cheesecake out of the Crock pot Express™ , set aside to cool down, and serve.

363. Apple Bread

Preparation time: **10 minutes** • **Cooking time:** 1 hour and 10 minutes • Servings: **6**

Ingredients:
3 cups apples, cored and cubed
1 cup sugar
1 tablespoon vanilla extract

2 eggs
1 tablespoon apple pie spice
2 cups white flour
1 tablespoon baking powder
½ cup butter
1 cup water

Directions:
1. In a bowl, mix the egg with the butter, apple pie spice, and sugar and stir using a mixer. Add the apples and stir again well. In another bowl, mix the baking powder with flour and stir. Combine the 2 mixtures, stir, and pour into a springform pan. Place in the steamer basket of the Crock pot Express™, add the water to the Crock pot Express™,
2. Cover, and cook on the "Beans/Risotto" setting for 1 hour and 10 minutes. Release the pressure, fast, leave the bread to cool down, cut, and serve.

364. Banana Bread

Preparation time: **10 minutes** • Cooking time: **30 minutes** • Servings: **6**

Ingredients:
¾ cup coconut sugar
⅓ cup butter, softened
1 teaspoon vanilla extract
1 egg
2 bananas, mashed
1 teaspoon baking powder
1½ cups flour
Salt
½ teaspoons baking soda
⅓ cup cashew milk
1½ teaspoons cream of tartar
2 cups water
Vegetable oil cooking spray

Directions:
1. In a bowl, mix the milk with the cream of tartar and stir well. Add the sugar, butter, egg, vanilla, and bananas and stir everything. In another bowl, mix the flour with salt, baking powder, and soda. Combine the 2 mixtures, stir well, pour into a cake pan which you've greased with some cooking spray and arrange pan in the steamer basket of the Crock pot Express™. Add the water to the Crock pot Express™,

2. Cover and cook on the "Beans/Risotto" setting for 30 minutes. Release the pressure, uncover the Crock pot Express™, take the bread out, set aside to cool down, slice, and serve it.

365. Chocolate Lava Cake

Preparation time: **10 minutes** • Cooking time: **6 minutes** • Servings: **3**

Ingredients:
1 egg
4 tablespoons sugar
2 tablespoons olive oil
4 tablespoons milk
4 tablespoons flour
Salt
1 tablespoon cocoa powder
½ teaspoon baking powder
½ teaspoon orange zest
1 cup water

Directions:
1. In a bowl, mix the egg with the sugar, oil, milk, flour, salt, cocoa powder, baking powder, and orange zest and stir well. Pour into greased ramekins and place them into the steamer basket of the Crock pot Express™.
2. Add the water to the Crock pot Express™, cover, and cook on the "Beans/Risotto" setting for 6 minutes. Release the pressure, uncover the Crock pot Express™, take the lava cakes out, and serve them after they cool down.

HERITAGE OF FOOD: A FAMILY GATHERING

To survive, we need to eat. As a result, food has turned into a symbol of loving, nurturing and sharing with one another. Recording, collecting, sharing and remembering the recipes that have been passed to you by your family is a great way to immortalize and honor your family. It is these traditions that carve out your individual personality. You will not just be honoring your family tradition by cooking these recipes but they will also inspire you to create your own variations, which you can then pass on to your children's.

The recipes are just passed on by everyone and nobody actually possesses them. I too love sharing recipes. The collection is vibrant and rich as a number of home cooks have offered their inputs to ensure that all of us can cook delicious meals at our home. I am thankful to each one of you who has contributed to this book and has allowed their traditions to pass on and grow with others. You guys are really wonderful!

I am also thankful to the cooks who have evaluated all these recipes. You're, as well as, the comments that came from your family members and friends were really invaluable.

If you have the time and inclination, please consider leaving a short review wherever you can, we would love to learn more about your opinion.

https://www.amazon.com/review/review-your-purchases/

About the Author

Patrick is a Chicago-based food writer, experienced chef. He is known for his culinary skills and his high standards. He has contributed food articles in Magazines and Blogs, growing out of his commitment to make it possible for everyone to cook, even if they have too little time. He enjoys combining the classic recipes with the modern cooking technology like Electric Pressure Cooker and home sous vide immersion circulator machine. The best results of his experiments he shares with the others - by writing books.

Made in the USA
Middletown, DE
22 January 2018